Haiti and the Uses of America

I0877580

Haiti and the Uses of America

Post-U.S. Occupation Promises

CHANTALLE F. VERNA

Rutgers University Press
New Brunswick, Camden, and Newark, New Jersey, and London

Library of Congress Cataloging-in-Publication Data
Names: Verna, Chantalle F., 1974– author.
Title: Haiti and the uses of America : post-U.S. occupation promises / Chantalle F. Verna.
Description: New Brunswick, New Jersey : Rutgers University Press, 2017. | Includes bibliographical references and index.
Identifiers: LCCN 2016025801| ISBN 9780813585178 (hardcover : alk. paper) | ISBN 9780813585161 (pbk. : alk. paper) | ISBN 9780813585185 (e-book (epub))
Subjects: LCSH: United States—Foreign relations—Haiti. | Haiti—Foreign relations—United States. | BISAC: HISTORY / Caribbean & West Indies / General. | HISTORY / Americas (North, Central, South, West Indies). | POLITICAL SCIENCE / Colonialism & Post-Colonialism. | HISTORY / United States / 20th Century.
Classification: LCC E183.8.H2 V47 2017 | DDC 327.7307294—dc23
LC record available at https://lccn.loc.gov/2016025801

A British Cataloging-in-Publication record for this book is available from the British Library.

Copyright © 2017 by Chantalle F. Verna
All rights reserved
No part of this book may be reproduced or utilized in any form or by any means, electronic or mechanical, or by any information storage and retrieval system, without written permission from the publisher. Please contact Rutgers University Press, 106 Somerset Street, New Brunswick, NJ 08901. The only exception to this prohibition is "fair use" as defined by U.S. copyright law.

www.rutgersuniversitypress.org

Manufactured in the United States of America

With heartfelt memories of

André Elizée (January 30, 1955–January 10, 2010)

and

Eddy Jean-Baptiste (March 14, 1972–February 22, 2011)

Contents

Preface

> We must have the dream. . . . and try to attain it at its maximum. . . .
> We must continue to fight, so we can arrive at what is possible.
> —Haitian scholar and activist Odette Roy Fombrun, 2002

A tremendous sense of hopefulness often accompanies moments of transition—beginnings and endings bring with them aspirations and expectations of what is to come. Ideas from the past or those newly inspired in the present can generate a sense of promising possibility. *Haiti and the Uses of America* is about the promise of the first two decades after the U.S. military occupation of Haiti, which lasted from 1915 to 1934, and the value of paying attention to the idyllic rhetoric during Haiti's earliest post-U.S. occupation years.

In doing so, I offer a perspective that is often absent from common narratives which explain U.S. involvement in Haitian affairs strictly as a product of U.S. imperialism, a function of a growing diaspora that emerged most notably during the dictatorships of François Duvalier (1957–1971) and his son Jean-Claude (1971–1986) and after changes to U.S. immigration laws in 1965. Unlike those who have taken up the task of investigating the pursuits and implications of a foreign, and particularly a U.S., presence in Haiti, I emphasize the complexity of interests some Haitians have had in U.S. involvement in Haiti and the consequences thereof. By implications and consequences, I do not mean specific, tangible results that came when some Haitians reached out to individuals and institutions from the United States. Rather, I am more concerned about understanding the roots and nature of ideas that ties to the United States could be positively promising in Haiti, and how those ideas began to establish themselves within various sectors of Haitian society, beginning with Haiti's professional and skilled urban residents. My aim is to provide greater historical depth and complexity to our understanding of the perspectives that inform Haiti's current ties to the United States.

My yearning for a more nuanced perspective came during the 1990s when I began wondering why some Haitians anticipated that U.S. involvement in the Haitian state's affairs could be a good thing, especially given critiques about occupation in the past and other forms of imperialism in the present. I had been observing and, with my own novice hopes, experiencing the roller coaster of expectations that came with the end of the Duvalier dictatorship in 1986. For many in Haiti and in the diaspora, visions of cross-class alliances in post-Duvalier Haiti held the promise of resolving many of Haiti's challenges. Sadly, highly contested elections and related violence thwarted that vision. Those challenges played out vividly when Jean-Bertrand Aristide, a Catholic priest turned populist politician, who in February 1991 had become Haiti's first post-dictatorship elected president, was ousted by a military coup several months later.

With the support of some Haitian lobbyists, in Haiti and from within many of Haiti's U.S.-based diaspora communities, the U.S. government imposed trade embargoes on Haiti and ultimately, in 1994, entered into an agreement with the military junta to secure Aristide's return to power. Fast-forward two decades, in Haiti's bicentennial year of independence (2004), another segment of Haiti's U.S.-based diaspora lobbied U.S. officials again. This time, the result was U.S. assistance for Aristide's removal from power during his highly contested second elected term. In 1994 and again in 2004, the U.S. government intervened militarily in Haiti, on both occasions under the auspices of United Nations missions.

Listening to competing views in news reports and in debates among family members, I reflected on the critiques I had heard when it came to previous interventions (including the one that facilitated Jean-Claude Duvalier's ousting in 1986) and I wondered: were the petitions some Haitians were making for intervention a good idea? I found myself frustrated knowing that the answer was very likely more gray than black and white. I wondered what it would mean if we (Haitians) acknowledged that the U.S. presence in Haiti was due to requests made by some Haitians. I pondered how we (Haitians) can critique foreigners for their presence in Haiti when that presence is facilitated by the invitations of a segment of the Haitian population. These were some of the reflections that led me to first think more critically about how some Haitians have viewed the United States. I started to ask: what lay beneath their decision to migrate to the United States? What factors led them to partner with individuals and institutions from the United States on a wide range of agendas? And, how could they reconcile nurturing connections between the two countries given their heavy critiques about how most U.S. officials took an authoritarian and racist approach to their missions in Haiti?

Moments when Haitians are faced with the question of whether to use their contacts with individuals and institutions based in the United States, and particularly the U.S. government, continue to unfold with each new day. In the wake of a devastating earthquake in January 2010, the U.S. government and a wide array of private entities were among the most visible foreign sources of assistance for immediate relief and ongoing efforts presented in the name of recovery. In an enthusiastic invitation to foreign investors, the U.S.-backed Haitian president Michel Martelly, elected in 2011, declared that Haiti was "open for business!" This slogan became a propaganda statement that helped to usher in new waves of foreigners, adding thousands of missionaries and other organizations that critics labeled "disaster tourists" and "disaster capitalists" to Haiti's local scenes. Reports on their engagement consistently critique the dismissive nature of most foreigners—including some members of the diaspora who return identifying more closely with non-Haitians than with Haitians. The foreigners facing such criticism are those who work in Haiti by asserting their authority and agendas with limited consideration for local leadership and initiatives. The consequences, however, seem to be a widening of opportunities rather than more closely regulated invitations. Such regulation generally comes from a handful of highly responsible entities who are committed to breaking the trend. One of the latest meanings of Haiti being "open for business" is the possibility of the U.S. government working with Haitians in the public and private sector to bring U.S.-farmed peanuts to Haiti when in fact efforts to enhance and promote Haiti's own peanut farming industry were already under way.

Speaking to the Haitian scholar-activist Odette Roy Fombrun in 2002, I asked her how there could be ongoing faith in the ideals of international cooperation, during the 1930s, 1940s, and even in the present, when the historical track record was so poor in terms of respect and benefits for most Haitians. She suggested that hope is greater than the failures and disappointments. Pushing toward the ideal on each occasion, she said, generates the possibility of another step forward. What this message suggests to me is that the results of that push can only be as good as the choices and actions of the men and women who live in a given moment, and whether those efforts align or fail to align with the ideal being pursued.

With a focus on the 1930s and 1940s, *Haiti and the Uses of America* is about a transitional period that infused tremendous hope and expectation among a broadening number of Haitians about the value of their contacts with individuals and institutions from the United States. Although the needs that the programs and initiatives were intended to address endure, so do expectations and attempts to be successful in this approach. Perhaps in gaining a glimpse of an early moment when a broad segment of Haitian society invested in and expected positive outcomes from their ties to the United States, we can understand why some of those hopes endure and better appreciate the choices to be made in order to witness favorable outcomes for all impacted by such efforts.

Note on Terminology and Language

The term *America* is used in several ways throughout the text, but most often to refer to the United States and in turn its citizens (Americans). I am highly conscious of scholarly and popular attempts to use alternative terms (e.g., U.S. Americans), in an effort to avoid privileging the United States before other countries in the hemisphere that could have equal claim to an "American" identity. To maintain consistency with the term that the contemporaries I study use, and in the absence of a satisfactory alternative that is linguistically fluid, I use the terms as described above. Also, as Walter Mignolo has already eloquently discussed in *The Idea of Latin America* (Wiley-Blackwell, 2005), the term "American" is in itself an idea. The attribution of "America" or "American" to other places and people in the Caribbean, North, Central, or South America is but an extension of that idea, in that it too privileges a more recent history above the indigenous one that precedes the first uses of the term *America*. In recognizing and writing about that history, however, there are several places in this text, most notably in chapters 1 and 3, where I make reference to this broader concept of "America" to discuss the articulation of a shared identity by individuals from across each of these geographical locations (e.g., Americas, inter-American, Pan-American). In fact, part of the larger argument of this book is how Haitian men and women sought to establish their central place in that "American" identity, as well as how they used that concept of shared identity to pursue various goals.

Unless otherwise specified, all translations in the text are mine.

Haiti and the Uses of America

Introduction

On November 28, 1944, Jean Price-Mars, one of Haiti's most widely respected public intellectuals and statesmen, addressed Nelson A. Rockefeller at the headquarters of the Haitian-American Institute in downtown Port-au-Prince. At the time, Price-Mars was president of the Institute and Rockefeller was U.S. president Franklin D. Roosevelt's Coordinator for the Office of Inter-American Affairs. Together, the Office and Haitian president Élie Lescot's administration, which Price-Mars represented, co-funded the Institute they had created in 1942. At the Institute, members of Haiti's privileged urban class had access to a library, meeting room, and art gallery; they could attend classical and folkloric music concerts, and take English language courses (plans for French classes were under way). Additionally, the Institute awarded study-abroad scholarships to young Haitians who were, as Price-Mars described it, "in a position to appreciate the value of North America's civilization and . . . who were in need of additional knowledge in any branch of intellectual or professional culture."[1]

In his formal address to Rockefeller that day, Price-Mars emphasized the importance of cultivating "cooperation between Haitians and Americans on a cultural front." Viewing culture as something more than the sharing of art and various traditions merely for their aesthetic value, Price-Mars celebrated the Institute as a site for the enrichment of one's mind. According to Price-Mars, each encounter between Haitians and Americans—whether through the arts, exposure to social customs, or educational enterprises—was a vehicle that could facilitate the mutual enrichment of both peoples as they were introduced or re-introduced to one another, as they became more familiar with each other's contemporary society and historic achievements, as they dialogued and learned from one another, and as they opened themselves to collaboration on projects of shared interest.[2]

When Price-Mars met with Rockefeller in 1944, he was fully committed to encouraging ties between Haiti and the United States by using what he called *rapprochement culturel*, a strategy he had relied upon when speaking about class issues in Haiti during the previous decades. Price-Mars believed that nurturing connections between Haiti's privileged, urban minority and its rural majority was essential to redressing the breakdowns in Haitian society that had made it possible for the U.S. government to usurp political, economic, and social control of Haiti through a military occupation that began in 1915 and ended in 1934. A decade after the occupation ended, Price-Mars argued that pursuing rapprochement culturel with the United States promised Haitians a way to overcome barriers from the past and to cultivate a relationship between Haitians and Americans that would yield concrete benefits for Haitians.

It is particularly striking that Rockefeller and Price-Mars met under cooperative conditions at the Haitian-American Institute when we consider better-known narratives about the two men, in the context of Haiti-U.S. relations (Figure I.1). Price-Mars is widely celebrated for inspiring an *indigéniste* movement during the 1920s, in which formally educated, urban Haitians claimed to defend their rural, working-class counterparts by protesting the social, financial, and political dominance of Americans in Haiti under the structure of military occupation. By contrast, Rockefeller was a member of one of the wealthiest philanthropic families in the United States at the time, and part of a capitalist elite with economic interests in Haiti who had come to establish financial control and pursue agro-industrial investments across the Caribbean and Latin America. In the face of mounting protests abroad and at home, as well as the financial costs associated with military intervention, U.S. officials employed cultural programs to soften

FIG. I.1 Nelson A. Rockefeller and Jean Price-Mars, seated across from one another, at the Haitian-American Institute in Port-au-Prince, Haiti, 1944. (Courtesy: Rockefeller Archive Center.)

their approach to pursuing commercial opportunities and to influencing political, economic, and social developments in the Western Hemisphere, thereby enabling the United States' international presence and influence through a structure other than occupation. It was within this context that Nelson A. Rockefeller created the Office of the Coordinator for Inter-American Affairs in 1940, during U.S. president Franklin D. Roosevelt's administration, and contributed significantly to this foreign policy tactic that gave rise to entities such as the Haitian-American Institute in Port-au-Prince (Figure I.2). Despite these realities, Price-Mars's views about rapprochement culturel encouraged him to preside over the Institute and to sit at the table with Rockefeller.

The encounter between Jean Price-Mars and Nelson A. Rockefeller points to the necessity of adding a layer of analysis to the history of Haiti-U.S. relations, which has been overly dominated by scholarly and popular narratives that emphasize (U.S.) domination and (Haitian) resistance. A more nuanced lens gives us room to take into account the fact that a segment of Haiti's educated, urban population—notably some officials, intellectuals, and members of Haiti's skilled and professional class—envisioned cultivating ties with the United States as potentially useful despite familiarity with

FIG. 1.2 Elements from dust jacket and title page, Coordinator of Inter-American Affairs, *Our American Neighbors* (Washington, D.C.: Public Affairs Press, 1945). (Design: Cameau Designs.)

and enduring concern about U.S. imperialism. A broader lens also forestalls the risk of assuming predetermined narratives where the inevitable and simple outcome of each encounter is the dominance of Americans over Haitians. U.S. power relative to Haiti has certainly been imbalanced and has negatively impacted Haitian society. However, the presence and influence of individuals and institutions from the United States in Haiti has not been without consequence for the United States or other parts of the world. Haitians have been more than victims or resilient agents in the history. They have been central players whose histories have not only been shaped by inter-American and international affairs, but who have also played a role in shaping those affairs. Seeing them in this way allows us to identify the historic moments, such as the first two decades of Haiti's post-occupation years, when new developments or an unexpected series of events could have or actually did unfold. It is an opportunity to see how far and wide Price-Mars's perspective carried, who else shared his views, and what some members of Haitian society anticipated that ties with the United States promised.[3]

Post-U.S. Occupation Promises

During the late 1930s through the late 1940s, a broad range of educated Haitian urban residents embraced the opportunity to cultivate ties with individuals and institutions from the United States and more than ever before publicly expressed appreciation for what ties with the United States promised. This practice led to a growing influence of individuals and institutions from the United States in the lives of Haitian citizens and in state-led plans for reforms in Haitian society. Haitians engaged in this practice anticipated an array of promising outcomes. They emphasized the possibility of improving one's economic or social status, as well as that of the larger society, by accepting scholarships to acquire skills through study in the United States or by welcoming American experts to oversee the training of Haitians and to pursue research in Haiti. They worked to institute reforms in Haitian governance and society through initiatives in education and public health, among an array of other areas. And they aimed to gain greater recognition for Haiti's significance in global affairs by promoting awareness of Haiti's cultural heritage, as well as its contributions to politico-economic matters of global significance. And while many of these pursuits and expectations were tied to the bilateral and multilateral agreements that Haiti's post-U.S. occupation officials entered into, they were not strictly driven by the interests of officials or standing administrations.

That is, in addition to state officials, Haitian participants were private citizens of a skilled and professional class that resided across Haiti. They were primarily in the capital city of Port-au-Prince, but also lived in the urban centers of Cap-Haïtien, Jacmel, and Saint-Marc (Figure I.3). They represented a range of the country's social and political categories, people who were dark-skinned (*noir*) and fairer-skinned (*mulâtre*), male and female, advocates of Haiti's folk culture (indigéniste), fond of foreign culture—most notably, American (Americanophile) and French (Francophile)—believers in socialist and communist reforms for Haiti's economy and society. They engaged in the era's activities individually, collectively, and sometimes at odds with each other.

Certainly, the Haitians most visibly engaged in internationalist activities that helped individuals and institutions from the United States gain further grounding in Haitian society were primarily members of a privileged segment of Haitian society. However, as historian Michel Hector has noted, far from being a homogeneous group, these middle- and upper-class Haitians were not necessarily unified in their perspectives or loyalties. They sometimes had fundamental differences of opinion.[4] Yet, most were attentive to the world beyond Haiti's borders and to the potential value of U.S. ties for their respective agendas. Consequently, a cross-section of Haitians with social and economic advantages participated in activities and promoted ideas that legitimized the place of individuals and institutions from the United States in the plans and activities that segments of Haitian society had access to.

The openness of a diverse range of Haitians to engaging with individuals and institutions from the United States was rooted

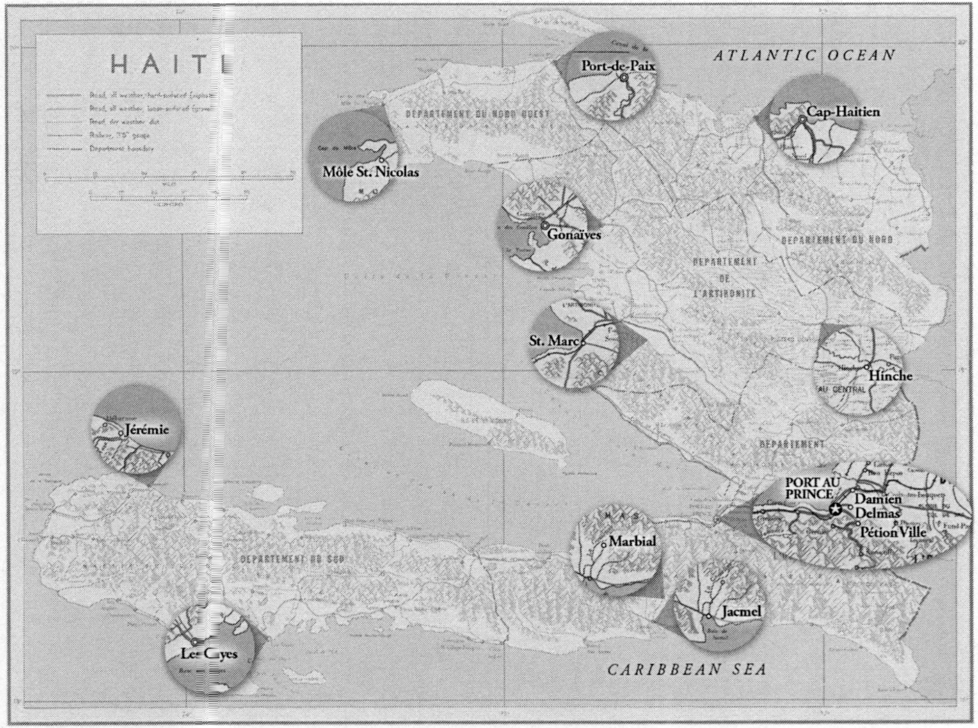

FIG. I.3 Map of Haiti featuring prominent cities. (Based on original UN Map 178/July 1949, Modifications by Cameau Designs.)

in the nineteenth century, when socially and economically privileged Haitian men and women looked abroad in anticipation that foreign resources and partners would benefit them when pursuing public and private goals. It was what historian Brenda Gayle Plummer has pointed to for the nineteenth and early twentieth century, and Glenda Sluga has illuminated for the post-1945 era: a cosmopolitan outlook. In their cosmopolitanism, segments of Haiti's population remained attuned to the relationship between domestic and foreign affairs—its advantages and challenges. Educated Haitian urbanites who tuned into the widespread circulation of inter-American and internationalist ideals in Haiti and around the world during the mid-twentieth century found in those ideals encouragement to include the United States in Haitian affairs more than ever before. Consequently, by the end of the Second World War, a generation of urban, educated Haitians came to use ties with the United States as a credible means of advancing plans for addressing their own social and economic needs, as well as those impacting other segments of Haitian society.

Haiti's first two post-U.S. occupation decades, the 1930s and 1940s, were a moment of transition between distinct eras and corresponding structures: from occupation to the end of occupation (*désoccupation*) in 1934, from an inter-American context to a more explicitly internationalist context after the Second World War ended in 1945, and from rule by mulâtres to noirs following a popular revolution in 1946. Within each of these moments, Haitians and Americans, particularly members of Haiti's professional class, had occasion to encounter one another and pursue their respective interests. Changing contexts gave rise to altered structures within which those encounters would take place. Still, those Haitians who were internationally engaged continued to consider a long-standing concern within Haitian society: what value, if any, was there in connecting with foreigners in general, and Americans in particular, when pursuing advancement of personal or national goals?

Haitians who were receptive to cultivating post-occupation ties with the United States included prominent figures such as Jean

Price-Mars, as well as Sténio Vincent, while he was president, educational reformer Maurice Dartigue, intellectuals and activists such as Dantès Bellegarde, Jeanne Sylvain, Max Hudicourt, and François Duvalier. They became part of a more ordinary professional class that began to grow in Haiti during the late nineteenth century. I say ordinary because not all of the men and women who appear in records from the 1930s and 1940s were prominent state officials, activists, or socialites. Their privileged status was less a function of the wealth they accumulated or prominent positions they held than tied to the knowledge, skills, or contacts they acquired. Educational and professional achievements positioned members of Haiti's professional class at the center of trends and developments that had the ability to impact Haitian society broadly. They worked in public offices, taught at national public schools, published and gave speeches, led civic or cultural associations, engaged in protest movements and reform projects across the island, traveled abroad, and welcomed the presence of foreigners in Haiti when they anticipated that such a presence could contribute positively to the advancement of private or state-sponsored goals. They were part of an evolving trend in post-U.S. occupation Haiti in which access to individuals and institutions from the United States generated social and economic privileges.

Haiti and the Uses of America draws attention to the existence and growth of a professional class in Haiti and encourages a discussion of Haitian society beyond the narrow binary of elite and non-elite, rich and poor. Indeed, an economically impoverished Black majority has existed in Haiti since the colonial period. But, those with a higher status in Haiti have not simply belonged to an economically wealthy minority. There has also been, particularly with the expansion of urban educational and labor opportunities during the late nineteenth century, a growing middle class and in that class, individuals who can be identified as noir and mulâtre.[5] During the post-occupation years, such opportunities for social and economic mobility also came to increasingly be associated with individuals and institutions from the United States. In this way, the post-occupation years were a turning point in Haitian history that popularized and expanded the instances in which Haitian men and women, across geographical areas and social classes, could use ties to the United States to elevate their status or the status of communities in Haiti. The post-occupation years helped to normalize the practice of looking to the United States to tap into resources for individual or national benefit. The focal point of such a practice would no longer be exclusively Europe.

Just as foreign elites, semi-foreign elites,[6] and native elites used ties to foreign metropolitan powers during the nineteenth and early twentieth century for economic, social, and political leverage in Haiti, the ties that individuals residing in Haiti made with individuals and institutions from the United States during the 1930s and 1940s created new avenues for personal advancement during the twentieth century. The affinities that Haitians built with U.S. culture, society, and institutions during the post-occupation years, the credentials and experiences that they acquired by participating in programs in conjunction with Americans, shaped elements of Haitian elite urban and rural culture, and created another avenue through which individuals could secure or advance their economic and social status in Haiti. In many ways, the opportunities reinforced existing class categories in Haiti. In other ways, they added new layers of prestige in which individuals could be associated with the United States. As the United States gained increasing status in world affairs, and as Haitian history unfolded in a manner that led Haitians to look to the United States (through migration or through institutional sponsorship) as a means of attending to individual, community, or state needs, the ties that Haitians had with individuals and institutions in the United States would offer them greater access to desired resources.

The Uses of America

Historiographical discussion of the interest a segment of Haiti's educated, urban elite had in engaging individuals and institutions from the United States has been absent in most texts about Haiti–U.S. relations. This is partly due to scholarly neglect in writing about the post-occupation period in historical accounts of Haiti and Haiti-U.S. relations. More so, however, it is due to the fact that the history of ongoing connections between Haiti and the United States during the 1930s and 1940s has been buried within writings about the legacy of U.S. hegemony during the occupation and the subsequent Good Neighbor Years. Works on the United States' foreign relations with Latin America and the Caribbean traditionally privilege the vantage point of individuals and institutions from the United States. Most scholars have helped us understand the ways that U.S. officials and citizens used policies and programs to present themselves as Good Neighbors who would end the practice of intervening militarily when concerns about political and economic developments across the region arose. Public figures and private citizens from the United States invested dollars, created programs, and pursued alliances around the world in order to gain control and influence over social, political, and economic developments globally. As historian Liping Bu has highlighted, Americans involved in these exchanges told themselves that these activities were the best way to "mak[e] the world like us [Americans]."[7]

However, understanding Haitian engagement with individuals and institutions from the United States in the wake of the occupation requires greater nuance. As the historian Frederick Cooper has suggested about the rise of economic development theories after World War II, it is essential that we acknowledge that some ideas were "a creation of neither the West nor the [Global] South, but . . . part of an historical process"—a dialectic. Paying attention to the ideas and activities of Haitians who engaged with Americans in pursuing technical, cultural, and educational programs during the 1930s and 1940s enables us to see that post-1945 international aid for development was a product of investments made by U.S. government and private entities, as well as partners and participants from the Caribbean and Latin America from the previous era. As opportunities with Americans became increasingly available in the United States and in Haiti or were funded with U.S. dollars, it became easier for the initiatives and ideas underlying them to appear to be strictly American. But, in reality, Haitians and other nationals were fully engaged in these processes. Documenting the processes as such shows that "the arrogance of the development idea came not from its assumption that one part of the world had something to offer another, but from the detachment of such a notion" from the men and women who asserted their own visions, and who sought to transform the political economic landscape of the world by participating in the emerging culture of international aid.[8]

As such, this book contributes to the trend in recent publications that highlights how public officials and citizens in the Caribbean, Latin America, and elsewhere engaged with and influenced the evolution of U.S. policy, rhetoric, and practices through their own petitions, protests, and forms of propaganda. Recent work by historians of U.S. foreign relations informs us that Latin Americans and Caribbean people were attentive to the U.S. government's proclaimed commitment to cease domineering forms of intervention in the affairs of other nations and to pursue more cooperative inter-American relations under the name of the Good Neighbor policy. Such works have examined U.S. foreign relations in places such as the Dominican Republic, Cuba, Trinidad, and Jamaica. The evidence and analysis in these texts reveal challenges U.S. officials faced when seeking to execute the Good Neighbor policy, such as overcoming the interventionist tendencies of earlier U.S. administrations and attempting to present U.S. officials as tolerant of racial differences. These works also document how the leaders and citizens of Caribbean nations evoked the rhetoric of U.S. Good Neighborliness in order to secure their respective interests, whether to secure employment or the support of the United States for decolonization from European rule. Other insights include greater awareness about the importance of the Good Neighbor policy for broader issues in international affairs, such as the political conditions that lend themselves to supporting authoritarianism, or how the political allegiance of these smaller Caribbean states was central to the waging of the more prominent Cold War.[9]

Seeing Haitians as complex historical actors does not require glossing over the often unequal character of Haiti-U.S. relations.

Rather, it is an opportunity to gain a more dynamic and less deterministic understanding of encounters between Haitians and Americans. As historian Gilbert Joseph has explained about the broader field of U.S.–Latin American history, "Turning away from dichotomous political-economic models that see only domination and resistance, exploiters and victims, Latin Americanists (like their counterparts in African, Asian, and European studies) are suggesting alternative ways of conceptualizing the role that U.S. and other foreign actors and agencies have played in the [Western Hemisphere] during the nineteenth and twentieth centuries." Such an approach allows us to see that although these encounters "are usually fraught with inequality and conflict, if not coercion," they are "*also* [ripe] with interactive, improvisational possibilities."[10]

By shifting our attention away momentarily from well-studied themes such as how others viewed Haitians, used and abused Haiti, and how Haitians reacted to this abuse, it becomes possible to account for Haitians as more than "objects" in the history of other people and places.[11] The Haitians who engaged with Americans during the post-occupation years were not simply capitulating to or protesting U.S. public officials or citizens who sought to implement American cultural agendas in Haiti. This is particularly the case in our understanding of Haitian mulâtres who benefitted from the racial prejudices of U.S. officials who privileged light-skinned Haitians over dark-skinned Haitians when making political appointments.

The political concessions (particularly financial) mulâtre leaders made to U.S. officials as Haiti transitioned from occupation rule to political sovereignty between 1930 and 1934 further reinforce the grounds upon which scholars have characterized mulâtre leaders as interrupting the nationalist agenda that mobilized diverse segments of the Haitian population in protest against the occupation.[12] As scholars of U.S.–Latin American and Caribbean history have written, "puppetry" is an inadequate means of explaining why or how some nationals facilitated U.S. involvement in their affairs.[13] Consequently, scholarly and popular perspectives which suggest that dark-skinned Haitians (e.g., Price-Mars) and mulâtres who aligned with indigénisme (e.g., Hudicourt), and to a lesser extent francophone identity (e.g., Bellegarde), were the only ones concerned with Haitian nationalism are no longer sufficient. There is room for further consideration of the collaborative stances mulâtres and other Haitians held toward the United States during the post-occupation years. And, as the first works on post-occupation Haiti have started to demonstrate, shared racial identity between African Americans and Haitians was only one basis of connection. Shared affinities regarding folk culture, inter-American ideals, capitalist and political interests led individuals from Haiti and the United States to enter into various forms of cooperation.[14]

Building on what classic scholarship by historians Brenda Gayle Plummer and David Nicholls emphasized, but that many have overlooked, these scholars of the post-occupation period reveal that political and economic interests generally trumped other bases of allegiance such as nationality and race. Consequently, there were opportunities for connections to become embedded in Haitian society, even while fervent critiques of Americans remained a reality in post-occupation Haiti. And, many critiques there were. Haitians and their international supporters protested against U.S. president Franklin D. Roosevelt when he refused to relinquish control of Haiti's finances at the end of the occupation, based on the argument that the U.S. government was securing the interest of U.S. bondholders. Further concerns arose in 1937 when Haitian president Sténio Vincent, members of his cabinet, and citizens publicly and privately questioned the soft stance that U.S. officials took against Dominican president Rafael Trujillo when anti-Haitian violence in the Dominican Republic led to the massacre of an estimated 20,000 people. And, in 1942, a new wave of protest emerged as Haitian citizens decried the displacement of Haitian farmers when a public-private venture, the Society for Haitian and American Agricultural Development, advanced under the administration of Haitian president Élie Lescot and U.S. president Roosevelt, launched an agro-industrial project to grow rubber plants, only to abandon the lands (by then devastated and unviable for farming) once wartime demands for rubber declined. Without relinquishing these concerns, numerous Haitian men and women stayed attentive to and engaged in the opportunities for making connections with Americans that they expected to yield advantages to them personally or for the projects they were committed to.[15]

Thus, if, as Brenda Gayle Plummer writes, the rise of nationalism during the occupation interrupted the cosmopolitan nature of nineteenth-century Haitian society, the post-occupation years were a time when cosmopolitanism and nationalism found fertile ground upon which to intertwine. Accordingly, Haiti-U.S. relations during the first two decades of Haiti's post-occupation period are best understood by paying attention to the ways that Haiti's politicians, intellectuals, professionals, and more ordinary citizens shaped and were shaped by regional and international contexts. The post-occupation period overlapped with the dynamic internationalist climate of the interwar (1917–36) and World War II (1937–45) years.[16] Alliances across the region (the Americas), and the world, gave rise to an era ripe with world-wide critiques of colonial empire and campaigns that stressed the merits of international cooperation. It was in this context that Haitian men and women were among the founders of and active participants in prominent international organizations such as the Pan-American Union, League of Nations, and the United Nations. Haitians who were open to articulating a cosmopolitan identity that encompassed a positive regard for the United States met with ample opportunities for their ideals to be reinforced. It was a time when a confluence of visions, activities, and events supported discussions in Haiti about the post-occupation period as a moment that held tremendous promise.[17] That promise entailed the hope that Haitians would be able to establish more equitable relations with Americans in order to generate foreign support for internal reforms across Haitian bureaucracies, opportunities for educational or professional advancement in Haiti and abroad, and diverse occasions for personal enrichment. Such developments make the post-occupation period a notable point on the historic continuum of Haitians who pursued ties with foreigners to educate and train themselves, and cultivate aspects of Haitian society in anticipation of greater social mobility, as well as economic, political, or cultural advances that could positively impact Haiti's international standing.

Accounting for a context beyond the bilateral dimensions of Haiti-U.S. relations offers an opportunity to better understand the evolution of relations between the two countries. The potential advantages of using a larger geopolitical framework are increasingly apparent due to the insights from a flourishing field on nineteenth-century Haiti. These works have shown that while Haiti may have been politically and economically embargoed by the era's major powers, diplomatic non-recognition did not prevent Haitians or foreigners who were interested in engaging with Haitians from interacting with one another. *Haiti and the Uses of America* brings to the fore twentieth-century evidence of the ideas Haitians embraced and the actions they took to assert a respected status for themselves in the world, as well as their contributions in the world. Doing so allows us to better understand that the place of Haitians in the development of international aid programs was not limited to the role of recipients, victims, or Cold War pawns.[18]

Making sense of Haitian involvement in building the post–World War II international aid system leads us to consider linkages between periods and processes that have been understudied or overlooked. This includes the fact that twenty-first-century ideas about the place of foreign experts and resources in a country's national reform plans are informed by the cosmopolitan outlook that Haitians have had as far back as their early nation-building period during the nineteenth century. Thus, *Haiti and the Uses of America* provides a narrative that places Haiti and Haitians at its center to encourage consideration of Haitian men and women as multidimensional actors who were not only the objects of the gaze, investigations, or the capitalizing ambitions and consumption of American officials, businesspeople, ethnographers, travel writers, or artists. Haitian officials, businesspeople, ethnographers, travel writers, and artists, among others, also considered the value of Americans in their affairs. They paid attention to, interrogated, sought to capitalize upon and consume people and things from the

United States. They actively explored how involving Americans in their plans might benefit them, their communities, their nation, and sometimes the world.

Chapter Outline

These themes and historical developments are examined in five narrative chapters. To discuss how and why Haitians were encouraged by the promises of the post-occupation years to pursue ties with the United States in order to attain personal, national, and/or international goals, this book begins by looking back at such practices during the eighteenth and nineteenth centuries. To establish the ways that inter-American exchanges laid the foundation for professional links to foreigners and for the kind of foreign involvement in national agendas which became a mainstay after 1945, the book ends after the Second World War.

Chapter 1 establishes that the links between cosmopolitanism and Haitian nationalism have roots in Haiti's colonial and early national period. The chapter draws on moments between 1791 and 1915 to present early evidence of Haitian statesmen and citizens who looked abroad, toward Europe and to a lesser extent toward the United States, to generate resources for state-led and personal goals, from the revolutionary period through the period immediately preceding the U.S. military occupation. These findings illuminate the fact that the post-occupation period was a turning point in the history of Haiti-U.S. relations.

Chapter 2 focuses on the occupation years to demonstrate that in addition to the well-known narrative of protest against U.S. occupation officials, some members of Haiti's educated, urban elite also expressed favor for the U.S. presence between 1915 and 1934. That favor was based on expectations about the ways that U.S. involvement in Haitian society could be potentially beneficial to Haitian political, economic, and social conditions. The chapter offers added insight as to why at the end of a nineteen-year military occupation, some Haitian officials and citizens expressed an interest in continuing rather than severing ties with Americans.

Subsequent chapters address the question, how did the idea that Haiti's ties to the United States could be beneficial, rather than detrimental, to Haitian society come to circulate more broadly in post-occupation Haiti? Chapter 3 highlights the ways Haiti's public officials, intellectuals, and other citizens participated in the campaign on behalf of Pan-Americanism, a regional ideal celebrating connections between independent nations in the Western Hemisphere. By establishing links between Haitian history and that of the Americas, those contributing to the circulation of Pan-American ideals served to normalize the perspective that U.S. involvement in and connection to Haiti could be beneficial for the Caribbean nation. These developments placed Haiti at the center of the international relations campaign rather than at the margins, where most scholarly accounts of Pan-Americanism tend to situate Haitians.

Chapter 4 extends this discussion with a focus on Haitian travel to the United States for advanced academic and professional training and Haitians welcoming Americans to come to instruct them in fields expected to contribute positively to Haitian governance and society. Such movement helped to normalize the place of individuals, institutions, and resources from the United States in the personal or national plans that Haitians made, particularly as concerned the professional status of middle- and upper-class Haitians.

In Chapter 5, a case study of Haiti-U.S. relations within the context of a United Nations Educational, Social and Cultural Organization (UNESCO) project that took place in Haiti's southeastern Marbial Valley extends the arguments in the previous chapter to a more international context. As Haitians and Americans turned their attention to the growing prominence of world-wide organizations more than inter-American organizations after the Second World War in 1945, the UNESCO project in Marbial illustrates how despite a shift in the structure of foreign influence and intervention, the interest that Americans had in Haiti and that Haitians had in the potential value of pursuing ties with foreigners, including Americans, endured. That local affinity reinforced and expanded the local relevance of a cosmopolitan sensibility and interest in securing a prominent position for Haiti on a world stage.

Finally, the book closes with an Epilogue that asks readers to consider: what were some long-term implications of this Haitian gaze toward the United States during the immediate post-occupation period? Some answers are presented through the history of Haitian migration to the United States and the efforts of Haitians to leverage their ties with Americans in order to pursue an array of goals. This evidence offers a final case for considering Haiti's deepening ties to the United States during the twentieth century, not merely as a product of U.S. imperialism or political conditions in Haiti, but also as a result of complex affinities that Haitian men and women have historically had for the United States.

1
The Promise and Peril of Foreign Ties, 1791–1915

In 1898, Haiti's foreign minister to Washington, D.C., Solon Ménos, proclaimed that to "fortify" Haiti's "moral and material position," it "sorely need[ed] and would be childish to neglect" being open to "the friendship of a great nation," what he referred to as "international intimacy." When Ménos spoke, his attention was explicitly directed toward the United States, who a decade earlier formally initiated a campaign of economic alliance with independent nations in the Americas. The result was increased trade between Haiti and the United States, which resulted in displacing France from being Haiti's leading trade partner. Further contributing to a decline in Haitian-French trade were French changes to their trade policy. When France began doubling tariffs on Haitian coffee exports and demanding a reduction in tariffs on their imports in Haiti, revenues that were central to Haiti's national treasury were negatively impacted. Ménos criticized France for having become "disdainful of [Haiti's] traditional bonds of friendship and culture." Ménos advocated for ties with the United States by declaring that the United States "usually wants to maintain . . . *good neighborliness.*"[1]

In trying to make a pragmatic case for forging ties with the United States, Ménos faced the dilemma of articulating whether it was possible to secure the perceived advantages of enhanced ties to the United States while explicitly rejecting local concerns about the implications of foreign, and particularly U.S. involvement in Haitian affairs. He himself relayed that foreigners were "the maker of [Haitian] discords . . . the shareholders and usurers of insurrections," and those who "nourished our civil wars." Yet, Ménos made his proposal that Haitians look away from their former colonizer, France, and toward the United States in the wake of contentious encounters between Haitian and U.S. officials since 1860 about leasing or ceding Môle St. Nicolas, a coaling station off the northwest coast of Haiti. What Ménos explicitly sought—the benefits of turning away from the colonial metropole (France)—was similar to the strategies employed by his contemporaries in places such as the Philippines and Cuba. Elites in these territories considered the advantages of shifting their commercial, political, and cultural ties away from their colonial power, Spain, and toward the United States. They did so even as the possibility of territorial occupation or annexation loomed large at the time, and eventually, became a reality. In the year that Ménos attempted to make his case for U.S. "good neighborliness," the U.S. military occupied the Philippines and Cuba, acquired Puerto Rico and Guam, and annexed Hawaii. In his petitions, Ménos explained that he "advocate[d] neither annexation nor protectorate, nor territorial concessions."[2] However, the United States' military interventions and territorial acquisitions in this period belied Ménos's attempts to deny the pernicious nature of U.S. expansionist ambitions.

Ménos's dilemma illustrates the historic challenge that Haitian officials and intellectuals had been grappling with since Haiti's early independence years: the challenge of whether foreign relations would impede or help Haitians advance their own goals. From the period of revolutionary war in colonial Haiti (Saint Domingue) and after the declaration of Haitian independence in 1804, leaders on the island pursued ties with France, with other European nations (most notably, Great Britain), and with the United States and the emerging states of Latin America despite continuous slights from across the Atlantic against the right and capacity of Haitians for self-rule. The decision of each Haitian leader to forge a specific type of tie was based on personal and strategic factors, and intended to reinforce particular agendas on the island. They pursued campaigns to secure political power, initiatives to educate individuals on the island, attempts to bolster the local economy, or efforts to contribute to contemporary international debates.

The profound desire to forge foreign ties on the island was rooted in Haiti's colonial history, its thirteen-year revolutionary war and declaration of independence from France. The existence of an independent Haitian state led by men of African descent challenged the principles that political and commercial leaders in France and elsewhere around the world relied upon to support the colonial system, and to secure their dominance in the world. By first making demands that led to the abolition of slavery in February 1794 and later declaring an end to colonial rule in 1804, Haitians called North Atlantic elites into question. They challenged the fact that these elites relied on the labor of enslaved Africans to fuel the lucrativeness of their economies *and* insisted upon racial hierarchies to impose order in their societies. Haitians made their demands by articulating their identification with and intent to expound upon contemporary discussions about individual rights. Moreover, Haiti's revolutionary leaders used military tactics that included assaults against the French, as well as the British and Spanish. Each of these European powers threatened re-enslavement and post-independence re-colonization of Haiti, and did so from the eastern part of the island (the territory of Santo Domingo/Dominican Republic).

In response to the insurgent stance that revolutionary Saint Dominguans and Haitians took, political elites from across the Atlantic World were quite calculated in their openness to forging ties with Haiti. The heads of France, Great Britain, and the Vatican, as well as Haiti's northern neighbor, the United States, delayed granting diplomatic recognition to the Haitian state. French recognition of Haiti came in 1825 on the condition that Haitians pay an indemnity for French property losses during the Haitian Revolution. Britain, as well as Denmark, the Netherlands, and Sweden granted recognition to Haiti immediately after

France recognized its former colony. Almost forty years later, the Vatican granted Haiti recognition with the signing of a concordat in 1860. And, as a result of political pressures from U.S. commercial agents and abolitionists during the U.S. Civil War, the U.S. government formally recognized Haiti in 1862. A protracted period of securing international diplomatic recognition meant that Haitians began their early national period grappling with severe international political and economic constraints. They faced the challenge of determining with whom it was possible to forge ties or with whom it would be best to do so. The reality was that that decision shifted with political circumstances; and, even when opportunities presented themselves, Haiti's leaders and intellectuals questioned the viability of particular alliances upon witnessing the pernicious practices of foreigners.[3] Thus raising the question: what place, if any, was there for foreign and, in the case of this particular chapter, U.S. involvement in Haitian affairs?

Nineteenth-Century Attempts at Good Neighborliness

The idea of "good neighborliness" preceded Ménos and the U.S. government's late nineteenth-century campaign for an economic and political alliance with independent nations in the Americas. From the outset of Haitian independence, Haitian leaders pursued "good" relations with their neighbors in the region and across the Atlantic, whenever possible, to secure economic and political autonomy on the island. They also pursued such ties to gain access to resources assumed to be beneficial for Haitian citizens and the state. Ultimately, these efforts were employed for the broader goal of demonstrating the potential of African and African-descended people for self-rule and full engagement in world affairs.

Transatlantic outreach was a prime means of challenging contemporary assumptions that Haiti's African-descended population was incapable of self-rule. From late 1803 through 1804, Haitian General Jean-Jacques Dessalines circulated proclamations across the Atlantic World to declare his commitment to an independent Haiti and to inform his audiences about the political principles upon which Haiti was founded. These proclamations reached newspaper audiences throughout the United States, as well as in Britain and the nearby British colony of Jamaica.[4] Such overtures continued despite political rivalries and turnover in Haiti. In 1806, Dessalines was assassinated and political power on the island shifted into the hands of two Haitian revolutionaries, Alexandre Pétion and Henri Christophe. Discord about which leader and political structure was best suited for the island led to the division and rule of Haiti as two independent states. From the city of Port-au-Prince, west across Haiti's southern peninsula, Pétion ruled his territory as a republic until his death in 1818. Meanwhile, Christophe ruled over Haiti's most prosperous port city of Le Cap south into Haiti's central plateau until his death in 1820. Although Christophe began his administration as a president, by 1811 he had declared monarchical rule over his territory. Despite these differences in governing structures, the leaders shared the view that there was value in forging ties with British abolitionists and the British monarchy, which held naval and commercial dominance in the world at the time.[5]

Without official recognition from Great Britain until 1862, Pétion and Christophe turned to private channels to pursue their interest in cultivating connections with the British. One such connection was with Robert Sutherland, a British merchant who was active and prominent in Haiti. Sutherland helped Pétion cultivate relations with the South American liberator, Simon Bolívar. Bolívar was the successor to Francisco de Miranda, who, responding to Dessalines's proclamations, identified Haiti in 1806 as an ideological and a strategic location to promote his own campaign for liberation in South America. Bolívar's connection with Pétion allowed him to secure refuge in southern Haiti, as well as arms, printing materials, soldiers, and funds to advance his campaign against Spanish colonial rule in South America. Pursuing close ties with Britain was also part of Bolívar's plans to establish sovereignty and international commercial opportunities for South America. Countering Spanish imperialism in the region, and securing ties with Britain for commercial and naval advantages were also a priority for Pétion. The re-institution of Spanish colonialism in Santo Domingo in 1809 and slavery in its provinces (re-established by the French, after Toussaint Louverture abolished it in 1801 during his occupation of Santo Domingo and the brief period of unification that lasted until French reoccupation in 1802) left Haiti susceptible from its eastern border.

Despite sharing anti-colonial sentiments and a desire to use international ties to bolster their political entities, the early connections between Bolívar and Pétion eventually faltered and led to the exclusion of Haiti from the most widely recognized first gathering of American states in 1826. It was evidence of the ongoing challenges Haiti's leaders would face in their pursuit of foreign ties. Bolívar had reached out to his neighbors, Haiti and the United States included, for support that would reinforce the revolutionary principles he fought for in South America; yet, given his political pragmatism, he eventually envisioned excluding Haiti and other states from a formal political union of American states. Bolívar sought to unify the newly independent nations of Spanish America in order to "present America to the world in an aspect of majesty and grandeur."[6] However, he also believed that it was necessary to present the newly independent Spanish American states as a culturally homogeneous and politically unified block whose alliance could offer a formidable defense for each nation's sovereignty and subsequent interests. Bolívar had explicit reservations about including states, such as the United States, Haiti, Brazil, and Mexico, that he felt would weaken the union's capacity to defend each nation. The exception to this rule for Bolívar was incorporating Great Britain (given its leading transatlantic status) into the union as a member or protector state.

It is in this context that Bolívar insisted on not inviting the United States *or* Haiti to the Congress of Panama (1826). As Bolívar described it, "The North Americans and the Haitians are foreigners to us, if only because they are heterogeneous in character." Bolívar had many other serious concerns that likely informed his reservations about affiliating with the two countries. He resisted domination, either by the United States, which he believed was culturally and hence, politically, superior to the South American states, or Haiti, which he saw as a "tremendous monster that . . . devoured the island of Santo Domingo." Bolívar's comment came in the wake of Haitian president Jean-Pierre Boyer's support of a military campaign in Santo Domingo to end Spanish rule on the eastern part of the island and his unification of the island under Haitian rule (1822–44).[7]

Boyer, who was Pétion's successor, supported anti-colonial campaigns in Santo Domingo to defend himself from domestic challenges to his authority launched from the eastern part of the island, as well as from threats of re-colonization by France or Spain, and from annexation by the United States. His action was similar to the unification strategy that Haitian revolutionary Toussaint Louverture had employed to extend and defend the abolition of slavery on the island between 1801 and 1802.

Such action led Bolívar to strategically avoid "a congress made up of diverse, weak, and conflict-ridden states [that] would have difficulty resolving American disputes or speaking with one voice to foreign powers." Bolívar resisted further identifying with African and mixed-raced peoples, whose presence in South America he already lamented as a cause of identity crisis and erroneously concluded had a poorer capacity for republican virtue. In his attempt to secure European support, and particularly Great Britain's mentorship and protection, Bolívar avoided allying with Haiti and the United States. His actions were likely in order to eliminate any postcolonial conflicts or penalties that might emerge by introducing former colonies of Great Britain and France into his political union. Bolívar's Pan-American commitment to ensure that his nation secured sovereignty, international respectability, and "access to the [international] bargaining table" shaped the choices he made when crafting a regional alliance.[8]

To challenge such marginalization, Haitian intellectuals such as Baron de Vastey and Émile Nau collaborated with Haiti's first political leaders to publicize the revolutionary currents and intentions of their political campaigns across the Atlantic World. Newspapers in the northern United States were, in fact, a major publishing site for the writings of several Haitian authors including Baron de Vastey who, in particular, was widely published, reprinted, and read in the early 1800s. Vastey served at the court of Henri Christophe, writing to defend Haiti, and more broadly, to defend Africans and the Black "race." With his words, Vastey promoted Black arts. He dedicated himself to responding to calumnious French writings. He decried the evils of the colonial system. He asserted the value of Christophe's administration. And, he made particular efforts to narrate the history of Haiti from a Haitian point of view. The writings that Vastey and his contemporaries produced are clear indications that elite Haitians did not see the United States as a threat but rather a "point of political comparison and departure."[9] Such a perspective was particularly possible because the United States had yet to establish its imperial prominence in the early 1800s. Vastey's contemporary, Émile Nau, wrote with a similar purpose during the nineteenth century. Nau emphasized that by developing Haiti's literary culture Haitians were developing their national culture. Nau wanted foreigners to read Haitian works as literature that was part of a larger hemispheric culture, as texts that had national *and* transnational value.[10]

By fostering ties with foreigners, Haiti's first leaders worked to challenge foreign detractors who dismissed the humanity of Haiti's citizens, the capacity of Haiti's leaders for self-rule, and by extension the legitimacy of the Haitian state. Haitian leaders sought to defend abolitionism, explore the best forms of governance on the island, pursue commercial ties, cultivate industry on the island, and defend the region from re-colonization. It would take more than a decade before Haitians began to make notable strides toward most of these goals, including securing formal recognition from foreigners, which came after 1825. Still, the connections yielded some modest results including frequent and favorable commentary about an independent Haiti, and particularly Christophe's kingdom, from several observers across the Atlantic.

Haiti's heads of state aimed to demonstrate Haiti's contribution to resolving the marginalization of Blacks and the discomfort of Whites living in the United States. Haitian leaders used transatlantic networks to promote African American emigration to Haiti, as a way to secure labor for the Haitian agricultural economy and to promote awareness about the unique circumstances for Blacks in Haiti. Haitian officials worked with White colonization agents and African American churches to arrange African American emigration to Haiti. Among the most notable moments of such campaigns were the 1820s, and then again between the 1850s and 1870s. These were decades when the question of whether African Americans could be fully incorporated into U.S. society was heavily debated and contested, particularly in the period leading up to the U.S. Civil War (1861–65) and in the subsequent Reconstruction Era (1865–77). Emigration to Haiti, which Jean-Jacques Dessalines had also proposed during his rule, was a way of providing African Americans with opportunities that were not available in the United States, given the constraints of racial hierarchies and the existence of slavery. Such plans involved connections with Prince Saunders, an African American man who had been working with the prominent English abolitionist Thomas Clarkson. Saunders's visit to Haiti culminated in his joining Christophe's royal court. In the decades that followed, several other Haitian leaders used their foreign networks to promote consideration of Haiti as a place of refuge for African Americans.[11]

By the end of the nineteenth century, Haitians had broader opportunities to generate cultural and commercial connections within the region of the Americas. A notable occasion was Haiti's participation in the International Conference of American States (1889–90). Plans for the conference included meetings in Washington, D.C., and a railway tour of the United States intended to expose attendees to the rise of industry and technology across the country. Although other U.S. officials had evoked or explored the idea of "good neighborliness" and inter-American alliances, this gathering was the most public of such efforts, initiated by U.S. Secretary of State James G. Blaine. Blaine was the first high-ranking official to formally pursue a Pan-American agenda in U.S. foreign policy. Considering it a matter of urgency to cultivate ties between countries in the region in order to establish profitable trade relations, Blaine advocated for an entity that would support such activities. His formal efforts began as early as 1881, when he invited Latin American republics to a "Peace Congress of the American States," arguing that "the time is ripe for a proposal that shall enlist the good-will and active cooperation of all states of the western hemisphere, both north and south, in the interest of humanity for the common wealth of nations."[12]

By the end of the 1880s, top U.S. officials and investors had committed dollars and resources to developing an infrastructure that supported close relations between Latin America and the United States. That infrastructure came through the hosting of conferences, beginning in 1890 with a conference that led to the creation of an association called the International Union of American Republics, whose agency was first called the Commercial Bureau of the Americas, subsequently renamed the International Bureau of the American Republics at the next meeting, and by the fourth meeting in 1910 designated as the Pan-American Union. It also entailed a major publication for disseminating information about the region's affairs, eventually known as the *Bulletin of the Pan American Union*, and regional meetings on an array of political, economic, and social topics.[13]

As an important follow-up to the first Conference of the Americas, Haitian commercial agents and diplomats accepted an invitation from U.S. officials to participate in the 1893 World's Fair Exhibition in Chicago. The exhibition was of particular relevance to the inter-American initiatives, because the fair was branded as the Columbian Expo in honor of Christopher Columbus's 1492 landing in the Americas. Given that Columbus's landing was recognized for having taken place on the island of Hispaniola (the territory which became Haiti and the Dominican Republic), the Haitian government took particular interest in participating in the expo. Strategically positioned in the "White City," so named because of the majestic and gleaming architecture of the white pavilions, the Haitian government welcomed visitors with an entryway to the Haiti pavilion that featured 1492 (date of Columbus's arrival), 1804 (date of Haitian independence), and 1892 (four hundredth Columbian anniversary). Inside, visitors found exhibits of agricultural products, art, literary texts, and national artifacts of historical significance such as the anchor from Columbus's celebrated *Santa María* and the sword of Haiti's leading revolutionary leader Toussaint Louverture.[14]

The Promise of Foreign Ties

While leaders on the island primarily pursued transatlantic ties for commercial trade and political alliances, they also heavily relied on such ties to meet educational needs on the island. Since the colonial period, class and social status on the island were linked to the connections one had to the outside world. Those privileged to travel abroad or to work with educators who came from abroad gained access to education and skills celebrated for having origins off the island. Toussaint Louverture set the tone of continuing colonial traditions on the island by relying on France to educate the island's residents. As governor-general of Saint Domingue, he created provisions in the constitution of 1801 to establish schools staffed by French educators. He provided government scholarships for island residents to study in France. And, like privileged colonial Whites and other free persons of color in Saint Domingue historically did, Louverture sent his two sons to France for advanced education. Louverture's revolutionary comrade Henri Christophe followed suit in 1802 by sending his son Ferdinand to Paris.[15]

During the early national period, Christophe and Pétion used British contacts to provide education, which they believed would generate economic advantages, reinforce national security on the island, and secure political recognition for Haiti. The most evident ties were those forged by Christophe and two prominent English abolitionists, William Wilberforce and Thomas Clarkson. Through correspondence and visits with the two, Christophe secured a range of resources from his relationship with these men. Wilberforce and Clarkson brought educators who followed the then innovative methods of English educator Joseph Lancaster to work for the two Haitian heads of state. Lancaster's model recommended a monitorial system of education as the best means of ensuring that members of a society's industrial class also gained access to education. Christophe succeeded in establishing elementary schools and a Royal Academy in territories under his jurisdiction. Additionally, Wilberforce sent at least two agricultural experts, along with two plows, to provide farmers in the kingdom with technical advice on increasing productivity on local plantations. By such means, Christophe sought to defend Haiti from re-colonization and the risk of a reinstitution of slavery. He lobbied to gain political recognition from the era's leading political entities (France, Germany, the United Kingdom, and the United States). He worked to capture fair access to the markets of those states. And, he aimed to secure material, human, and financial resources to support his investments in developing Haiti's naval force, public works infrastructure, and legal, educational, and cultural institutions.[16]

By the mid-1820s, these efforts to demonstrate Haiti's civility and to secure a more reputable position for Haiti in international affairs became increasingly tied to Haiti's connections to France and the Vatican. The cultural exchanges that Haiti had forged with Britain and the United States during the early nineteenth century and efforts of Haitian leaders to de-emphasize or cautiously approach ties with France began to subside. Between 1825 and 1860, Haiti's executive officers did much to reinforce the place of France as Haiti's most important international ally. Increasingly, it became difficult for other foreigners to establish as significant a cultural presence in Haitian society. The bond with France was both financial and cultural. In 1825 Haitian president Jean-Pierre Boyer agreed to pay an indemnity to French property owners for lands and other assets damaged or lost during the revolutionary war, in exchange for diplomatic recognition and, thereby, a degree of insurance against re-colonization. In order to pay the debt, Boyer arranged for a loan from a French bank. Then, in 1860, Haitian president Fabre Geffrard signed an agreement (concordat) with the Holy See that resulted in the Roman Catholic Church's recognition of Haiti and the Haitian state's granting of "special protection of the government" to the religion in Haiti. As part of the agreement, the Church assigned clergymen from France to staff schools and religious institutions in Haiti. These clergymen not only represented the authority of the Catholic Church in Haiti but also independently carried out the administrative and instructional tasks in Haitian schools. Geffrard agreed to pay the salaries of these educators and provide curriculum guidelines via the Ministry of Public Instruction. These schools became the primary means of educating young Haitians and eventually the nation's most prestigious educational institutions.[17]

The predominance of French instructors in Haitian schools, and France's international reputation as a premier source of knowledge and culture during the nineteenth century fueled a Francophile outlook among most Haitian statesmen and intellectuals. For example, when it came to Haiti's cultural, educational, or intellectual affairs, the Haitian statesman Anténor Firmin, who passionately lobbied for Haitian trade with the United States, was convinced that Haiti ought to maintain its attachment to French culture. As he described it, the French language was the "best vehicle of human thought."[18] Historian Watson Denis distinguishes Francophilia from the francophone culture that previous scholars have discussed when writing about elite Haitians. Rather than simply drawing attention to the French basis of traditions and culture in Haiti, Denis describes Francophilia as a preoccupation with the consumption of French culture and the practice of elevating all things French to a superior status. He argues that the inclination of elite Haitians toward France was a strategy elected throughout the nineteenth century, particularly after 1860, to elevate Haiti's own identity in the world and apart from other emerging nations, such as the United States.[19]

The perspective expressed by Firmin and shared by other Francophile Haitians that France was a cultural and scientific mecca was one that loomed large in the plans and aspirations of statesmen and intellectuals across the region. Scholars and members of the general public usually emphasize Haiti's colonial ties to France as the basis of the prominence of France in Haitian culture. Yet, we gain an even more accurate understanding of such ties by acknowledging that the importance that Haitians attributed to France was a strategy employed across the Atlantic World. During the nineteenth century, educated elites in the Americas viewed France as the preeminent source of refined knowledge and social customs. For example, in Brazil, in addition to looking toward Lisbon, the Portuguese monarchy looked toward France for "models of aesthetic refinement for the new court," following a period of "fervid anti-French patriotism" after the Napoleonic Wars. Similarly, intellectuals in Mexico and Argentina validated France as a source of inspiration in plans for governance and establishing cultural traditions during their early nationalist periods. It was within this broader intellectual current of ideas that Haitian intellectuals celebrated France as a nation-building resource.[20]

Given that contemporary views about Africa were unfavorable and that the presence of African elements persisted in Haitian culture, Haitian intellectuals and politicians remained focused on Europe even as they proudly acknowledged Haitian self-governance as proof of the capacity of African-descended people. During the 1880s, Haitian intellectuals wrote prolifically to defend against deeply embedded beliefs that African-descended people were inferior and to challenge detractors who questioned the viability of an independently ruled Haitian state. However, their arguments aimed to distance Haiti from the Africa that was under colonial rule during the late nineteenth century by emphasizing pride in a glorious African past. Given the expanding colonial exploits of Europeans across the African continent and European justification of such action by arguing that Africans needed the political supervision and intellectual guidance of Europeans, the imperative of defending the legitimacy of the Haitian state intensified in the 1880s. Writing in 1884, the Haitian theorist Louis Joseph Janvier declared, "Haiti doesn't need to be protected by anyone to develop" in his volume, *Haïti aux Haïtiens*.[21] The following year, Anténor Firmin countered the positivist arguments that French writer Count Arthur de Gobineau made about the inferiority of African-descended people in *The Inequality of the Human Races*. Contributing to the emerging field of anthropology, Firmin published *The*

Equality of the Human Races, arguing against the widely held idea that humanity could be classified into inferior and superior races, with African-descended persons being inferior to Europeans. Haitian author René Depestre has described these nineteenth-century writers as constituting a "pre-negritude movement."[22] Turning to apologist arguments, writers such as Janvier, Firmin, and Hannibal Price erroneously argued that African culture and society had atrophied in the nineteenth century as a result of the continent's geographic isolation. To defend their own legitimacy and ensure their inclusion in contemporary world affairs, they emphasized that by contributing to the world's contemporary civilization, Haitians could demonstrate the capacity of African-descended people to achieve their full potential and a respected standing in the world.[23]

But, by the late nineteenth century, some members of Haiti's political and intellectual class were outspokenly critical of the focus on Europe and, particularly, their peers' reliance on France for the education and training of young Haitians. Démesvar Delorme (1831–1901), who served as Minister of External Relations and Minister of Public Education and Cults during Haitian president Sylvain Salnave's administration, argued explicitly for the need to develop Haitian schools rather than having to send Haitian students abroad to study. Two decades later, in 1889, the Haitian legislator Léger Cauvin presented similar objections to the Constituent Assembly at Gonaïves. By the 1900s, a few more Haitian educators acknowledged the value of applied education, as opposed to the classical liberal arts traditions that dominated the Haitian education system. These advocates saw vocational education as a way to improve Haiti's agro-industry by educating the country's peasant majority whom they anticipated would contribute to the fueling of industrialization in Haiti. They were not, however, simply reacting to the models that they viewed from abroad. Rather, they considered such models as part of a longer tradition of seriously questioning how they might address the internal and external factors impacting the evolution of Haiti's political economy.[24]

By 1906, the Haitian educator Fleury Féquière was lobbying for Haitians to embrace vocational models like those taught at Hampton and Tuskegee Institutes in the United States for Haiti's educational system. "I do not preach hatred of France to my fellow citizens, as some perhaps believe that I do," Féquière stressed in his collection of essays entitled *L'éducation haïtienne* (1906). He emphasized to his compatriots, "[we have] a real interest in knowing [the United States of] America, because there are Blacks in America and . . . we can see in [their experience] the expansion of a solid education instituted to make these men prepared for all of life's struggles." Féquière argued for a more objective approach to addressing the needs of Haitian society. While acknowledging concerns about U.S. imperialism, particularly the U.S. customs receivership in the Dominican Republic at the time, Féquière also called into question abuses that were internal to Dominican and Haitian bureaucracies. "We should not form a pretext to arguments about the benefits of imperialism," he wrote. In this way, Féquière sought to be generous in his praise and heavily tempered in his criticisms. He relayed his appreciation for the educational opportunities African Americans had in the United States. He noted that he felt further encouraged by observing French educators who traveled and had their own appreciation for pedagogical developments taking place in the United States. Such admiration, he stressed, was explicitly tied to the increasing prominence of the United States in agricultural, industrial, and commercial affairs worldwide.[25]

Féquière found a fellow supporter in Jean Price-Mars, who as inspector of public instruction (1912–13) also celebrated the model of technical training African American students were receiving in the United States. Price-Mars's own appreciation of the U.S. model was fueled by the insight he gained after hearing Booker T. Washington speak in France, and later on, visiting Tuskegee in 1903. Price-Mars had met the African American educator during the latter's speaking tour in Paris where he proclaimed the strides that African American, Native American, and foreign students were making because of the vocational and technical training they were receiving at schools such as the Tuskegee Institute, which Washington founded and directed. Price-Mars had traveled to Paris in 1899 as a young scholar funded by the Haitian government to complete his medical degree. While abroad, he ended up taking courses in other fields such as sociology and anthropology, and serving as a Haitian diplomatic representative, first in Paris and then in Berlin. Washington's ideas resonated with Price-Mars, because he saw them as a way to improve the social condition of Haiti's rural majority and to introduce educational reforms that he believed could benefit the Haitian economy. In 1904, Price-Mars traveled to the United States as one of Haiti's representatives at the 1904 World's Fair (Louisiana Purchase Centennial Expo) in St. Louis. While there, Price-Mars wrote Washington to arrange a visit at Tuskegee to study the educational model more carefully.[26]

Although most young Haitians continued to attend schools with classic curricula in Haiti, it appears that public officials such as Féquière and Price-Mars were not the only ones who were open to the pedagogical orientation being used in the United States. As revealed by historian Frank Guridy, students and parents from Port-au-Prince were among the thousands around the world writing to Washington to express interest in studying there. By 1908, students from Haiti, Cuba, Togo, and the Philippines, among other territories, helped to constitute an international presence at Tuskegee. Tuskegee records list Joseph Adams as the first Haitian student to enroll at the Institute in that same year. And, as a class photo from that year reveals, another Haitian student enrolled at that time was Alexandre Lavaud (Figure 1.1). Like the Haitian educators who advocated on behalf of the Tuskegee model, it was not that these students and their parents were unaware of U.S. imperialist practices or the prejudices that may have narrowed the range of educational opportunities available to them (e.g., learning carpentry rather than architecture or entrepreneurial skills). Rather, as Guridy argues, they recognized the chance to study at Tuskegee as one of the beneficial "opportunities created by the emerging imperial structure."[27]

FIG. 1.1 International representation in the 1908 class of Tuskegee Normal and Industrial Institute. Left to right and back to front: 1. Sierra Feijoo Saturnino of San Juan, Puerto Rico; 2. Edward Andreas Anthony of Lomé, Togo; 3. Bethuel Aldrick Pusey of San Andrés, Colombia; 4. Alvin. J. Neely of Newberry, South Carolina; 5. Malcolm Iwane Kawahara of Saga-shi, Japan; 6. Alexandre Lavaud of Port-au-Prince, Haiti; 7. Luís Delfín Valdés of Havana, Cuba. (Image created by A. P. Bedou, New Orleans, 1914. Courtesy: Tuskegee University Archives, Tuskegee University)

The greatest impediment to "good neighborly" campaigns and educational cooperation during the nineteenth century was the pernicious role foreigners continued to play in Haitian nation-building efforts, even after they recognized Haiti diplomatically. Haitian leaders continuously faced the challenge of finding a delicate balance between inviting foreign support and defending against foreign abuses. Writing in 1891, Ménos's contemporary Hannibal Price lamented that for "too long" Haiti's development had "been retarded and compromised by the . . . revolutions and disturbances ceaselessly stirred up by foreign merchants or by bankers eager to gorge themselves with Haytian gold, and to fish profitably in troubled waters."[28] Price's observations were based on the decades of collusion between foreigners and Haitians interested in securing political office or other advantages on the island.

Financiers from abroad seeking political favors and preferred terms of trade typically used their funds to tip the Haitian political landscape to their advantage by financing armed groups, known as *kakos*, formed to overthrow existing governments. In 1867 and 1889, U.S. commercial agents provided funds that facilitated the ousting of Haitian presidents Sylvain Salnave and then Floral Hyppolite from office. The influence of foreign financing, in this case and others, was backed by what Brenda Gayle Plummer has described as "a show of force." That is, ships from the United States and Great Britain, Germany and France circulated along the coast of Haiti during periods of civil uprisings, relaying the message that such disturbances could at any moment lead to a foreign intervention.[29] Such aggression, combined with the speculation, commercial smuggling, false customs declarations, and fraud engaged in by corrupt foreign officials who resided abroad and in Haiti, as well as the strategy of marrying Haitians that German commercial agents, in particular, employed to secure Haitian national rights, were some of the ways that foreigners came to occupy a pernicious place in Haitian society. Added to potential concerns about the financial exploits of Americans in Haiti, there was the fact that by the late 1890s, many

Haitians were familiar with the disparaging ways White Americans treated people of color, whether abroad or on U.S. soil.[30]

Recurring proposals throughout the nineteenth century for the Haitian government to lease or cede Môle St. Nicolas, a coaling station off the northwest coast of Haiti, to the United States, epitomize the fragility of Haitian efforts to enter into agreements with Americans that would not compromise Haitian sovereignty or integrity. As early as the 1860s, Haitian politicians (those in office and those seeking to secure power) used the Môle as a negotiating tool in their conversations with U.S. officials. The value of the Môle lay in its strategic naval location, for geopolitical reasons and for the purpose of expanding the United States' commercial reach across Latin America and the Caribbean. Territorial concessions to foreigners, however, were a contentious matter in Haiti, just as acquiring foreign territories, particularly those inhabited by persons of color, was unpopular in the United States. Moreover, U.S. officials such as James G. Blaine tied bold demands to their proposals, for instance requiring that the Haitian government allow U.S. officials to represent Haiti in Europe. In April 1891, when both Haitian and U.S. officials involved in deliberations over the Môle seemed to be equally interested in reaching an agreement, U.S. officials interrupted the potential accord by approaching the talks in an aggressive and dismissive manner. Rather than seeking a mutual point of agreement with the current administration, U.S. officials attempted to coerce the Haitian government into ceding the Môle based on an offer made by earlier Haitian administrations. Guided by racial prejudices, the officials from the United States presumed that they did not need to take the perspective of the Haitian government seriously. In the face of popular suspicions of U.S. interests and protests against Haitian officials who appeared to be yielding to American dictates, Haiti's Minister of Foreign Affairs at the time, Anténor Firmin, withdrew his support for the proposal to lease the Môle. Negotiations over the Môle repeatedly ended at an impasse.[31]

By the early twentieth century, commercial and financial developments led to a shift in which the Haitian government's debts were transferred from French to American lenders. In this way, Haiti's political leaders consummated their economic dependence on the United States. Between 1903 and 1911, U.S. imports to Haiti increased two-fold through the work of Syrian and Lebanese merchants, to whom U.S. creditors and State Department officials had provided U.S. dollars and passports to promote U.S. commercial interests and counter the growing French, German, and British commercial presence in Haiti. Even more significantly, during the first decade of the twentieth century, American financiers at the New York City–based National City Bank gained control over 40 percent of the Banque Nationale de la République d'Haïti's (BNRH) titles. In 1911, the National City Bank's vice-president, Roger L. Farnham, became vice-president of the BNRH. By 1912, the BNRH board was composed entirely of citizens of the United States. U.S. commercial contracts also proliferated in Haiti, most notably the 1910 agreement between the Haitian government and U.S. investor James P. McDonald. The investment was intended to fund the completion of a railroad project that a group of Haitian businessmen initiated in 1905. The track between the Haitian capital, Port-au-Prince, and the northern city of Cap-Haïtien, was planned as a way to encourage fig-banana developments on both sides of the railroad track in the central region known as l'Artibonite. Protests by residents of farming communities along the railway line, and dissatisfaction with the execution of the plans, led the Haitian government to stop making payments toward the project. As a result, the U.S. company began making claims against the Haitian state. The project became infamous as the Haitian state's debts increased for a project that did not fulfill its intended purpose.[32] The cost of a foreign presence in Haitian affairs was at odds with Haitian interests.

In response to the persistent threat of European and U.S. power in Haiti, a group of elite Haitians turned to cultural nationalism to defend Haitian sovereignty. Two among this group were the poet Oswald Durand and the composer Occide Jeanty who addressed their concerns about a possible military intervention by producing works that relied heavily on elements from Haitian folklore. As was the case during the period immediately following Haitian independence, not all segments of the Haitian population eagerly allowed European influences to trump local customs in Haiti. These cultural nationalists theorized that by valorizing Haiti's peasant culture and its African roots, they could defend the integrity and hence the sovereignty of the Haitian nation. Aware of the central role that Haitian peasants and laborers played in the Haitian economy at the turn of the twentieth century, Haiti's cultural nationalists argued that if Haiti's leaders acknowledged the value of what was local, they would be less likely to make compromises that could adversely affect the nation.[33]

Cultural nationalism that focused on Haiti's rural majority and folk culture remained on the margins of mainstream nationalist discourse until the late 1920s; but, curiously enough, when those ideas became more popular, they also became the very ground upon which a new generation of elite Haitians would find reason to forge ties with Americans. Keenly aware of the racial biases and the imperialist practices of their northern neighbor, and more in tune with the economic and cultural leadership of Great Britain and France across the Atlantic during the nineteenth century, few of Ménos's peers responded favorably to his call to reconsider their traditional bonds with France, in favor of closer relations with the United States. Throughout most of the nineteenth century, interest among elite Haitians for cultivating ties with the United States, particularly cultural ones, remained a minority phenomenon. It would take nearly three decades before Ménos's vision of rapprochement with the United States would come to fruition.

2

"With the Spirit of Friendship"

U.S. Occupation, *Indigénisme,* and Haitian Nationalism, 1915–1934

In 1931, a young professional and emerging public reformer named Maurice Dartigue published a schoolbook called *Géographie locale*. Discussing the need for such a schoolbook several years later, Dartigue emphasized that the book was intended to counter what he saw as a paradox in Haiti's educational practices. Namely, Dartigue decried the Haitian practice of relying on France for its textbooks. He argued that this made Haiti a "spectacle of a so-called nation 'independent and free' for more than 100 years. . . . [One that] has textually copied a system of another country [France] which is . . . completely foreign to our lives. We use books to study animals and plants some of which the children have never seen and which 99% will never see. As grown ups we have access to books about our country but our children have access only to books that refer to the rivers of France."[1]

The lessons in *Géographie locale* mirrored the early educational experiences of Jean Price-Mars, whose writings and speeches inspired the *indigénisme* movement of the 1920s in which young Haitian leftists embraced the idea that knowing about Haiti's local, folk culture was an integral way of defending against the U.S. military occupation of Haiti that began in 1915. When Price-Mars was a child growing up in an upper-middle-class family in northern Haiti, his father used Haitian folk tales to teach his son and other children in the community a wide range of lessons. Among those lessons was instruction about the local topography, which served as a window onto learning Haitian geography. Price-Mars advocated the technique of grounding instruction in Haitian realities as a way of encouraging members of the Haitian elite to consider the importance of learning about, and supporting, the education of rural Haitians.[2] It was in accepting a sense of connection to Haiti's rural majority that Price-Mars and other indigénistes strove to counter the conditions that U.S. government officials used to justify their authoritarian presence in Haiti.

Despite the parallels in the pedagogical approach in *Géographie locale* and Price-Mars's indigéniste message, Dartigue's primary sources of training as a professional and a reformer came through his affiliation with U.S. occupation officials. To date, records and recollections about Dartigue and Price-Mars do not reveal an intimate relationship between the two men. Furthermore, Dartigue did not identify as an indigéniste and he did not involve himself in protests against the occupation. Rather, he was deeply steeped in the Service Technique, a bureau that U.S. occupation officials created to circumvent working with Haitian officials in the existing Ministry of Public Instruction. Thus begging the question: How do we account for the overlapping agendas? And, what are the implications of such an overlap?

Existing narratives about the occupation suggest that there were two types of Haitians during the occupation: puppets—individuals who yielded to U.S. authorities—and protestors—individuals who resisted the dominance of U.S. officials over the Haitian state. Yet, the parallels in Dartigue's activities and the agenda encouraged by Price-Mars suggest that there was greater complexity to the ways that Haitians related to the presence of Americans in Haiti. The professional training and opportunities that Dartigue acquired through the Service Technique enabled him to establish a career for himself that was focused on reforming the Haitian state and society. One reading of Dartigue's involvement with the occupation bureau is that it was motivated by personal gain and the promise of social mobility. Another, however, is that such cooperation was strategic and emerged out of a belief that the resources of the occupied state could be deployed in the service of reforms that worked in tandem with indigéniste ideology. That layered understanding of Dartigue allows us to consider the ways Haitians could view their engagement with the occupied state, namely individuals, institutions, and ideas from the United States, as being in alignment with Haitian national interest. It was in this way that two agendas that in many ways were at odds with one another during the occupation also worked in sync. Consequently, by the time the occupation came to a close, Haitian officials who had been strategically engaged with Americans on behalf of goals that echoed the indigéniste agenda found ground to argue that there was a place for Americans in plans for post-occupation Haiti.

Establishing U.S. Authority in Haiti

The U.S. occupation of Haiti began when U.S. Marines landed on Haitian soil on July 28, 1915 and subsequently declared a mission to establish peace, governmental order, and to defend the lives and financial interests of Americans in Haiti. By the time of their arrival, U.S. officials were already entrenched in the use of military force as the way to protect their geopolitical and commercial prominence in the region, having occupied Cuba, the Dominican Republic, Mexico, and Nicaragua. In the summer of 1915, members of U.S. president Woodrow Wilson's administration used the assassination of Haitian president Vilbrun Guillaume Sam and the pretext of protecting U.S. lives and assets on the island to declare the right to establish an occupation force in Haiti. They expressed concern about political turnover and violence in Haiti without regard for the fact that commercial investors from the United States contributed to that turnover by funding politicians who mobilized armed groups (*kakos*) that claimed control across various regions in Haiti, and ultimately state power. In exchange for their financial support, these investors secured the economic favor of the politicians who secured their place in office.

The arrival of U.S. Marines was also an opportunity for Haitians who had a stake in the pacification of kakos to advance their own interests. Large-scale land proprietors and members of the commercial class were among those who welcomed the arrival of U.S. Marines. Without dismissing concerns about U.S. authoritarianism, these elite Haitians anticipated with caution how the foreign presence could be helpful. They were eager to see an end to the political violence that was disrupting production and trade. And, they hoped for more sustained control of regional or state power. They desired such conditions to advance Haiti's commercial activities. These converging interests led U.S. chargé d'affaires Robert Beale Davis and Haitian Secretary of Foreign Relations and Public Instruction Louis Borno to sign a treaty that authorized U.S. control of the Haitian state on September 15, 1915.

Similar to the very first treaty between Haitian and U.S. officials, signed in 1864, the language of the 1915 treaty emphasized amity. The 1915 treaty stressed that working together in "the most cordial ways," Haitians and Americans would have an opportunity to strengthen their relationship. The treaty proposed that Haiti–U.S. cooperation would serve to defend Haitian national sovereignty and support progressive development on the island. Set to expire ten years after its 1916 ratification, the treaty positioned Americans as the experts who would help Haitians establish a national guard and regulate Haiti's national finances, sanitation, public works, and agricultural affairs. Many of those arrangements would be established through at least seventeen subsequent bilateral agreements, signed through the final agreement to withdraw U.S. military troops from Haiti in 1934.

Some members of the Haitian elite had a favorable outlook about the American presence in Haiti at the start of the occupation. Two influential groups—commercial agents and Catholic clergymen—composed of foreigners residing in Haiti, as well as local Haitian elites, were early supporters of the occupation. Commercial agents of Syrian and Lebanese descent residing in

Haiti benefitted from the commercial contracts the U.S. presence brought. Haiti's French Catholic clergymen helped to spread the news about the United States' projects and missions by communicating with Haitians across the countryside, particularly to attack Haitian Vodou. Because they were concerned about the relationship between Haitian Vodou and kako resistance to the U.S. presence, occupation officials helped to pillage sacred sites, suppress local religious practices, and restrain the privileges of Haitian civilians. U.S. occupation officials worked with Haitian officials to eliminate rural forms of authority (known as the *chef de section*) and suppress bands of anti-occupation kakos by creating a gendarmerie based in Port-au-Prince. This national guard centralized traditional forms of military control while creating employment opportunities that helped to establish a new middle class. The occupation officials accepted Haitians as executive officials in the occupation government or bureaucrats overseeing the reform of civil service agencies.[3]

Yet, in many ways, it soon became apparent that shared assumptions about what aspects of Haitian society needed reform and the importance of defending Haitian sovereignty did not necessarily translate into shared perspectives about the approach Americans ought to take when fulfilling their supervisory role. As Brenda Gayle Plummer has described it, the breakdown came from "the question of who would administer and benefit from needed reforms."[4] The openly racist attitudes of many U.S. occupation officials negated the favorable opinions that some Haitians initially had about the potential contributions of U.S. citizens to Haitian society. The prejudices of U.S. occupation officials confirmed concerns some Haitian intellectuals had prior to the intervention about the racist and imperialist tendencies of Americans in their relations across the region. U.S. officials were heavy-handed when working within Haiti's ministries, which led to a continuous battle with Haitian officials who sought to benefit from American assistance without relinquishing control of their bureaucracies. U.S. occupation officials reinstituted a forced labor system to build roads and to support counterinsurgency missions against kakos across the island. These chain gangs, known as *corvée*, dated back to the colonial period and therefore were viewed by Haitians as particularly degrading. The conscripts were roped when working and detained under conditions reminiscent of the slave society that Haitians had proudly abolished.[5] Besides eliminating the resistance of kakos, the roads were intended to facilitate the occupation officials' surveillance operations and mobility across the island for military and commercial purposes.

Other abuses included excluding elite Haitians from popular social clubs, intercepting incoming and outgoing telegrams, censoring Haitian periodicals and arresting Haitian newspaper editors, and weakening a protectionist property rights law that Haitian officials had introduced at the time of independence to defend Haiti from recolonization. When revising the Haitian constitution in 1918, occupation officials used Article 5 to introduce a clause that extended the privilege of owning real estate to "foreigners residing in Haiti and to societies organized for the purposes of residence and agriculture, commercial and industrial or educational enterprises." U.S. officials used the new provision to justify their right to own property and become involved in Haitian education since the treaty authorized U.S. involvement in agricultural and commercial affairs.[6]

While Haitian and U.S. officials shared an interest in reforming the country's schools, tensions surrounded the proposed approach to executing such reforms. Consequently, there was ground for protest and varying degrees of consensus between Haitians and Americans about the extent to which Americans would be involved in Haitian affairs. Upon their arrival in 1915, various U.S. officers began by conducting health surveys and redirecting public health activities generally reserved for the poor to serve the U.S.-led Haitian gendarmerie. Eventually, care for the larger public was reinstituted by working with private institutions such as local hospitals and a branch of the American Red Cross that came to Haiti in August 1915. At the School of Medicine, Norman T. McLean, the U.S. sanitary engineer, sought to prioritize laboratory studies. The curricular changes that U.S. officials proposed countered the wishes of Haitian administrators and medical professors by reducing the school's traditional focus on clinical training.

To assert their respective priorities, American and Haitian officials resorted to making changes that gave occupation officials autonomous authority over Haitian institutions. In the case of Haiti's health services, the first change was to move the School of Medicine and the clinical courses to different buildings. By July 31, 1918, McLean carried out the flagrant act of closing the School of Medicine, declaring a need for reorganization. He then used the facility to house a newly created School of Nursing. An important institution for training and expanded professional opportunity for Haitian women was established at the cost of dismissing the authority of existing medical professionals. A smallpox outbreak later that year led officials to reopen and reorganize facilities to accommodate the public need for vaccines and treatment. By February 1919, Sudre Dartiguenave, who had been head of the Haitian Senate when the marines arrived and was elected by that same senate to serve as Haitian president under the occupation, signed a law establishing the Service National d'Hygiène. Similar to the approach U.S. officials employed in the Philippines and in Puerto Rico, an occupation bureau was charged with overseeing the colonized state's public health services and medical education institutions.[7]

While Haitian officials and U.S. occupation officials agreed upon the types of reforms needed for Haiti's school system, the conflict between them arose over plans for executing the changes. The reforms that U.S. Marines traveling across the countryside proposed were consistent with issues identified by Haitian ministers of public instruction and heads of state who were in office before and during the occupation. Shared concerns about the problems most in need of attention included the paucity of rural schools, the poor condition of the few schoolhouses that did exist, and a poorly trained, underpaid teaching staff. Haitian president Dartiguenave initially welcomed the opportunity to benefit from the experience and advice of a U.S. educational expert on how best to proceed. Officials went searching for an expert who had experience with a large school system, and with a French, Creole, and Catholic background. They selected Lionel Bourgeois, a former county superintendent of schools from Louisiana, who arrived in Port-au-Prince on September 11, 1917. After making his own investigations, Bourgeois emphasized the need to improve the salaries, ensure the training, and follow through on the supervision of Haiti's teaching staff. He believed that greater authority ought to be extended to the Americans, so as to enable their ability to carry out reforms in Haiti without their authority being questioned. Haitian Minister of Public Instruction Dantès Bellegarde concurred with Bourgeois's recommendations; however, he disagreed strongly with Bourgeois's approach to achieving the reform. Whereas Bourgeois recommended that twenty-six inspectors from the United States travel to Haiti to oversee the implementation of reforms, Bellegarde argued that occupation officials ought to recruit French educational experts.[8]

These diverging perspectives on how to best staff the reforms led to tensions in executing the agreed-upon agenda. In Bourgeois's opinion, the way to resolve the situation was to secure greater U.S. authority. Minister Bellegarde was concerned that American experts, having been socialized to view Blacks as capable of little more than menial labor, were not in the best position to support the education of Haiti's citizens. As was the case when dealing with the field of health, U.S. officials resisted any challenges to their authority concerning general education. This point of conflict resurfaced throughout the next decade, as U.S. occupation officials continued to present Haitian officials with plans for educational reform that relied on American experts and refused to support the preference of Haitian officials for French experts. U.S. officials asserted their power over the situation through their control of the Haitian budget. When Bellegarde attempted to implement his own plan for increasing teacher salaries, the U.S. financial advisor, responsible for approving Haitian requests for budget allocations, denied the request for funds.

Meanwhile, the U.S. financial advisor simultaneously fulfilled the requests of U.S. officials who began developing the Service Technique de l'Agriculture et de l'Enseignement Professionnel, an occupation bureau for education which opened in 1922. The Service Technique consolidated six existing Haitian schools that had offered industrial training for girls (the École Élie Dubois), boys (École Industrielle, École du Bâtiment, and École J. B. Damier), correctional education for boys (Maison Centrale), and technical studies in agriculture (École d'Agriculture). Service Technique programs focused on training professionals who would in turn instruct Haiti's largely rural population in techniques of farming, sanitation, and disease control (in plants, animals, and humans), and in industrial trades. Its aim was consistent with educational programs that Haitian officials had already started to put in place. Still, Haitian officials criticized the Service Technique because it drained resources from Haiti's other national schools and privileged a vocational curriculum above the classical curriculum that was traditionally at the core of Haiti's education system. On fiscal and ideological grounds, Haiti's Minister of Education Bellegarde argued against investing in educational programs that reinforced the idea of Haitians as laborers.[9]

Besides the anger felt within Haiti's ministries, Haiti's rural and urban residents had become increasingly resentful of the violence and political heavy-handedness that U.S. officials relied on to establish their authority on the island. Haiti's urban elite also faced harassment. Their social mobility was suppressed through summary arrests, the imposition of curfews, exclusion and segregation at local social clubs, and censorship of writings against the occupation. As a result of these conditions, rural and urban residents joined or supported the expansion of kako movements against occupation officials. The armed groups eventually garnered popular recognition as a twentieth-century revolutionary force against foreigners who challenged Haitian sovereignty. Members of the urban elite also began to speak and publish to domestic and international audiences, to express their outrage at the conditions of the occupation. In 1919, public concern in Haiti, the United States, and elsewhere around the world reached a critical point when occupation officials murdered Charlemagne

Péralte. A formally educated militant leader, Péralte had been leading resistance movements against U.S. control since the marines arrived. After his capture and murder, his corpse was placed against boards, as if crucified, and then photographed. Contrary to official expectations that circulation of the image would become a tool to deter further revolts, the images reinforced popular views of Péralte as a martyr.[10]

Mounting protests in Haiti, the United States, and abroad since the beginning of the occupation, but particularly in 1919, led to a 1921 U.S. Senate investigation into the occupation and a subsequent reorganization of the occupation in 1922. The authoritarianism and violence of occupation officials in Haiti were in tension with worldwide discussions on behalf of national self-determination taking place during the late 1910s. The political ideal was one that U.S. president Woodrow Wilson had popularized as part of peace negotiations after World War I and that many Haitians were committed to using to advance their arguments against the atrocities of the occupation. Through varied political actions, such as becoming a founding member of the League of Nations, and the emergence of nationalist organizations like the Union Patriotique in alliance with the U.S.-based National Association for the Advancement of Colored People, Haitians remained attentive to the ways that a climate of internationalism could help them hold the United States to its claims that it was a leader in modeling ways to achieve peace and progressive development in the world. Anti-imperialism protestors in the United States pressured U.S. foreign policy officials to avoid the social, economic, and political costs of colonial rule. The culmination of protests led the U.S. Senate's investigating committee to recommend that legal rather than military authority be at the head of the occupation, through the appointment of a high commissioner, and that more bureaucratic approaches be used in carrying out the terms of the treaty. In these ways, the U.S. Congress sought to temper the range of anti-imperialist protests challenging the integrity of the United States' moral authority.[11]

Subsequent to these power struggles, a quietly growing rapprochement between elite Haitians and occupation officials began to take place during the 1920s. This occurred as elite Haitian students and professionals gravitated toward the occupation bureaus that U.S. officials relied on to circumvent Haitian political opposition to their plans for reform, and as Haitian elites responded to what they saw as a more cooperative approach to fulfilling the treaty mission. Part of what facilitated the arrangement was a bureaucratic change. When the occupation began in 1915, the Ministry of Public Instruction was attached to the Ministry of Foreign Affairs. In 1922, Louis Borno, whom U.S. officials selected to replace the increasingly non-compliant Dartiguenave as Haitian president, reassigned the education portfolio to be attached to the Ministry of Agriculture. This bureaucratic restructuring supported the claims of U.S. occupation officials that their efforts to increase the focus on technical and vocational training in Haiti's education system was directly related to the mandate to improve conditions for the development of Haiti's agricultural economy.[12]

During this period, opportunities to work in these occupation bureaus allowed Haitians who were already of a professional class or had an interest in a professional career to work with American experts in Haiti and through study abroad. Consequently, these individuals were personally exposed to what ties to the United States could mean for their professional development and socioeconomic mobility. Advanced training in the health field was foremost among these opportunities. The U.S. High Commissioner John H. Russell solicited the Rockefeller Foundation Heath Board for assistance with missions in public health, sanitation, and medical education taking place under the Service d'Hygiène. Beginning in 1923, the U.S.-based philanthropy was able to advance its own interest in epidemic and tropical diseases by surveying hookworm and malaria in Haiti, and subsequently implementing control efforts in Haiti during the decade that followed. The foundation's work in occupied Haiti expanded to the field of medical education in 1926. They began with a survey of the medical school. Then, between 1927 and 1930, the foundation provided fellowships (*bourses*) for twelve members of the Haitian faculty and administration to pursue advanced studies at medical institutions in the United States and Canada.[13] Occupation officials expected that when scholarship recipients (*boursiers*) completed their studies they would return to Haiti and continue working with the relevant missions.

Similarly, Haitians affiliated with the Service Technique had the opportunity to study in the United States. In particular, students enrolled in the occupation bureau's teacher training courses in the School of Agriculture were affiliated with Teachers College, Columbia University. At the time, Teachers College was the institutional home of the pragmatist educator and philosopher John Dewey. It was also home to the Department of Rural Education, where Mabel Carney, a widely respected author in the field, had been teaching and directing the program since its inception in 1918. Carney had a reputation for supporting all of her students—Black and White. Maurice Dartigue was in his early twenties by the second phase of the U.S. occupation. He had come from Les Cayes with his family to Port-au-Prince, as a child, when his father became Minister of Agriculture and Public Works. In the capital city, Dartigue completed his secondary studies at Collège St. Martial and began a degree at Haiti's Faculty of Law before joining the first class at the School of Agriculture (1924–26) when his father died. Dartigue was among those who benefitted from Carney's mentorship, as well as the tutelage of occupation officials in Haiti. At Columbia, Dartigue took the Rural Education seminar with Carney. The few records pointing to Dartigue's relationship with Carney reveal that they shared exchanges beyond the seminar. On at least one occasion, Carney invited Dartigue and other Rural Majors to her home for a luncheon discussion. And, later on, Carney wrote letters of recommendation so that Dartigue could secure additional funds to continue with his studies at Columbia, where he completed a master's degree during the 1930–31 academic year (Figure 2.1).[14]

FIG. 2.1 Maurice Dartigue (first man seated to the right) in front of the International House (dormitory) with classmates and friends, including his future wife Esther Dartigue (seated to his right), New York City, 1931. (Courtesy: John Dartigue.)

By affiliating with the Service Technique, Dartigue was able to improve his economic situation and launch his professional career. Funds from the Haitian national budget went toward fifty incentive scholarships of $20/month for ten months when students enrolled in the program. This was a timely resource for twenty-one-year-old Dartigue, whose family was in financial distress after his father's death. The ability to generate income through his studies and by working in various positions following his enrollment at the school, while also establishing his credentials as a professional in the field of education, was of tremendous value to Dartigue. Beginning in 1926 and until 1929, Dartigue served as an assistant to occupation official Carl Colvin and later as a school inspector. From 1928 to 1931, Dartigue also served as a teacher in education and social studies in the Rural Normal School. In January 1928, Dartigue also became the first director of the Farm School of Chatard, a post-primary agricultural boarding school. In 1930–31, he was responsible for supervising the School of Agriculture's experimental farms. From 1931 to 1934, he conducted surveys and studies in the rural education division of the School of Agriculture. During this time, he continued his work as an inspector, specifically for rural and farm schools. In the course of a decade, Maurice Dartigue went from a first-year student in the field of agricultural education to one of Haiti's leading bureaucratic experts in the field, particularly later, as Minister of Agriculture, Public Instruction, and Labor (1941–46).

The professional experiences of Maurice's father, Manto Dartigue, also seem to have informed the younger Dartigue's decision. Like many educated Haitians, Manto worked in numerous capacities. He worked as a lawyer, as the proprietor of a sugarcane plantation, and in a series of political posts (Cayes representative to the national legislature, governor of the South of Haiti). He refused other official positions (a second mandate in the legislature, nominated successor to President Oreste Zamor), and traveled out of the country, first to work on the building of the Panama Canal (circa 1904/05), and later moving with the family to Curaçao for several months (circa 1914/15). Witnessing his father's experiences in Haitian governance, as a planter, as an individual who traveled abroad for timely opportunities, and someone who did not bequeath economic security to his family from his private legal practice, Maurice Dartigue may have been particularly open to the opportunities at the School of Agriculture.[15]

For other students, the incentive that their work would help usher in reforms within Haitian society was explicitly instrumental to their commitment to study at the School of Agriculture. Max Vieux was also a member of the first class of the agricultural school established under the Service Technique. Prior to studying at the School of Agriculture, Vieux pursued post-secondary studies at the École Industrielle des Bâtiments (Industrial School for Buildings) for four years, and then at the École des Sciences Appliquées (School for Applied Sciences) for studies toward an engineering degree for fifteen months. When the Service Technique began offering agricultural courses, Vieux decided to redirect his studies, preferring agriculture because of his familial ties to the field. His uncle was a businessman who owned a farm. His father owned a coffee factory outside Port-au-Prince in Rivière Froide, where Vieux lived as a young child. Vieux recalled that his classmates in the School of Agriculture were other middle- and upper-class students who came from provinces across Haiti. As Vieux described it, the added appeal of studying at the School of Agriculture for him, as well as other students, was that the program was not focused strictly on a liberal arts curriculum, but on scientifically oriented subjects that would prepare them to work as agricultural professionals. A generation of elite Haitians was getting to experience how ties with individuals and institutions from the United States could benefit their personal goals in life and allow them to contribute to the larger society.[16]

The link between career development and civic contributions that Haitian professionals could experience while working with the occupation bureaus, and the simultaneous resurgence of Haitian cultural nationalism during the 1920s, suggests why it became possible for a broader spectrum of elite Haitians to identify ground for engaging with individuals from the United States on behalf of social reforms in Haiti during the occupation. The ability to recognize those connections requires a reconsideration of the ways scholars to date have written about the significance of indigénisme during the occupation.

Jean Price-Mars has been most widely recognized as promoting an indigéniste outlook among Haiti's educated urban elite during the occupation. By generating a more profound awareness among his fellow educated Haitian urbanites of Haiti's working and rural majority, Price-Mars intended to create appreciation among elite Haitians for the majority's contributions to Haitian society, particularly through folk traditions and a sense of responsibility among elite Haitians for the life conditions of rural and working-class Haitians. Price-Mars believed that nurturing such cross-class connections was essential to redressing the breakdowns in Haitian society that made it possible for the U.S. government to usurp political, economic, and social control of the sovereign state.

Locally, the lectures and writings of the well-traveled Jean Price-Mars, a statesman, ethnographer, and public school instructor, inspired many of his students and influenced the discussions taking place in an array of literary and activist clubs. In *La Vocation de l'élite* (1919), Price-Mars called upon Haiti's educated elite to take an active role in defending national sovereignty and advancing the country's socioeconomic conditions. A significant part of that responsibility, according to Price-Mars, lay in improving the quality of life of Haiti's rural residents. Drawing upon the work of nineteenth-century Haitian intellectuals and cultural nationalists, Price-Mars aimed to stimulate a greater appreciation for and sense of commitment to Haiti's rural communities among the urban elite by emphasizing that there was yet-to-be-recognized value in the Haitian folklore that flourished in the countryside. In 1928, Price-Mars consolidated his views on these themes with the publication of the influential *Ainsi parla l'oncle*, an ethnographic survey of Haitian folk customs. Younger Haitian intellectuals and activists became interested in Haiti's rural culture for both its anthropological value and for the political reasons that Price-Mars advocated. Price-Mars's ideas were most influential among young Haitian students from this period, and on the rise of leftist movements in Haiti such as Noirisme, Socialism, and Marxism.

At the center of scholarly discussions about indigénisme and related movements is an emphasis on these developments as movements that were strictly in opposition to the efforts of a mulatto elite that was affiliated with U.S. occupation officials.[17] However, closer consideration of the rhetoric advanced by Haitians who affiliated or associated with the occupation reveals that the line between indigénistes and those working with occupation officials was not so stark. In fact, there are echoes and explicit connections between the two that allow us to see why those open to U.S. involvement in Haitian affairs saw themselves as committed to Haitian interests. The ideas driving receptiveness to indigénisme paralleled the progressive arguments about uplift—where elites helped to facilitate social and economic changes among other groups (urban and rural poor, Native Americans, African Americans)—that had inspired reform initiatives in the United States since the late 1890s and which U.S. occupation officials drew upon to carry out their mission in Haiti.[18]

Maurice Dartigue, first as a student and then as an employee of the Service Technique who took an increasingly important role in educational, agricultural, and labor reform initiatives in Haiti, falls within the group of mûlatre Haitians that existing narratives suggest were committed to ideas and efforts that countered the indigéniste outlook that Price-Mars encouraged. Yet, Dartigue's call for reforms during and after the occupation not only echoed those of his tutors from the occupation. They also echoed contemporary indigénistes who aimed to get members of Haiti's educated, urban elite to recognize that their failure to attend to the importance of Haiti's rural residents to Haitian nation-building led to the conditions that allowed for U.S. intervention in 1915.

In his capacity as director of Rural Education (1931–41), Dartigue spoke about the importance of using schools to promote a sense of community among all citizens. In 1928, he asked a group of first-year students taking pedagogy courses at the School of Agriculture, "what is the aim of the public primary school?" The majority replied, "to teach reading and writing to the children of the poor." As a way of encouraging an alternative mode of thinking, Dartigue published a textbook for the Service Technique entitled *Les problèmes de la communauté* (1931). The main focus of the text was the development of a civic consciousness among Haitian teachers and students. Its tone reinforced the ideas about uplifting the masses that informed the approach taken by occupation officials to carry out their mission in Haiti, and that also lay at the core of what indigénistes espoused. Stressing the importance of universal access to education through public schools, Dartigue argued that "an extensive amount of education among a small group does not facilitate the development and grandeur of a country." Rather, such a national status would be due to instruction across social classes: "a community [benefits] from the education of its majority." Dartigue's idealist vision positioned Haitian schools as the place where the "principles of communal life" would be found—"different individuals with different goals and desires grouped together," "children from all [of Haiti's] social classes, all on equal footing before the rules of the school, with the same opportunities to show their value and advance according to their own efforts."[19]

Dartigue also stressed the importance of nationalizing Haitian pedagogy by moving away from the prominence of French influence in Haiti's schools. Besides his call for lessons based on Haitian topography in *Géographie locale*, Dartigue emphasized the value of providing an education that moved beyond a classical academic focus. He argued against the production of graduates who became "candidates for a public function." He advocated on behalf of "practical" training intended for "social, political and economic amelioration of the country." Acknowledging that there were efforts, during the nineteenth century, to provide rural education in Haiti, Dartigue noted that the obstacle to this mission during Fabre Geffrard's administration was overreliance on French instructors. He praised efforts to train more Haitian instructors in Haitian schools, the site where students ought to be able to learn about "the Haitian milieu and what makes it operate" without "disdain." Student exposure to foreign cultures, Dartigue proposed, should be for the purpose of having "access to the world cultural heritage," and to use acquired knowledge to bring "changes and ameliorations" to the local milieu.[20] Based on the various initiatives Dartigue would pursue in the decades ahead, it is clear that he saw value in using the knowledge he garnered under the tutelage of U.S. occupation officials and their U.S.-based affiliates to cultivate his vision of a national community in Haiti.

That there could be synergy between the agenda of occupation officials, that of Haitians who supported them such as Dartigue, and the indigéniste ideas that Price-Mars advocated is further evidenced by an address that Price-Mars gave in October 1929 to students at the School of Agriculture. It is a rare but explicit indication that Price-Mars could be, at once, direct in his critique of American interactions with Haitians and supportive of what such interactions offered to his compatriots. In his speech, Price-Mars empathized with student concerns about the policies of occupation officials. However, he also made clear his support for the Service Technique's curriculum by reasserting his appreciation for models of vocational education from the United States. In his opinion, the occupation bureau programs reinforced the idea that elite Haitians ought to use their knowledge in service to the Haitian majority.

These were two positions Price-Mars advocated well before the occupation, but that the budding nationalist identity of the 1920s allowed him to make more successfully. Although indigénistes were not the only Haitian nationalists who expressed a concern for the majority, they, unlike other nationalists, lobbied against the elite's preoccupation with France and French culture as Haiti's preeminent source of knowledge, by celebrating the folk elements of Haitian society. In this way, indigénistes reinforced the efforts of occupation officials to challenge the long-standing centrality of France and more broadly, Europe, in Haitian plans for their society. And, they also began to embrace more explicitly their responsibility to the Haitian peasantry.[21]

The resonance between U.S. occupation officials' understanding of the relationship between the elite and the rural population with that of the indigéniste movement is also evident in nationwide protests mounted by students and employees of occupation agencies in late November 1929. Scholars of the occupation have noted that the strike began when privileged students at the Service Technique protested American director George Freeman's announcement that incentive scholarships would be reduced, to accommodate a corresponding allocation for students who agreed to complete field work and not solely academic work. Freeman defended his actions as a means of accommodating the increasing number of students seeking admission. Yet, he was also reacting to boursiers who had been paying local laborers to complete the manual training portion of the curriculum. The boursiers argued that subcontracting manual labor allowed them time and energy to focus on their academic studies.

Scholars have also emphasized the fact that the Haitian president at the time, Louis Borno, was also the target of protests. Critiques of Borno were multifold. Despite resisting the authoritarianism of occupation officials during the first years of the occupation, Borno came to support occupation bureaus, such as the Service Technique, administered by U.S. officials. Moreover, Borno and U.S. officials interfered with the fall 1929 election calendar, due to fears of the outcome. In the end, Borno announced that the election was cancelled. By working in political conjunction with U.S. officials, Borno subjected himself to heavy criticism.[22]

Considering that students protested against occupation officials and the Borno administration in 1929, it is worthwhile foregrounding that the student protests did not challenge the idea that there was a place for the expertise of U.S. personnel and institutions in Haitian society. Rather, they primarily challenged the approach taken by U.S. occupation officials. For example, soon after the strike began, Kent Melhorn, director of the National Public Health Service, noted that students from the School of Public Health who joined the strike told him that they did so not because they were dissatisfied with him or their program but in solidarity with the other students. Students at the Medical and Law Schools and at public and private schools across the country all joined the strike in sympathy, adding to the intensity of protests. The message to Melhorn, besides potentially serving as a means of ensuring immunity against any backlash, provides evidence that the protests were not a simple critique of American involvement in Haitian education and professional training. Similarly, Max Vieux recalled that during his days as a student at the School of Agriculture, he welcomed the opportunity to pursue the agricultural training, but was frustrated with the use of instructors from the United States who spoke only English. Vieux criticized the use of translators in such a context as ineffective. Haitian student dissatisfaction with the educational programs and bureaucracies installed by occupation officials was more about the implementation of the U.S.-sponsored programs rather than the programs themselves.[23]

The student strikes took on larger significance during the first week of December 1929, as mounting political dissatisfaction and economic hardship across the country led to widespread protest. With each new day, politicians, businessmen, customhouse workers, French Catholic clergy, and other residents across the country capitalized on the protests to advance their own critiques of President Borno and U.S. officials in Haiti. The Borno administration had introduced constitutional amendments that expanded the power of the president. Soon after, Borno announced and U.S. officials confirmed that popular legislative elections originally scheduled for 1930 were being cancelled. Alongside these political developments, a poor coffee crop in 1928, declining coffee prices, and excise taxes on alcohol and tobacco in 1929 led to discontent among Haiti's rural residents.[24] The competition of the large-scale agricultural producer HASCO (the Haitian American Sugar Corporation) and standardization proposals that impacted the economic viability of small-scale sugar and coffee production led to further critiques of the Borno administration.

During the first half of December 1929, authorities employed strong-arm tactics to regain control across the country. Things took a particularly violent turn on December 6 when fifteen hundred peasants gathered to voice their concerns in the southern town of Marchaterre, located outside the southwestern city of Les Cayes. The crowd met with twenty U.S. Marines who, sensing a threat, responded with fire, ultimately killing twenty-five and wounding seventy-five others. Borno and Russell quickly declared martial law to establish order in Port-au-Prince. Use of the Haitian Garde, the national armed force that U.S. officials mounted as another occupation bureau under the auspices of the treaty, only aggravated public sentiment about the U.S. presence in Haiti.

The Road to Haiti's Second Independence, 1930–1934

At the dawn of 1930, the protests taking place in Haiti drew local and international attention, bringing the question about what, if any, value there was in Haiti-U.S. ties to the fore. Haitians who were hopeful about continued Haiti-U.S. cooperation had to contend head-on with how they could reconcile what they valued about U.S. involvement in Haitian affairs with their commitment to upholding their personal dignity and authority over Haitian national affairs.[25] Some three decades after Solon Ménos wrote about the advantages of an intimate relationship with the United States, the issue of whether ties with the United States could work in service of Haitian national interests or whether such ties were simply an imperialist strategy by U.S. policymakers that only threatened Haitian sovereignty resurfaced with new urgency.

On the U.S. side of the matter, U.S. president Herbert Hoover invoked the language of Good Neighborliness to declare his desire for a new era in U.S. foreign relations that would set his presidency apart from that of his predecessors. As High Commissioner John H. Russell—who presided over the marine forces in Haiti—pushed for increased authority, President Hoover expressed an eagerness to cease responding to civilian protests with military action. Consequently, the Hoover administration began to explore strategies for tempering the political climate in Haiti and to pursue a successful end to the treaty mission.[26] Before his presidential inauguration, Hoover had notable opportunities to cultivate and convey his vision of the United States' role in the world. He served as one of President Woodrow Wilson's delegates to the peace talks at the end of World War I. In 1921, he was appointed secretary of commerce and within days issued a public statement on the importance of inter-American trade for the United States. Similarly, three days after his election as president of the United States, Hoover announced his plans to embark on a Goodwill Tour across Latin America, which took him to countries in South and Central America.[27]

To gesture toward a shift in U.S. practices abroad, Hoover responded to the 1929 strikes by acknowledging, during his first annual address to Congress, the need to facilitate a peaceful withdrawal of troops in Haiti and by appointing two commissions to investigate the character of the U.S. occupation in Haiti. "We still have marines on foreign soil—in Nicaragua, Haiti, and China," Hoover began. "In the large sense we do not wish to be represented abroad in such manner," he continued. Specifically discussing the estimated seven hundred troops in Haiti, Hoover relayed his administration's sense that "the solution . . . is still obscure." Thus, he petitioned congress for an appropriation of funds to commission a study of conditions in Haiti. "It is my desire to establish more firmly our understanding and relationships with Latin American countries by strengthening the diplomatic missions to those countries. . . . I know of no expenditure of public money from which a greater economic and moral return can come to us than by assuring the most effective conduct of our foreign relations." For Hoover, pursuing the end of the occupation (*désoccupation*) through diplomatic means was the best course for fulfilling the treaty, set to expire in 1936.[28]

Congressmen and politically engaged citizens in the United States drew parallels between the American occupation in Haiti and that of the British in India, the Japanese in Korea, and the obstacles to voting that African Americans faced in the United States, to impress upon Hoover the need for a new course of action in Haiti. Hoover's approach to addressing the situation in Haiti and political pressures at home, however, led him to face even further critique. The congressional commission charged with investigating conditions in Haiti began as a five-member body headed by William Cameron Forbes, former governor-general of the Philippines, which the United States had occupied in 1898. The commission, comprised entirely of Whites, excluded African Americans. The composition of the Forbes Commission mirrored precisely the type of racism and paternalism that Haitians and Haiti's sympathizers in the United States and elsewhere around the world had been protesting during the occupation years. The Forbes Commissioners lamented that among the Haitians testifying before the commission, only two expressed appreciation for the work of occupation officials. In an effort to address critiques in Haiti and abroad about the make-up of the commission, Hoover appointed an all-Black commission, headed by Tuskegee president Robert M. Moton, charged specifically with investigating Haiti's system of public education. Moton had previously been on the radar of U.S. occupation officials who a decade earlier unsuccessfully sought out his expertise for educational reform efforts in Haiti. After their studies, both the Forbes and Moton commissions advised that with some bureaucratic modifications,

Americans could play a constructive role in the development of Haiti's state and society.

While outspoken Haitians primarily expressed their desire to see a swift end to the U.S. military occupation, it was soon apparent that this view did not necessarily translate into a desire to completely sever ties with the United States. Those who believed that Haiti could benefit from continued occupation were in the minority. More commonly, politically engaged Haitians sought to take full advantage of the Hoover administration's movement toward a policy that emphasized a more cooperative foreign relations strategy and that sought to showcase inter-American relations as a model for resolving imperial conflicts in Europe. Such a policy, for elite Haitians, meant a more public opportunity to hold U.S. officials accountable to their public pronouncements in favor of bilateral relationships in which two nations interacted on more equitable terms.

Haitians attuned to the political climate recognized that 1930 was a moment when they were well positioned to use their international ties to attain nationalist goals. By drawing attention to the ways that Dantès Bellegarde and Louis C. Lhérisson sought to use the commission hearings to hold U.S. officials accountable to their political promises, historian Millery Polyné has provided illustrative evidence of this strategy. As educators and administrators, Bellegarde and Lhérisson had ample opportunity to become familiar with the significance of U.S. involvement in Haitian affairs. More than a decade earlier, Bellegarde had experienced such difficulty obtaining the support of U.S. officials for his preferred approach to implementing educational reforms that he remained vigilant in challenging American approaches. Addressing the Forbes Commission, Bellegarde expressed his faith in a redefined relationship by stating that he "'knew that [Hoover] was against the military imperialists' because of the comments [he made on May 2, 1927 as] . . . U.S. Secretary of Commerce at the Third Commercial Pan American Conference in Washington, D.C." At that meeting, Hoover spoke in "conflict" with the policy of U.S. president Calvin Coolidge's State Department when he critiqued loans for military purchases or war purposes as being a threat to peace. Bellegarde saw the commission meetings as an opportunity to advance the international ties to which, in his capacity as a Haitian diplomat and intellectual, he had long been committed. At a private gathering for the Moton Commission, Lhérisson stressed his belief that "Hoover's emphasis on nonintervention and military withdrawal from Haiti and Latin America, as well as 'systematic intellectual exchanges' and increased commercial investment, could provide a space for egalitarian agreements to ignite the Haitian economy, and in turn, ameliorate Haitian schools."[29]

The challenge for Haitians who were receptive to the Good Neighbor rhetoric of the 1930s, a period charged with nationalist protest, was identifying a politically acceptable place for Americans in their country. In the wake of the commission investigations, the Hoover administration agreed that Haitians should conduct elections that would reestablish the legislative and executive branches of their government, which U.S. officials had disbanded in 1917. Haitian men, the only citizens with the right to vote in 1930, would go to the polls to cast their ballots for legislators. Next, the newly elected members of Haiti's National Assembly voted for a Haitian president from within the legislative body. Candidates for the assembly ran the gamut from those well known for staunchly protesting the occupation to those who viewed it as in Haiti's "best interests."[30]

The fall of 1930 was becoming a pivotal moment in elite Haitians' imagining of the role they would accord to the United States in their national affairs and of the conditions under which they would allow the United States to assume that role. One month prior to the election, Eugène Roy, whom Haitian and U.S. officials had selected to replace the unpopular Louis Borno as the interim president of Haiti, explained that whoever was elected would necessarily take a conciliatory stance. Advising the outgoing U.S. High Commissioner John H. Russell, Roy stated that "any President coming into office will have to cooperate with the United States Government officials. . . . [T]hey might cry 'a bas' [down] to the Americans . . . when not in office, but . . . upon taking up the reins . . . they would find conditions entirely different than they had assumed, and would have to assist."[31] This was Roy's perspective from the inside. His words were reinforced, albeit with a slightly different tone, four days before the election by the editors of the conservative Haitian daily *Le Nouvelliste*, who declared: "There will be neither 'red' nor ultra-nationalists in the next Houses . . . no ANTI-AMERICAN, but only anti-conventionists and anti-occupationists." In the wake of "the severe challenges experienced [under U.S. military rule], the new Representatives of the People can only be . . . patriots, committed to work towards the liberation of their homeland, to free her from all trusteeship, above all to make her prosperous, respected, and swollen with pride." The editors noted that if Americans honored the principles of the Good Neighbor Policy then they, "beginning with President Hoover," ought to be among the first supporters of Haitian nationalism.[32]

When the results of the election came in, nationalist candidates won the vast majority of seats in the National Assembly. They elected assemblyman Sténio Vincent to the presidency. Vincent was a founding member of L'Union Patriotique, Haiti's most prominent elite anti-occupation organization. Vincent had been an adamant critic of U.S. encroachments on Haitian political and economic sovereignty and argued during his campaign for an immediate end to the occupation. These views had generated financial and electoral support across class lines for Vincent's candidacy.[33] The election of Vincent and other nationalist candidates led the editors of Haitian dailies to declare with certainty the triumph of nationalism and "the end of the American regime in Haiti." In the opinion of *l'Elan*'s editors, Haiti's nationalist officials were "the irreconcilable enemy of the Convention [the 1915 Treaty]," and these same nationalist were assumed to be "the party that will not cooperate with the Americans."[34] Just what the nationalist win meant for the future of Haitian ties with the United States remained unsettled.

Contrary to the nationalist rhetoric that challenged cooperation with Americans, very early on Vincent and his administrators did seek to sustain ties with Americans, and for reasons beyond the political constraints that Roy anticipated and that most scholars have highlighted. Haiti's newly elected officials expressed interest in cooperating with Americans because they believed such ties could prove advantageous to their plans for building a cadre of professionals for Haiti's bureaucracies. Thus, even though Haitian Minister of Foreign Affairs Pauléus Sannon insisted on promptly replacing U.S. officials in the government with competent Haitians, he also remained open to retaining a few U.S. experts. Writing to the U.S. State Department, Sannon proposed a plan to "Haitianize" his nation's bureaucracies by stating, "In every service or branch of service where there is a Haitian assistant who is discharging his duties with competence, he is qualified to replace the American supervisor." Transferring power in this way, he argued, was "the only practical means of preparing the way in time for the liquidation of the Treaty and of carrying out the intentions of the two interested Governments." Yet, in Sannon's very first Haitianization proposals, he petitioned for co-direction in the fields of engineering and sanitary works, particularly in agricultural and industrial development, as well as in the highly contested financial advisor's office.[35]

In the fragile transition between the protests of 1929 and negotiations of the 1930s, Vincent and his administrators carefully couched their requests amid favorable recollections of interactions between Haitians and American during the 1920s, with little to no commentary on any aspects of the relationship that might merit redress during the post-occupation years. For example, Maurice Dartigue, who after completing his studies quickly rose up the administrative ranks in the Service Technique and ultimately became Vincent's director of Rural Instruction in 1931, advocated on behalf of American contributions to reforms in Haiti. He emphasized the importance of tempering "puerile politics," and stressed that acknowledging whatever Haitians had gained during the occupation was an important strategy for acquiring long-needed resources for Haitian advancement. Perhaps based on his own experience and position, as well as his success moving through the ranks, Dartigue advanced uncritical arguments that solely praised the work of U.S. occupation officials. For example, he argued that they trained an "efficient" army and set up "laws . . . regulations and administrative principles that . . . kept [Haiti's public] services from falling into anarchy, inefficiency and misappropriation of funds." That vantage point was based on Dartigue's understanding of the United States' Pendleton Act of 1883, which established a merit-based system for government employment, as a model for the Haitian civil service system and the professionalization of Haitian administrators. However, he did not publicly acknowledge awareness about how prejudices had marred that process.[36]

Besides the contributions of U.S. officials, the Vincent administration looked to private sources of support from the United States. Cognizant of the support U.S. occupation officials received from the Rockefeller Foundation, Rulx Léon, Vincent's general director of the National Public Health Service, appealed to the foundation for "further aid in building, courses, or study trips." Léon was among the Haitian medical professionals working with the Service d'Hygiène who traveled abroad in 1922, with funding from the Rockefeller Foundation. Based on their own positive experiences, members of the Vincent administration advanced their plans for Haiti-U.S. cooperation with little caution about the critiques that had emerged in the preceding years.[37]

To defend their efforts to legitimize the role of American expertise, funds, and policies in plans for post-occupation Haiti, Vincent sought to redefine what had stirred criticism during the occupation as a nationalist and cosmopolitan agenda at the dawn of a new era in Haiti's history. In July 1934, he did just that while welcoming Hoover's successor, U.S. president Franklin D. Roosevelt, who sailed into Haiti's northern port city of Cap-Haïtien. Roosevelt's visit was part of his own Goodwill Tour across Latin America. The tour was designed to promote an image of the United States as the "good neighbor" intent upon establishing a new era in its relationships within the region—even as his administration refused to relinquish financial control over Haiti and other territories where the United States maintained financial receiverships.[38]

Before Roosevelt took office, Vincent and other Haitian elites were concerned about the impact of his presidency on Haiti. As assistant secretary of the navy, Roosevelt had been in Haiti in 1917, at the start of the occupation. As a result of this visit and subsequent bragging about his authorship of the revised Haitian constitution (a claim he later refuted as a being a misquote, when it was used to critique him), Roosevelt became widely known for his interference in Haitian affairs.[39] Because of this history, Vincent had made efforts to secure an agreement with the Hoover administration to end the occupation before Roosevelt was inaugurated as president. Once Roosevelt was in office, both heads of state recognized the importance of carefully narrating the meaning of the transition to the post-occupation years. Haitian dailies reported with much fanfare the fact that this was the first time an American president set foot in Haiti.[40] Haitians had a basis upon which they could shift their view of Roosevelt from being a foe to a friend.

Vincent impressed upon his Haitian audience that cordial ties with the United States were not only natural but also essential to Haiti's achievement of economic and foreign policy goals. As Vincent attempted to negotiate commercial accords with Roosevelt, he presented his proposals as favorable to the export of Haitian goods. He emphasized that to send products such as coffee and bananas to the United States was to access "un débouché [p]resque naturel" (an almost natural outlet).[41] Roosevelt's own words suggested that the burden of "good neighborliness" rested with Haitians themselves, with little reference to the actions of Americans or the United States' role in Haiti's recent past. In a speech during his time in Cap-Haïtien, Roosevelt declared his hope that when the occupation had ended, Haitians would look back on the occupation officials "with the spirit of friendship" and happiness, "remembering that they tried to help the people of Haiti." Sustaining that outlook, Roosevelt explained, would allow for "closer relationships of commerce" and what he assumed Haitians "desire[d] far more than commerce . . . a spirit of understanding and a spirit of friendship between not only [Haitians and Americans] but also [the] two Governments."[42]

FIG. 2.2 Postcard featuring parallels between Haitian presidents Jean-Jacques Dessalines and Sténio Vincent to promote the idea that the end of the occupation was Haiti's second independence. (Courtesy: Jean Fouchard Family Collection.)

However, the Roosevelt administration's retention of the financial receivership in Haiti and refusal to grant Haiti full economic sovereignty fueled political contentions in Haiti and abroad. Protestors questioned Vincent's level of commitment to advocating on behalf of Haiti's national interest and challenged his reputation for being a nationalist. In response to such protests, Vincent emphasized that his administration was firmly on the path to Haiti's "second independence" (Figure 2.2). Hosting Roosevelt in the north of Haiti at Vertières, where Saint-Dominguan revolutionaries won the final battle of the Haitian Revolution, Vincent pointed to a connection between the present and the past, declaring that "this second Vertières, very peaceful this time . . . is unfolding in the same setting as the first, in the midst of the same countryside that saw the last great feat of arms of our forefathers, in November

1803." As a challenge to anyone who might question his nationalist credentials, Vincent referred to himself as Haiti's "Second Liberator." Moreover, by highlighting that Haiti's transition to independence was being secured through cordial diplomatic relations—as opposed to the war that had preceded independence in 1804 and the diplomatic isolation that followed—Vincent defined 1934 as an auspicious moment.[43] The exact nature of that promise, and the extent to which a broader set of Haitians would be receptive to sharing in that vision, in spite of tensions from the past and points of disagreement in the present, is the history that unfolded during the post-occupation period.

3

Pan-Americanism in Port-au-Prince

Historical Memories and Urban Activities, 1934–1945

On September 8, 1934, less than one month after U.S. Marine troops left the shores of Port-au-Prince, the Haitian weekly *Le Temps* announced the upcoming broadcast of a one-hour concert featuring Pan-American themes on the U.S. Navy's shortwave radio channel, NAA.[1] These navy concerts had been aired periodically from an Arlington, Virginia–based station since at least 1929. After the occupation ended, the radio broadcast was one of numerous opportunities Haitian officials, intellectuals, and other members of the urban elite, particularly those residing in Port-au-Prince, had to be exposed to the idea that Haiti's ties to the United States were natural, could be cordial, and were of value to Haitians. Thinking about the nations across the Americas as interconnected and their relations to one another as something that held significance for the world was not new. It was rooted in similar politics from as far back as the late eighteenth century, but most notably from the nineteenth century.

In the mid-twentieth century, efforts in favor of inter-Americanism were distinct from earlier initiatives in that they penetrated more deeply into the society at large, much further than diplomats, individuals engaged in commerce, and a select group of intellectuals. In the years between the two World Wars, and particularly during the final years of the Second World War, diverse members of civil societies across the Americas participated in various ways in the Pan-American campaign. Foreign policy shifts initiated by U.S. presidents Herbert Hoover and Franklin Delano Roosevelt propelled the campaign, coupled with significant amounts of time, funding, staffing, and other resources expended by the U.S. State Department, other U.S. government agencies, and their private affiliates. These efforts accelerated during the Second World War (1937–45),[2] as U.S. officials sought to use Pan-Americanism to bolster wartime defense. The possibilities of securing the political allegiance of Latin American nations as part of the Allies, capturing economic opportunities that opened up as war in Europe blocked off traditional markets, and promoting new modes of stimulating foreign appetites for American culture and commerce, all undergirded American interest in Pan-Americanism.[3]

As in the past, however, Haitian engagement in the inter-American campaign was not mere acquiescence to the influence of U.S. foreign policy and practices. Neither was it detached from the critiques Haitians and others had made of the racist and authoritarian politics of the preceding decades. Much like their predecessors, members of Haiti's post-occupation urban elite sought to capitalize on the Pan-American fervor of the World War II years, using it to advance ideas and agendas to which they had long been committed and that were of particular relevance to their current circumstances. Consistent with the regional principle, elite Haitians understood that Haiti's relationship with the world at large and its regional neighbors, including the United States, was of great importance to Haiti's status in the world and, consequently, to accessing opportunities for Haitian society.

While they maintained a variety of affinities, agendas, and circumstances, the most vocal advocates of mid-twentieth-century Pan-Americanism for Haiti widely embraced several common themes: (1) that Pan-American ideals were at the core of Haiti's founding principles and national identity; (2) that the 1930s and

1940s was a historical moment when they could redress foreigners' past infractions toward their country; and, (3) that they could use the inter-American campaign to demonstrate Haiti's historic and contemporary role as a noteworthy contributor to global society. And, in ways that were distinct from previous manifestations of Pan-Americanism in Haiti, a greater segment of Haiti's cosmopolitan residents participated in the cultivation of these ideas. The pervasiveness of these ideas during the 1930s and 1940s meant that broader segments of Haitian society, including young schoolchildren, had opportunities to develop identities and perspectives about their society that were intimately connected to the larger world. In this they were akin to citizens around the globe who during this period were also developing an international identity within a variety of local interests and affiliations.

A "Moral" Case for International Cooperation

Haitian politicians and intellectuals viewed the Pan-Americanism of the 1930s and 1940s as an historic opening in their long-standing commitment to use international relations as a means of establishing a balance of power with the United States. Yet, recognizing that the moment was not completely devoid of the very hierarchies that they were working to overcome, they employed language and engaged in activities intended to help them access financial opportunities, defend Haitian political sovereignty, and secure a central place for Haiti in historical and contemporary understandings of international affairs. To safeguard potential gains in the near future, they most often expressed grievances in the context of the past and pursued opportunities for redress by emphasizing the possibilities of the present.

As Haitian minister to Washington, D.C., Élie Lescot lobbied for access to financing opportunities from the United States with political caution. Public platforms based in the United States such as Pan-American Union meetings and its *Bulletin* did little to encourage a critical stance.[4] Therefore, when writing to President Vincent in 1938 in preparation for a CBS News interview, Lescot said: "I am not of the opinion . . . that we would enter into many details [during the interview], for example speaking of the Fiscal Agency; this would not be for the moment good politics." Lescot was scheduled to appear on May 22 in the third of a series of Pan-American broadcasts on economic cooperation with foreign ministers from Honduras and Guatemala. His reservations reveal his understanding of the broadcast as a public relations event that featured Haiti as an engaged member in inter-American affairs, not a public space for contested political discussion. Lescot's cautious comments were likely tied to his hopes of securing assistance from the Export-Import Bank. The Roosevelt administration created the public financing entity in 1934 to stimulate the U.S. economy through foreign trade agreements. Four years after Haiti regained its political sovereignty through military *désoccupation*, Haiti's financial désoccupation had yet to take place. A U.S.-appointed fiscal representative continued to oversee Haiti's national finances, and the repayment of occupation-era debts financed by U.S. bondholders remained set to expire in 1947. Yet, Lescot advised Haitian president Vincent that "We could only in exposing our needs, discuss our hopes in mutual economic assistance—a normal logic of the Good Neighbor policy."[5]

Finding a balance between harshly critiquing U.S. foreign policy toward Haiti and expressing Haitian expectations, even a sense of entitlement, was a true challenge for any Haitian who dared to speak out within inter-American forums. Regardless of how willing or adept Haitians speaking publicly were about critiquing contemporary U.S. foreign policy toward Haiti, they frequently articulated their perspective in ways that focused on themes of moral redress, accountability, and positive expectations about the political moment. The Haitian educator and statesman Dantès Bellegarde, for example, described the long road to achieving the ideals of international cooperation and particularly the process of building a viable international organization, as one of "continual creation." He emphasized that the process depended on the "confidence and . . . good will" of nations, their "spirit of peace," and "sincere desire to collaborate." Central to this process were not only "political disarmament by the reduction of military forces and economic disarmament by the reduction of tariffs" but also the "higher work" of "moral disarmament . . . by the suppression of that hate and distrust that poison the life of nations."[6] Circa 1939, Haitian intellectual and statesman Jean Price-Mars declared that by fulfilling the era's Pan-American ideals, leaders from the United States and Latin America could redress the assaults they had waged on Haiti in the past. He noted that when the world's leaders failed diplomatically to recognize Haiti's independence in 1804, they "heavily handicapped Haiti's economic, social, and political development" and expressed the hope that current leaders would offer Haiti "the Christian charity and human fraternity" that Haitians had historically extended to their neighbors.[7] Similarly, in a pamphlet entitled *Toussaint Louverture: le précurseur de l'amitié américano-haïtienne*, Lescot advocated for Haitian gains in the twentieth century by referencing the fact that U.S. leaders ultimately defended the legitimacy of a slave society during the nineteenth century when they refused to support Louverture during the revolution, despite the international alliances he forged with the United States and England, when seeking autonomy from metropolitan France (discussed in Chapter 1).[8]

Haitian and American advocates of inter-Americanism during the interwar and Second World War years argued that addressing the foreign relations challenges Haiti historically faced could be central to building a model of regional cooperation, which could be instructive elsewhere in the world. In Price-Mars's words, Haiti could be a "test case" for actualizing the era's ideals. Pointing to initiatives on behalf of founding the United Nations, the leftist political activist Max Hudicourt declared, "[I]n spite of all the past failures of international efforts to preserve the peace, from the Hague conference of 1907 down to the League of Nations, the world today can and must establish a true peace in which the priority of the national interests over the common welfare of all people—the cause of the past failures—will be completely rejected." He further explained that it was his positive outlook about the postwar period "that warrants my relating the problems of Haiti, the problems of a small, oppressed people, to the question of world security and peace. Were there no hope for a new concept of international fellowship, it would be foolish and rash of me to presume to discuss the difficulties of my country at this hour."[9]

Writing for the inter-American organ *Voz de Haiti en las Americas*, Joseph Montllor, a member of the U.S. Office of the Coordinator for Inter-American Affairs and Haitian American Rapprochement Committee, argued that as a war brought on by Fascism and Nazism engulfed the globe, inter-American exchanges could be considered, in the hemisphere and abroad, as "signs of national virility rather than as symptoms of weakness and of the inability to assimilate." Montllor's earliest commitment to inter-Americanism took place when he was a graduate student at Columbia University in 1939 and continued when he helped organize his university peers into a permanent Conference of Latin American students. He leveraged those ideals in his career as a U.S. foreign service officer. Through his work, he helped to create publications such as *Voz de Haiti* and radio programs like "Le quart d'heure de Frère Hiss," which captured the attention of broad audiences in Haiti.

From Alejandra Bronfman's brief historical sketch of radio in Haiti-U.S. relations, we know that "Le Frère Hiss" featured scripted conversations in Haitian Creole between two fictional characters (Frère Hiss, a peasant, and Maître Jasmine, an urban intellectual) to relay weekly news about the war and its local significance. The show, produced in 1942 by the U.S. government, with the support of Haitian writers and actors, and commercially broadcast on Haitian station HH3W, is reported to have become a popular hit among Haitian audiences. In the years that followed, listeners sent letters and group photos to Nelson A. Rockefeller (U.S. Coordinator of Inter-American Affairs) revealing a regular audience across the city and as far north as Port-de-Paix. From these records and a survey of the local scene carried out by the Secretary of the local committee to explore the veracity of the letters, we learn that groups of five, ten, and in some places, hundreds of "peasants" were gathered on several Saturdays around small radios in barbershops and at storefronts. The success of this 1940s Haiti-U.S. broadcasting effort, made possible through a commercial radio culture that Haitian broadcasters stimulated during the 1930s, was a notable shift from the critiques occupation officials faced when they attempted to use radio to broadcast government-sponsored education to rural and urban audiences during the 1920s. Thus, with programming that emphasized the relationship between issues of concern in Haiti and events taking place abroad, Montllor described programs in rapprochement as a way to "overcome . . . obstacles that face[d] not only the Americas but the world as a whole."[10] For Montllor, like Hudicourt, Price-Mars, and others working toward rapprochement, individuals and governments around the world needed to recognize that their nation's strength could be enhanced through cooperation rather than through domination and resistance.

Haitian Historical Memories

Haitian intellectuals and officials commonly used Haitian history to advance their view that Haiti held a rightful and logical place at the center of the mid-twentieth-century campaign for Pan-Americanism. Referencing particular historical moments, they emphasized the interconnection between Haitian history and world history, the contributions of Haitians to the development of an inter-American approach to nation-building, and Haiti's significance in the evolution of regional and global politics. The three historical narratives frequently evoked were (1) the role free men of color from Saint Domingue played in the Siege of Savannah (1779–82), a decisive moment for Americans in the War of Independence; (2) the relations between Haiti and the world during the Haitian Revolution (1789–1804); and (3) the aid Haiti's presidents Jean-Jacques Dessalines and Alexandre Pétion, respectively, gave to Francisco de Miranda and Simón Bolívar as the latter led campaigns for South America's liberation from Spanish colonial rule (1806–19).

Prominent individuals like Bellegarde and Price-Mars, as well as lesser-known figures such as educator Max Gustave Chaumette, were among those who kept such narratives circulating during the mid-twentieth century. Between 1937 and 1944, Chaumette, an instructor of history and geography at the Collège Vertières, a secondary school in Port-au-Prince, spoke and wrote widely to demonstrate how, since the colonial period, Haitians had epitomized the Pan-American ideal. Making reference to the contributions of Saint Dominguans in the Battle of Savannah, as well as the alliances Haitian revolutionaries sought to forge with Americans during the revolutionary war in Saint Domingue and at the time of Haitian independence (discussed in Chapter 1), Chaumette proposed that the principle of inter-American alliance was already in play prior to formal Pan-American initiatives during the nineteenth century. As he put it, "The Pan-American ideal circulated in [Haitian] veins and [Haiti's ancestors] engraved it onto American soils with our blood well before the ideal was conceived . . . and revealed."[11] Although scholarly debates persist about which free people of color from Saint Domingue traveled to and fought in the battle of Savannah, the fact that a unit of soldiers did travel and participate in a revolution that challenged colonial rule provided Haitian Pan-Americanists with powerful evidence. Haiti's ancestors set a precedent during the eighteenth century for Haitian-American alliances.

Narratives about the link between Haitian history and Pan-American history most commonly circulated in educational settings and among formally educated audiences. For several years, Chaumette addressed students, administrators, faculty, and distinguished guests at annual Haitian Pan-American Day celebrations. He compiled materials to author and publish at least three books: *Considérations historiques sur le panaméricanisme* [Historic Considerations on Pan-Americanism] (1937), *Haïti et les problèmes panaméricains* [Haiti and Pan-American Problems] (n.d.), and *Le panaméricanisme à travers l'histoire d'Haïti* [Pan-Americanism throughout Haitian History] (1944).[12] Dantès Bellegarde promoted awareness of the Pétion-Bolívar connection during a Pan-American Day speech at Collège Simón Bolívar, a high school in Port-au-Prince. He later published the speech in one of Haiti's most prominent scholarly journals, *La Revue de la Société d'Histoire et Géographie* and in the Pan-American Union's regional publication, the *Bulletin of the Pan American Union*.[13] The two publications allowed Bellegarde to reach notable audiences. *La Revue* was the organ of a Haitian research group founded at the Lycée Pétion in Port-au-Prince in 1923. The roster of members included Bellegarde and other widely known and respected instructors from the lycée who had created their society to extend lessons they shared with their students to Haiti's reading public among urban elite circles, to promote awareness about Haitian history and society. The *Bulletin* meanwhile helped Haiti's intellectuals extend their reach outside the country. As the organ of the Pan-American Union, the *Bulletin* circulated amid readers in the twenty-one member republics. Besides being read in diplomatic, school, and university settings, public libraries subscribed to the *Bulletin*.

Writing textbooks was another way to impress messages about the international significance of Haitian history upon local schoolchildren. In 1938, René Piquion and Love Léger published a new edition of *Histoire d'Haïti*, a standard text in Haitian schools. The authors included the aid that Pétion extended to Bolívar among the facts mentioned in the textbook. In discussing the end of the U.S. military occupation as a key moment in Haitian history, the authors also highlighted the role of U.S. president Franklin D. Roosevelt and his use of the Good Neighbor Policy to emphasize how Pan-Americanism served to redress tensions in Haiti–U.S. relations, and in turn contribute to peaceful resolution of conflict in the world.[14] Outside of Haiti, Fritz Louis Dorsainville, who traveled to attend West Virginia State College, did his part to convey these narratives about Haitian history to his contacts abroad, by giving a speech to students, faculty, administrators, and visitors at his host institution.[15] These types of initiatives led President Vincent to publicly describe Haiti's citizens, particularly statesmen, diplomats, professors, technicians, and businessmen, as the members of society who were ultimately responsible for the advancement of Pan-American principles.[16]

Some Americans made it clear that they were willing to acknowledge the connections between Haitian history and Pan-American history, and were equally interested in drawing links to contemporary politics. A year before the occupation ended, U.S. Minister to Haiti Norman Armour proclaimed in 1933 that it was a "grand satisfaction for the people of the United States to remember the material assistance given by the Haitian people to the American cause of liberty." Just over a decade later, in 1944, U.S. State Department officials joined Haitian president Élie Lescot and members of a Haitian Coordination Committee to celebrate the unveiling of a plaque commemorating the participation of free men of color from Saint Domingue in the American Revolution. U.S. Secretary of State Cordell Hull spoke at the event, held in Saint Marc, the port city from which the Saint Dominguan participants departed for Savannah. In his comments, Hull referred to the events in Savannah as evidence of the freedom that both nations recognized and represented. He expressed hope that Haiti and the United States would collaborate once more in the postwar period.[17]

The key for some Haitian advocates, however, was to show that Haiti's role in modern history was not simply limited to ushering in the independence of individual states across the region; rather, Haitians were central to the evolution of the modern world's political values and systems. By identifying the relationship between Haitian and other independence struggles across the Americas, Price-Mars countered the idea that Haitian history was abnormal, of marginal importance, or of interest only because of its racial dimensions. He emphasized how Saint Domingue's revolutionary break from France was similar to revolutions elsewhere in the hemisphere, particularly in that the revolutions and the republics that came of these revolutions were all shaped by "doctrines that ennobled the eighteenth century." Moreover, Price-Mars noted that while foreigners typically characterized Saint Domingue's revolutionaries as brutes, delinquents who lay outside world civilization when recounting the revolutionary events leading up to Haiti's independence, they overlooked the fact that in addition to republican ideals, violence was central to all major revolutionary struggles in the Americas. Overall, Price-Mars sought to emphasize that in each of these struggles the fight against colonialism was an effort

FIG. 3.1 "The MOST EXCITING chapter in Pan-American history was acted out here . . . the great court at La Ferrière, citadel of the Emperor Christophe of Haiti, the Negro ruler who successfully defied and defeated the forces of the great Napoleon. (Inset) One of the hundreds of cannon that defended the fortress. Field expeditions of the Smithsonian explore such historical monuments, preserve the details of their eventful stories." Undated. (Courtesy: Frank R. Crumbie Collection, Box 5, Scrapbook 5, p.17, University of Florida George A. Smathers Libraries, Special and Area Collections.)

to escape class oppression and the privilege of a few.[18] Price-Mars's protégé, a young lawyer and ethnographer named Kléber Georges-Jacob, also sought to challenge those who might denigrate or minimize the broad significance of Haiti's history. In his 1943 homage to Toussaint Louverture, Georges-Jacob asserted that as a revolutionary leader, Louverture "does not pertain solely to the Blacks of Saint-Domingue. He belongs to Africa, America, all of humanity" and "the Haitian struggle was a human struggle that transcended the boundaries of towns, nations and races" (Figure 3.1).[19]

In these ways, Jacob and Price-Mars sought to promote awareness that the Haitian Revolution was more than a revolution in which Blacks eliminated and trumped White rule. They advanced interpretations of Haitian history in which race was not the sole and central factor shaping the revolution in Saint Domingue and the efforts to establish the Haitian nation. By presenting universal narratives about Haiti's revolutionary history, Jacob and Price-Mars aimed to present Haitian history in a manner that would allow others to broadly recognize and appreciate the significance of the revolution and by extension, Haiti, in the world. To discuss Haitian history beyond a racialized lens was not to neutralize or overlook the racial dimensions of Haiti's early history. Rather, it was intended to convey that Haiti's history was of positive consequence for Whites as well as Blacks. Historical memory became a means of defending the case for alliances and cooperation.

As compelling as these universalizing narratives of Haitian history could be, tempering the contexts of race and power also led to romanticized interpretations of the past and present.[20] Élie Lescot, who rose to the Haitian presidency in 1941, was particularly plagued by the challenge of addressing the complex tensions between the ideals and actual circumstances that informed early relations between Saint Domingue/Haiti and the United States. In an attempt to justify his commitment to strong Haiti-U.S. ties and Haiti's full participation in the Pan-American campaign, Lescot drew parallels between Toussaint Louverture and Franklin D. Roosevelt in a Pan-American Day Speech entitled "Toussaint, Precursor of Haitian-American Friendship." The speech was printed in pamphlet form and similar references to Louverture as an early supporter of Haiti–U.S. ties appeared on the front page of the April 7, 1942, issue of *Le Matin*. The focus on Louverture during the week of Pan-American activities overlapped with the anniversary of Louverture's death while imprisoned at Fort de Joux, France. Comparing Roosevelt's "sage politique de bon voisinage" (wise good neighbor politics) to the politics of earlier U.S. presidents John Quincy Adams, Thomas Jefferson, and Abraham Lincoln, Lescot presented the United States as the "Grand Ami d'Haïti" (Haiti's great friend). He went so far as to describe these U.S. statesmen as individuals who were all driven by an "ideal of Christian humanity."[21] In actuality, each of these presidents had reservations about Black rule born of a slave revolt and the viability of a society in which Blacks and Whites coexisted peacefully. The positive references these U.S. leaders made about Haiti were rooted in national self-interest. As discussed in Chapter 1, Adams and Jefferson, as well as several of their successors, pursued ties with revolutionary Saint Domingue and independent Haiti during the eighteenth and nineteenth centuries in order to secure access to commercial markets and political advantages. The existence of an independent Haiti was of value to other U.S. leaders, like Abraham Lincoln, because it served as a possible colonization site that would facilitate the removal of free people of color from the United States.

But Lescot also had interests, as did earlier Haitian statesmen and leaders elsewhere in the region. Preoccupied with maintaining good political relations with the Allied Forces during the Second World War, and securing prospective commercial advantages that came along with such ties, Lescot used historical references to evoke Louverture's role not only as the precursor in Haiti's domestic affairs, but also in Haiti's ties to the United States and England. He did so by emphasizing that "the Black leader showed himself disposed to conciliate . . . to establish navigation and allow American ships to enter [Haitian] ports . . . to facilitate [Haiti's] commercial expansion." Lescot aimed to tap into Anglo-American alliances to secure commercial opportunities for Haiti. It was a strategy similar to that employed by Christophe and by Pétion during the nineteenth century, as well as by Trinidadian nationalists in the 1930s and 1940s, to name but a few examples.[22]

The strategy behind sanitized references to early Haiti-U.S. ties is also apparent if we consider that Haitians who spoke about ties between Haiti and the world generally did not reference international engagements that could be read as exclusively race-based alliances. Thus, in comparison to the frequent references that Haitian officials and intellectuals made to the contributions of Saint Dominguans to the Battle of Savannah and the aid given to South American revolutionaries, they generally failed to note that Haitian presidents Henri Jean-Pierre Boyer and Geffrard invited African Americans to emigrate to Haiti during the 1820s and 1860s.

Nor did they speak about individuals from the British Caribbean who sought exile in Haiti as they struggled for liberty and rights during the nineteenth century.[23]

The challenges that mid-twentieth-century Haitian Pan-Americanists met were similar to those of their nineteenth-century predecessors: seeking inclusion but facing the problem of how they or others viewed Haiti in relation to Africa and blackness. As Brenda Gayle Plummer describes, "Pan-Africanism . . . [was] a way of stepping out of a discourse that did not privilege blackness, [and] Pan-Americanism . . . [was] a way of subordinating . . . particularisms in a manner that left the nation state intact." During the nineteenth century, Haitian politicians such as Anténor Firmin affirmed "blackness" but did not embrace "Africanity." Given that Pan-Americanism had historically been "constructed as white throughout the Americas," Plummer argues, Haiti represented a curious "anti-thesis" to the two ideologies.[24] Whether Haitians recounting historical moments were conscientious or not in sustaining such silences around race, these discrepancies suggest that invoking historical memories was not simply an opportunity to demonstrate Haitian pride, but also a choice based on assumptions about what would appeal to potential officials, donors, and lobbyists at the risk of alienating an audience or oversimplifying the history. By selectively evoking race, Haitian Pan-Americanists aimed for full inclusion even as their silences prevented that genuine possibility with each historical omission.

Pan-Americanism as Elite Urban Culture

As occurred elsewhere in the region, mid-twentieth-century Pan-Americanism was not only the domain of diplomats, commercial agents, politicians, and intellectuals, as was common during the nineteenth century. The expansion of Pan-American activities and circulation of Pan-American ideals also became a notable part of Haiti's social landscape across various cities, and particularly in Port-au-Prince, during the 1930s and 1940s.[25] Haitian journalist Max Charlmers implied as much when he wrote that the

Pan-American movement "owe[d] its vitality to the permanence of democratic aspirations found in the citizens of the Americas' twenty-one republics," of which Haiti was proudly one.[26] They drew on Pan-American themes to animate local schools, clubs, and a wide array of public venues. In a period when Haitian men and women continued to criticize U.S. policies toward Haiti, such as the enduring financial supervision and the pursuit of agro-industrial projects that inflicted hardship on the Haitian economy, many members of Haiti's urban elite also engaged fully in cultural activities they believed upheld the inter-American and more broadly, internationalist principles being widely discussed during the 1930s and 1940s.[27]

Dynamic engagement with Haitian history and Pan-American ideals, Jean Price-Mars suggested, was a means of facilitating *rapprochement culturel*, that is, the process of helping Haitians and Americans to better know one another, their respective societies, and their outlook on life. For Price-Mars, the urgency of a strategy of rapprochement culturel lay in his belief that it could eliminate factors that undermined the positive potential of the United States' participation in Haitian affairs. He understood "the goal of cultural cooperation between Haitians and Americans" to be "to dissipate the misunderstandings and errors of the past." Eliminating the "indifference" and the "prejudicial tendencies" Haitians and Americans had toward one another, Price-Mars argued, was essential to overcoming Haiti's historically tainted relations with the United States which in turn were an impediment to Haiti's national development. In his opinion, inter-American activities were about cultivating peace, justice, and human fraternity and challenging what he described as the weak, envious, and animalistic tendencies of the human mind.[28] In sum, by tackling human prejudices through cultural relations, Price-Mars saw a way to support the development of Haiti-U.S. relations on an equal footing.

Elite Haitians demonstrated their interest in cultural connections by creating and participating in a number of bilateral cultural institutions during the 1930s and 1940s. State-sponsored and private clubs of this nature were part of several intellectual circles that elite Haitians created to discuss their cultural interests and, for many, to debate the best ways of addressing contemporary challenges. These cultural spaces emerged in conjunction with other movements—such as surrealism, feminism, and affirmations of folk culture, which resonated with negritude (a global variation of Haiti's indigéniste movement)—that were popular in Haiti, as well as elsewhere in the world, during this time.[29] In an editorial appearing in the Haitian daily *Le Matin* on February 3, 1943, the Port-au-Prince–based lawyer and author Lallier C. Phareaux described his own appreciation for rapprochement culturel, explaining that by exchanging knowledge, individuals in Haiti and abroad could become more familiar with one another, develop greater sensitivity for one another's concerns, and garner a greater appreciation of what one could offer the other.[30]

Earlier in the post-occupation period, U.S. officials demonstrated concern about how Haitians viewed them. Yale University professor Charles T. Loram recognized that concern, especially when considering Haiti's historic relationship with France. Loram, who was widely respected in the field of education for his work on rural schools in South Africa, advised State Department officials that cultural programs could help them in their mission. He stressed that in addition to the technical and scientific collaborations already underway, U.S. officials ought to "do something along the cultural lines, not to counteract French influence, but to show a side of our [U.S.] cultural life totally unknown by Haitians."[31] In this context, U.S. Legation officials in Port-au-Prince took note of arguments by Haitian scholar Charles F. Pressoir about the advantages of Pan-Americanism versus Pan-Latinism for Haitians. Pressoir was responding to a French lecturer who advocated Pan-Latinism, that is, solidarity among societies with Latin-based languages and cultures, as a model for resolving current conflicts in Europe. Pressoir emphasized that because of Haiti's "geographic and economic situation vis-à-vis the United States," Pan-Americanism was more in the country's self-interest than Pan-Latinism. Moreover, Pressoir emphasized that beyond culture, human interests were what joined people together, seeing "continental necessities, historic circumstances, common anxieties, and the aspiration for peace" as the Western Hemisphere's binding interests. In other words, he stated, "Pan-Americanism does not signify for us [Haitians] exclusion but rather the development and adaptation of Latinism."[32] By speaking of French and U.S. traditions as complementary resources, Loram and Pressoir reinforced the idea that there was room for incorporating a greater American cultural presence within Haiti's social fabric.

In the years that followed, the U.S. State Department and private entities across the United States made sizable investments in intercultural relations with Haiti. It was in this context that Lallier C. Phareaux celebrated L'Institut Haïtiano-Américain, the institute co-sponsored by the Haitian and U.S. governments to promote Haitian-American cultural exchanges. Phareaux featured the institute as a prime example of how institution building could facilitate the process of rapprochement culturel. The Haitian poet René Bélance, who was in his early thirties when the Haitian-American Institute opened on July 4, 1942, saw the cultural center as a vibrant site for improving cross-cultural ties. Bélance, who had migrated to Port-au-Prince from the southern town of Corail for his studies, described the Institute as a place where Haitians, Americans, the French, and members of all social groups, and particularly students who attended local lycées, congregated and participated in activities that encouraged rapport. Because the institute was primarily focused on Haiti-U.S. ties, the activities that took place there encouraged the incorporation of U.S. culture into the social spaces of Haitian artists, intellectuals, and youth. Bélance found it to be useful in challenging the tradition of Haitian nationalism with its concomitant negative attitude toward Americans.[33]

Still, elite Haitians welcomed cultural relationships with any foreign country they expected would contribute positively to their intellectual and cultural sensibilities, and for some, their country's political economic affairs. Haitians tuned into the internationalist climate of the interwar and postwar years eagerly pursued ties with Great Britain, nurtured the Haitian-French connection, and also sought ties with countries in the Western Hemisphere.[34] By 1943, Haitian elites formed social groups such as the Société Bolívarienne and the Société des Amis du Mexique. Dantès Bellegarde, who wrote and spoke widely about the Pétion-Bolívar connection, was a member of the Bolívarian club and it was his fellow members in that club who asked him to speak publicly on the topic (Figure 3.2). Max Mossanto, president of La Société Bolívarienne—founded for the express purpose of advancing Haiti's ties with American republics—used radio and print media to communicate to a broader public his ideas about the evolution of Pan-Americanism and its contemporary significance for guarding and developing Western civilization. In a speech broadcast on radio station HHBM, and subsequently reprinted in *Le Matin*, Mossanto argued that prejudice and hatred had slowed down the "evolution" of Pan-Americanism. He pointed to the activities of the era as evidence of increasing efforts to enhance

FIG. 3.2 Holiday card featuring the "Fathers of Pan-Americanism" from Haitian Consul Charles B. Vincent. Undated. (Courtesy: Frank R. Crumbie Collection, Box 5, Folder 3, "Business Cards," University of Florida George A. Smathers Libraries, Special and Area Collections.)

cultural understanding among the American republics. As a sign of positive change, he referenced an upcoming conference of the Inter-American Caribbean Union in Port-au-Prince.[35] (Connections across the region included the British Caribbean. In 1948, a Jamaica-Haiti Institute operated at 21 Avenue John Brown in Port-au-Prince.) However, beyond serving as an opportunity for cultural connections the conference was a gathering that provided a platform for attendees to discuss the merits of economic cooperation between Caribbean territories, and its relationship to contemporary plans for federation in the British Caribbean. As described by the African American educator and scholar Rayford Logan, the meeting in Port-au-Prince was a key opportunity for the individuals involved to make positive strides to securing their economic self-sufficiency.[36]

While many cultural manifestations of Pan-Americanism began as part of official efforts to honor the contemporary inter-American political order, Haiti's urban residents of several generations were also clearly engaged with them. Public markers were the most explicit indication to private citizens that the internationalist order was reshaping their society. Over the course of several years, officials renamed streets in Haiti. A major roadway between the suburb of Pétion-Ville and Port-au-Prince was designated Avenue Panaméricaine.[37] Other streets acquired the names of Pan-American "heroes," that is, individuals from the United States and elsewhere across the Americas celebrated for their contributions to advancing inter-American ideals.[38] U.S. Senator William H. King, the outspoken critic of his country's military occupation of Haiti, was honored when Avenue des Dalles in Port-au-Prince was given his name. King's street was located between Avenue Charles Sumner and Avenue John Brown in recognition of two Americans who had campaigned for U.S. diplomatic recognition of Haiti and the abolition of slavery, respectively.[39] In June 1938, the already popular Franklin Delano Roosevelt gained further recognition with the dedication of a boulevard in his name linking Port-au-Prince with the neighborhood of Carrefour.[40] The Haitian government also graced two major streets in Port-au-Prince with Simón Bolívar's name. The first was the road to the mountains of Kenscoff; the second was the downtown road that had been known as Rue de la Réunion.[41] Another street in Port-au-Prince was designated Avenue José Martí, after the nineteenth-century Cuban revolutionary leader.

While Haitians who referenced or traveled along these streets in their everyday lives may not have changed the way they spoke of these streets, the widespread physical markings in Port-au-Prince did not go unnoticed. At least one act of protest reveals a level of awareness among members of the public about the political names given to Haitian streets. During the fall of 1937, in the wake of the massacre of thousands of Haitians residing in the Dominican Republic and the repatriation of thousands more, protestors in Port-au-Prince defaced a local street sign that bore the name of Dominican president Rafael Trujillo. Sténio Vincent renamed the street as one of a series of public demonstrations that he and Trujillo had used to promote the idea that there were cordial ties between the two heads of state, that both were committed to inter-American solidarity, and that such diplomatic ties were effective in resolving inter-island matters such as regulation of the border. The heads of state used Pan-American performance and pronouncements to gain political advantages. For example, in 1938 Trujillo renamed a street in the Dominican Republic after Vincent in a "public attempt" to remedy the tensions following the massacre.[42]

As part of the effort to keep Pan-American ideals circulating in Haiti's public spaces and among various audiences, Haitian officials incorporated inter-Americanism into the experience of Haitian schoolchildren. The most prominent way of doing so was by assigning the names of other American republics to Haitian elementary and secondary-level schools. The outside walls of Port-au-Prince's schools were marked with signage that identified the buildings as the National School of the "Republic of the United States of America," the "Republic of Ecuador," and the "Republic of Chile" (Figure 3.3).[43]

In addition to school renamings, there were school activities that enabled young Haitians to generate their own sense of connection to the Pan-American campaign. Well into her seventies, Jacqueline

FIG. 3.3 Haitian Public School, "École Nationale République de l'Équateur," Rue Faustin I, Delmas 41, Port-au-Prince, Haiti, 2013. (Photography by and courtesy of: Nadève Ménard. Design: Cameau Designs.)

Levy proudly recalled personal connections to Pan-Americanism from her youth, including her elementary school's affiliation with Argentina. In 1940, she and her classmates learned the Argentinean national anthem. Levy was nine at the time; yet, more than sixty years later, she voluntarily broke out into the anthem with passion and joy as she reveled in the memory. Levy also remembered with pride that she was one of four classmates whose "Dear [Pan-American] Sister" letters were selected for mailing abroad. Even students who attended schools without a formal Pan-American designation were encouraged to consider the significance of Haiti's inter-American relations for their cultural development. Charles Manigat, who attended elementary school in the northern port city of Cap-Haïtien, recalled how his school director, Louis Mercier, discussed the topic of Pan-Americanism as one of many themes eloquently presented at the start of every day.[44]

Annual Pan-American Day celebrations gave Haitians across generations an opportunity to cultivate a sense of national pride that was linked to an affinity for ties across the Americas. As did other members of the Pan-American Union, Haitian president Vincent pronounced April 14 as a national holiday in 1931. The holiday was created in May 1930 by members of the Union to commemorate its founding at the end of the first International Conference of American States in 1890.[45] In Haiti, like elsewhere in the region, all public services were suspended, and schoolchildren and other members of the Haitian elite were encouraged to join public officials in celebrating the holiday. Levy recalled that her lessons on the Argentinean national anthem were part of her school's preparations for a Pan-American Day celebration.[46] In 2009, Max Chaumette Jr., son of the prolific author of Pan-American texts, still had fond memories of marching in annual Pan-American Day parades and of the many years his father spent speaking and writing about Pan-Americanism's significance for Haiti.[47] Young Haitian schoolchildren also gathered as local Boy Scouts to participate in saluting the flags from the twenty-one American republics, a lecture on the goals of Pan-Americanism, a closing film on scouts across the Americas, and a campfire gathering at Lycée Pétion.[48]

Activities organized in 1940 were particularly festive, to honor the fiftieth anniversary of the founding of the Pan-American Union. Haitian schoolchildren joined the nation's highest-ranking public officials and foreign diplomats in a series of political, cultural, and religiously inflected events. Both Haitian and foreign officials were recognized with the "Order of Pétion-Bolívar," which commemorated the assistance Haitian president Alexandre Pétion had extended to Simón Bolívar during his campaigns to liberate South America from Spanish colonial rule. The honor had been established in 1939 "for the purpose of recognizing, in a very special manner, the eminent services rendered to the cause of Pan-Americanism by foreign chiefs of state, career diplomats, and other individuals from Haiti and abroad."[49]

In a cultural extravaganza coordinated by Haiti's first women's organization, La Ligue Féminine d'Action Sociale, for the 1940 celebration, young Haitians paraded in assigned national costumes and performed on the stage of the capital city's downtown Rex

Théâtre. The event showcased Haiti's cultural heritage, as well as the cultures of nations across the Americas, including Panama, Mexico, Venezuela, and the United States.[50] Women such as Jacqueline Wiener-Silvera and Lina Fussman-Mathon who were leaders of Haiti's rising cultural performance scene during the 1930s and 1940s played a central role in coordinating cultural events for the Haitian state. Wiener-Silvera, who led one of the few theatrical companies in Haiti at the time, directed a student presentation featuring the heroic historical figure Princess Anacaona, to honor Haiti's indigenous ancestors. Fussman-Mathon, a classically trained pianist who added prominence to her name by leading choral and dance performance groups, directed Haitian primary schoolchildren in a performance of folkloric songs and dances, including a tribute to the African American educator Booker T. Washington, and a cappella renditions of Negro spirituals which were internationally recognized at the time. Fussman-Mathon's work with the children was part of her collaborative efforts with elite artists, such as the German-Haitian pianist Werner Jaegerhuber. Members of Haiti's musical elite combined their appreciation for European classical music with their interest in the collection, arrangement, and adaptation of Haitian folk music.

Such efforts were a response to Jean Price-Mars's call to enhance the awareness that elite Haitians had of Haitian Vodou and folkways. By extension, Fussman-Mathon and her collaborators hoped to garner international appreciation for Haiti's musical culture.[51] The schoolchildren also displayed paintings and costumes representing the "Indian and Spanish North American" cultures of Mexico. Theatrical skits, sometimes accompanied by music, featured student performances of the history and current events of North, South, and Central America.[52] Young women from Sainte Rose de Lima boarding school performed a skit in honor of this first Catholic saint of the Americas who served as their school's namesake.[53] The following year, President Vincent maintained the religious dimension of celebrating Pan-American Day by gathering with national and foreign officials at the cathedral in Port-au-Prince for a *Te Deum solennel* (a formal hymn of praise).[54] Official gatherings were a space within which local culture and Pan-American ideals came together.

Haitian residents who were unable or uninterested in attending any of these events in person could still experience Pan-American Day activities taking place in Port-au-Prince, as well as elsewhere across the region. Besides broadcasts from the United States, such as the Pan-American concert hosted by the U.S. Navy in 1934, Haitian radio stations and newspapers featured local stories and commemorative programs. In 1942, the Ligue presented an evening radio broadcast on HHBM in honor of Pan-American Day featuring music, poetry, messages from schoolchildren, and an address from Haitian women to women across the Americas.[55] As with other commemorative events, these radio programs were intended to publicly salute the Americas, honor prominent figures in Pan-American history, and promote recognition of Haiti's role in the history of the region and the political ideology of inter-Americanism.[56] Haitian newspaper editors dedicated space to articles on the history of the Pan-American Union and published quotes from "famous Americans" such as U.S. president Franklin D. Roosevelt, Latin American revolutionary leader Simón Bolívar, Brazilian president Gertulio Vargas, U.S. Under Secretary of State Sumner Welles, and Mexico's Secretary of State for Foreign Relations Ezequiel Padilla.[57] They also published monthly "inter-American calendars," prepared by the Press Division of the United States' Office of the Coordinator of Inter-American Affairs, which noted annual celebrations and important dates in the history of the Americas.[58] Other dates recognized by the Haitian government included the day of American Culture (October 13), Pan-American Health Day, and the date Saint Domingue's free people of color departed to participate in the Battle of Savannah (May 4). Taken together, these inter-American activities aimed to weave local and regional threads in the history and contemporary manifestations of Pan-Americanism into Haiti's everyday urban affairs.

Provocative reflections on moments in Haitian history, consideration of Haitian history's significance for the contemporary political and economic order, and the emergence of a vibrant and internationally conscious urban social scene provided elite Haitians with numerous occasions to explore what types of connections might help them redress past abuses in Haiti-U.S. relations. However, more than gaining an opportunity to reflect about the past as a means of forging new pathways into their future, these men and women also had occasion to become familiar with the ideology of inter-Americanism insofar as it could provide contemporary context for a more positive outlook about the United States and other countries, and it could add value to contemporary Haitian society. Through speaking, writing, and coordinating a range of cultural activities, Haitian politicians, intellectuals, and social elites helped Pan-American and international themes become further embedded in the fabric of twentieth-century Haitian national identity, society, as well as Haiti-U.S. relations. It is to the ways that travel between Haiti and the United States during the 1940s for cultural and professional purposes reinforced these developments that we turn next.

4

La Nouvelle Coopération

Cultivating Knowledge through Haiti-U.S. Ties, 1936–1948

In 1944, thirty-year-old Henri Télémaque boarded a Pan American Airways flight departing from Port-au-Prince to Miami. Télémaque was en route to Washington, D.C., for postgraduate training in statistics at the U.S. Census Bureau. While working as an employee of Haiti's National Office of Public Health, the young statistician caught the eye of Chester Young, a White American statistician who had come from the United States to help the Haitian government prepare a national census. In a 2001 interview, Télémaque recalled how Young praised his work ethic and proposed that he travel to the United States for further professional training. That trip ultimately allowed Télémaque to spend time in Washington, D.C., New York City, and New Mexico over the course of seven months.

But initially, Télémaque hesitated to say yes to Young's invitation. It had been fifteen years since his last period of formal study. Télémaque wasn't even sure he was interested in staying on at the Haitian Public Health office. He was entertaining the possibility of leaving public service to work with his brother full-time at a "promising bakery" he had started, inspired by the success of a Port-au-Prince–based pastry business that his mother had taken on to support the family after his father died. Perhaps more significantly however, Télémaque was concerned about subjecting himself to the racial hostilities he anticipated meeting while in the United States. What finally allowed him to accept Young's offer was his sense that regardless of his professional future, visiting the United States would allow him to garner additional knowledge, which he considered to be valuable for the experience, if nothing else. Télémaque decided to travel. Determined to circumvent the barriers and assaults he feared he would meet as best as he could, he became one of at least seventy Haitian *boursiers* (scholarship recipients) who traveled to and studied in the United States in 1944.

In addition to arranging travel abroad for professionals such as Télémaque, Haiti's Ministry of Education offered apprenticeships in manual arts recognized for their aesthetic, hygienic, and industrial economic value. One such program began in 1944, under the auspices of the Inter-American Educational Foundation, of which Haiti was a founding member. Urban and rural Haitians studied weaving, fiber work, and ceramics under the direction of specialists from the United States. The first participants were fifty rural schoolteachers who took part in a summer school training session also hosted by the Haitian Ministry of Education. That group soon expanded to include "a group of 13 boys, from the city [of Port-au-Prince] and other parts of the country, who came to receive training in general education and specifically to learn a trade." This group of thirteen "boys" (men who were as young as high school students and as old as recent college graduates) continued training in the manual arts beyond the "close of summer school . . . until the opening of the fall session of the Normal School." Marcus Douyon, who had graduated from college in 1944, was one of those "boys." In 1945, Douyon began studying ceramics under the direction of Glen Lukens, a White American professor who in August 1945 began a faculty appointment at Damien, the site of the Service Technique, the occupation-era training institution for agricultural and manual studies. The Haitian and U.S. governments sponsored Lukens's position in order to develop local manual industries.[1]

The coordinators and advocates of these opportunities, referred to broadly as "intellectual cooperation," viewed these types of interaction between Haitians and Americans as integral to Haiti's national interest. They expected that the programs could develop the capacity of Haitian citizens to contribute positively to innovations in the Haitian economy and society. They saw the programs as a way to command respect for Haitians as citizens within the inter-American and broader international order. They celebrated these initiatives as a viable way to encourage reforms and innovations in Haiti's social, economic, and political affairs. And, they also drew attention to the ways that participating Americans had an opportunity to further advance their own knowledge and build their respective fields of expertise.

As Haitians agreed to travel to the United States for advanced training at an unprecedented rate, as they welcomed Americans to work in Haiti as experts, and as they adopted elements of U.S. society such as American English as assets that could bolster one's status and access to employment, they were conceding that there was a legitimate place for the United States in the everyday Haitian experience. As with the performances, renaming of public sites, and cultural gatherings in Haiti on behalf of Pan-Americanism discussed in the previous chapter, the coordinators and participants of intellectual cooperation between Haiti and the United States—boursiers likeTélémaque and apprentices like Douyon—helped popularize the idea that Haiti's ties to the United States could be beneficial and not strictly detrimental for Haitian society. In this way the United States became further integrated into local understandings about what would enable Haitians to succeed in local endeavors, be they of personal or national concern. Because of this, a greater number of Haitians could also recognize individuals, institutions, and ideas from the United States as a source of enrichment for Haitian society beyond its francophone tendencies, and even a factor that encouraged some aspects of African-based folk traditions on the island. From such a vantage point, Haitian public officials or private citizens could discuss ties to the United States as something that was compatible with the nationalist ideals that emerged at the end of the occupation. For some, the greatest advantage of this perspective was that such gains in turn might help Haitians secure a more respected and, by extension, prominent place in the world.

Programs and Possibilities

Regional and international alliances during the interwar and Second World War eras made it possible for Haitian citizens to travel to many countries, but especially to the United States (Figure 4.1). These opportunities for intellectual cooperation were particularly stimulated by the efforts of Haitian bureaucrat and educational reformer Maurice Dartigue. From his own experiences as a boursier during the occupation, and subsequently as a leading public official, Dartigue was aware of the opportunities to fund and host intellectual exchanges through inter-American networks, and particularly the U.S. government, as well as private foundations, universities, and corporations based in the United States. Between 1930 and 1944, he became the leading advocate for intellectual cooperation between Haiti and the United States. As a result of his efforts and contemporary international agreements, at least seventy Haitians received funding to study or train in the United States in 1944. Those numbers were significantly greater than similar exchanges in previous years. According to the Institute of International Education, the prominent entity that worked with governments and host institutions to arrange such exchanges, between one and ten students from Haiti traveled to the United States under its auspices during the period 1923–37. By contrast, those numbers increased to eighteen students (1939–40), fifty-one (1942–43), sixty-one (1944–45), and fifty-four (1945–46). The Haitian government numbers likely varied from those of the Institute given that Haitian men and women traveled in various capacities. For example, individuals like Jacqueline Latour who traveled to study voice at Mills College, a women's college based in California, arranged and covered their own expenses. Additionally, from the fall of 1943 through 1944, approximately eight Haitian

FIG. 4.1 "[Haitian Public School] Supervisors in front of the Library of Columbia University," New York City, 1933, in Maurice Dartigue (Service national de la production agricole et de l'enseignement rural), *L'œuvre d'éducation rurale du gouvernement du président Vincent 1931–1936* (Port-au-Prince: Imprimerie de l'État, 1936). (Courtesy: John Dartigue.)

professionals traveled to non-U.S. institutions in Canada, Cuba, Venezuela, Chile, Mexico, Argentina, Trinidad, and England.[2]

The wartime alliance between the United States and Great Britain also facilitated travel across the Americas. A man named Polynice Dorsinville, for example, received a scholarship from the Standard Fruit and Steamship Company to travel to Trinidad where he studied Tropical Agriculture at the Imperial College of Agriculture. At the time, the Trinidadian college was the British Empire's "recognized centre for postgraduate training in tropical agriculture." In another instance, two Haitian men, Dr. Constant Pierre-Louis and Paul Lizaire, both received awards from the British Council. Dr. Pierre-Louis's scholarship allowed him to pursue postgraduate surgical studies in England, while Mr. Lizaire traveled to Nottingham to study English Language and Literature at University College.[3]

The Haitian government entered into numerous agreements, co-founded organizations based on professional identities and interest groups, and collaborated with civil institutions whose affiliates were enthusiastic about inter-American and international alliances as a means of advancing their respective missions. The opportunities in the United States were substantial because the Roosevelt administration made sizable investments in intellectual cooperation as a part of its defense and foreign policy agendas. Wartime concerns fueled such opportunities because public officials and private citizens across the region sought to improve postwar economic or political conditions by eliminating factors that they understood led to war. Immediately following the First World War, the New York City–based Institute of International Education (IIE) encouraged the U.S. government to expand exchanges that had been taking place with European and Asian societies since the nineteenth century by funding exchanges with the Americas. The Roosevelt administration recognized this strategy as an opportunity to concretize its claims that the United States was a Good Neighbor, to further establish itself as a leader in international affairs, and to advance inter-American relations as a model of postwar international relations.[4]

In one of the earliest initiatives, signed in Buenos Aires in 1935, the Haitian government agreed with its regional partners to exchange two graduate students annually and one or more instructors biannually from each signatory nation. Louis Mars, son of Jean Price-Mars, was one of the first to participate in a faculty and student exchange that his father had arranged with Fisk University and U.S. philanthropic foundations. As a visiting professor with a nine-month appointment, the younger Mars taught a course entitled "Problems in Psychiatry and Culture" at Fisk. The elder Price-Mars also arranged exchanges that enabled scholars from Haiti's Institute of Ethnology, which he co-founded in 1941, and prominent institutions such as Northwestern University and the University of Chicago, to pursue their research.[5] These types of exchanges enabled U.S.-based scholars such as the anthropologists Melville Herskovits (University of Chicago) and Alfred Métraux (Yale University) to advance their research agendas by working in Haiti, expose their graduate students to field research, and generate publications that contributed to their prominence, as well as the study of African-derived cultures in the Americas.[6]

Most Haitians traveling to pursue advanced studies and professional experiences at this time did so courtesy of public-private partnerships between entities in Haiti and the United States. Partner offices from the U.S. government included the Department of Agriculture, the U.S. Public Health Service, and most notably, the Office of the Coordinator for Inter-American Affairs. Local government offices also contributed funds. During the 1941–42 academic year, New York City Mayor Fiorello LaGuardia awarded a scholarship to Félix Morisseau-Leroy, then a young Haitian educator and writer. Morriseau-Leroy used his *bourse* to study the principles, organization, and administration of secondary instruction at the City College of New York and Columbia University.[7]

In the private sector, American and Haitian corporations supported the programs by providing in-kind donations and funds or hosting travelers. This is a practice that historian Paul A. Kramer has referred to as "corporate internationalism."[8] It was part of a renewed effort by corporate heads to restore the positive reputation of the role of corporations, particularly on the heels of economic depression during the 1930s. Partner corporations were able to use their funds to guide the training of Haitians they had already hired or might hire in the future. Pan American Airways (Pan Am), for example, presented at least one round-trip ticket annually to each of the twenty participating American republics, for use by student travelers. The Haitian boursier Emmanuel Torres traveled to Miami courtesy of Pan Am to study aviation mechanics. This opportunity appears to be distinct from a recruitment effort that led at least six Haitian men, the majority of whom were members of the Haitian military, to travel for training at the Tuskegee Institute beginning in 1943. These Tuskegee trainees were among the U.S. Army Air Force's group of African-American military pilots who fought in World War II. Other boursiers like Paul Boncy pursued studies outside of the aviation industry. Boncy flew to Bloomington, Indiana, also courtesy of Pan Am, in 1943 to study bacteriology at Indiana University. He received additional funds from the Haiti office of the prominent American agro-industrial firm, the United Standard Fruit Company. In 1944, Maison O. J. Brandt, a Haiti-based firm, owned by Jamaican entrepreneur Oswald Brandt, sponsored Raymond Riboul's travels to Philadelphia to study industrial textiles at the Philadelphia Textile Institute. Meanwhile, the lighting utility firm, Compagnie d'Éclairage Électrique de Port-au-Prince et du Cap, sponsored several boursiers including Franck Lauture, who went to Rockford, Illinois, where he studied electricity at the Central Illinois Electric and Gas Company. These companies, as well as other entities such as hospitals and printing companies, played a significant role in facilitating travel between Haiti and the United States during the post-occupation years. Each of these opportunities for sponsored travel improved the prospects of those who were thus able to travel to the United States.[9]

By the final years of the Second World War, a greater emphasis was placed on in-country-based programs. Haiti, the United States, and five other American republics entered into an agreement with the Inter-American Educational Foundation (IAEF), a government-controlled non-stock-membership corporation created in 1943 by Nelson A. Rockefeller, the U.S. Coordinator of Inter-American Affairs (CIAA). Their intention was to facilitate "long-standing plans for hemispheric cooperation in the solution of basic educational problems" during the war and postwar period. Among its goals, the IAEF was charged with assisting the CIAA to implement its programs, and extending joint efforts among the ministries of education, as well as special ministry departments in the partner republics, and a "Special Representative of the Foundation." Their work effort targeted promoting literacy and language acquisition, as well as skilled and professional education. To carry out this work, the foundation arranged and sponsored the travel of educational specialists from the United States to work with Haiti's Ministry of Education, and supported visits by distinguished educators, supervisors, and teachers from Haiti to the United States for lectures, studies, and participation in national, state, and local education programs.[10]

The Haitian government was one of IAEF's core partners. In 1944, IAEF received $50,000 from Haiti to complement IAEF's $172,000 allocation for the Caribbean nation. The financial investment IAEF made in Haiti during its first few years was about average, compared to the entity's investments in other Latin American republics. The median expense for Haiti between 1942 and 1949 was $184,500. Other country totals were between $55,000 (Panama) and $570,000 (Brazil) during the same time frame. Haitian access to IAEF funding lasted until 1949, when total expenses for Haiti dropped to $0. IAEF staff members were very engaged in Haitian society during the years 1944, 1945, and early 1946. The following year, the Haitian government and the IAEF agreed to terminate the program, release project-related assets in Haiti, and make "arrangements for . . . future continuation and operation under other auspices."[11] The trajectory of the IAEF was not unlike that of its occupation-era predecessors, as well as subsequent initiatives (such as the Marbial project discussed in Chapter 5). Funding, structures, and priorities would shift, but the practice of incorporating foreign resources and expertise into Haitian society would continue as Haitians and Americans aimed to determine a sustainable and successful approach for each cooperative mission.[12]

Contending with Enduring Tensions

The flourishing of such opportunities did not necessarily generate a positive outlook among Haitians about Americans or American society. Nor were concerns from the preceding decades about involving Americans in Haitian affairs, particularly as related to education or broadly speaking, knowledge, absent from the minds of educated Haitian urbanites. Rather, the willingness of some Haitians to advocate for or participate in intellectual cooperation between Haiti and the United States during the post-occupation years was a means to address or at least attempt to circumvent tensions in the bilateral relationship. And it was the post-occupation context that made it possible for Haiti-U.S. ties to appear palatable to a broadening range of Haitians, even those who might not be concerned with political matters. Intellectual cooperation opened up the possibility for *rapprochement culturel* between Haiti and the United States.

As had been the case for Henri Télémaque, whose story was told at the opening of this chapter, the existence of White racial prejudice toward African-descended people could easily temper the enthusiasm of Haitians who were potential boursiers. Racial segregation and the violent behavior that American military officers relied upon to carry out their occupation mission was a vivid and recent example of what interactions with prejudiced Americans could mean for Haitians.[13] To this should be added the fact that through public news reports and the personal relationships that some elite Haitian urbanites had with African Americans, Haitians were aware of the disdain many White Americans felt for Blacks.[14] That those sentiments could turn into disparaging and sometimes deadly incidents makes it no surprise that Télémaque or any other Haitian would be tentative about participating in any sort of intellectual exchange or professional development opportunity with Americans.

Thus, the decision of Haitian men and women to travel to the United States suggests that boursiers such as Télémaque had some degree of confidence that something about themselves or the post-occupation context could temper such harsh realities. Traveling with a great degree of anticipation about how he would deal with the Jim Crow context of racial segregation, Télémaque's first experiences in the United States confirmed his initial reservations.

Arriving in Miami, Télémaque found himself insulted as he prepared to board a connecting train headed to Washington, D.C. He looked at the two signs intended to direct him to where he would board at the Miami station. One read, "Whites only"; the other read, "Dogs and Blacks."[15] Such signs, listing dogs alongside Blacks, Chinese, Mexicans, and women, typically displayed across the United States, associated dogs with various groups of people targeted for exclusion. Cream-colored in complexion, Télémaque decided to take his chances at passing for White and as he recalled it, he boarded the train without incident. His success at circumventing at least one Jim Crow regulation continued later on during the train ride when he was seated at an empty table in the dining car, and joined by a group of White passengers who decided to sit next to him.

Whether Télémaque was aware of it or not, alternative enforcement regulations and practices in Florida during the 1940s may help explain his ability to travel without anyone confronting him about his presence. In the wake of occupation-era protests, U.S. public officials made efforts to allow visitors from the Americas to have a favorable experience when traveling to the United States. This is particularly noteworthy since Haitian boursiers to the United States were hosted at diverse institutions, not simply predominantly Black institutions, in every region of the United States. By attempting to shield Latin American and Caribbean visitors of color from Jim Crow practices, these officials sought to demonstrate the principle of "Good Neighborliness."[16] Visitors of color who spoke a foreign language (most often, Spanish—which Télémaque happened to speak) or who were able to present a foreign passport avoided some of the daily prejudices that African Americans experienced.

Outspokenness was one way of instructing Americans about the need to be mindful of the respect Haitians participating in the programs expected. After spending time in Washington, D.C., at the U.S. Census Bureau and several months in New York City at Columbia University, Télémaque learned that his itinerary was to include a trip to the southern United States (Alabama, specifically).

He immediately protested to his supervisor, the chief statistician, who assured Télémaque that the experience would be fine, based on the sensitivity of his supervisors at the next host institution. Télémaque persisted in his protest and it appears to have paid off. After New York, Télémaque went west to New Mexico instead, where he spent time in three different cities including Albuquerque. Being outside the southern United States, where Télémaque anticipated he would encounter more profoundly discriminatory experiences, New Mexico's demographics and Télémaque's training in English and Spanish led him to feel more comfortable about his new destination. Through his protests, Télémaque encouraged his host to remain attentive to the concerns he had and to the level of respect he expected while visiting the United States.

Skepticism about working with Americans also emerged among members of the Haitian Garde, when the Vincent administration contracted with the U.S. government to provide training in Haiti during the post-occupation years. One of the most visible ways that Haitian and U.S. officials negotiated the end of the occupation between 1930 and 1934 was by replacing U.S. military officers with Haitian military officers. In the midst of that process, the Vincent administration arranged for ongoing training and support from the U.S. military. One such instance took place in 1939 when Haitian minister to Washington, D.C., Élie Lescot, welcomed two U.S. colonels (Samuel Heidner and George Hatton Weems) to Haiti. The arrival of these officers led to an uproar among more senior members of the Garde and some members of the general public.

Lescot challenged the protests by calling them uninformed skepticism about American involvement in internal Haitian affairs and contrasting the protestors' views with his uncritical optimism about the post-occupation era. Expressing his frustration to Vincent, Lescot wrote, "the worries of the senior Gardesmen . . . are not justified. In Haiti, people must put it well into their minds that the United States is very much sincere when it proclaims its Good Neighbor Policy. They have, among all others, eloquently proven that in all that concerns us."[17] Unreceptive to the criticism he faced for supporting military cooperation during the post-occupation years, Lescot declared to members of the Haitian Garde and the general public that anyone who criticized this initiative had a "*peuple's*" level of consciousness (i.e., a popular and therefore, in elite parlance, a less elevated mindset) about inter-American affairs and national security matters. Claiming greater wisdom, presumably from his political experience, Lescot sought to demonstrate that an alliance with the United States was a means of defending domestic and regional interests. In particular, Lescot described military cooperation with the United States as a means of ensuring a trained Haitian Garde and encouraging U.S. investment in Haiti. To further justify his initiative, Lescot pointed to the example of an air force base that the Cuban and U.S. governments were collaborating on.[18] Along those lines, in 1941, Lescot arranged for Haitian officers to be trained by a U.S. aviation mission in Haiti. As he saw it, training and infrastructure development through cooperation with the United States ought to be considered consistent with, not at odds with, Haiti's national interest.

Perhaps as a strategy for lessening concerns and enlisting greater support for cultivating military ties with the United States, by the early 1940s the Vincent and Lescot administrations arranged for members of the Haitian Garde to travel to the United States for advanced training. Guardsmen were significantly represented among those pursuing advanced studies abroad during the early 1940s. Being selected for study abroad was one way that Haiti's military class garnered social prestige. And, while most trained in military fields, a few guardsmen pursued studies in other areas. Major Luis Maximillien, for example, accepted a scholarship from the U.S. government to study medicine and health services at the Medical Field Service School at Carlisle Barracks in Carlisle, Pennsylvania, during 1941–42. And Lt. Léon Désiré Paris studied motor transport services at the U.S. Army Motor Transport School at Fort Holabird, near Baltimore, also with support from the U.S. government. Other Haitian military officers traveled for mechanical instruction and pilot instruction, for example.[19]

Haitian officials working in other bureaus where occupation-era collaborations had taken place also pursued post-occupation cooperation that enabled Haitian professionals to work with or travel to train with other professionals based in the United States. A distinguishing characteristic of the post-occupation initiatives seemed to be that the collaborations could take place across institutions, as opposed to through a centralized, U.S.-directed occupation administration. This may have offered Haitian officials some leverage in cases where their priorities did not match those of their prospective funders. Such was the case during the 1930s and 1940s when Haitian officials petitioned the Rockefeller Foundation (RF) for assistance with medical education and disease control. Because the foundation's greatest focus at the time was on public health missions, RF officers responded favorably to proposals from the National Service for Public Health for aid in disease control. The RF allocated $1,750 for an updated malaria survey in 1935 and followed up with a $10,000 allocation for control work that began in 1939 and continued through 1943. In addition to working in the capital city of Port-au-Prince, the foundation extended its disease control efforts into the southern provinces of Jacmel and Petit-Goâve until 1943.[20] Writing to a colleague in 1940, one RF officer spoke to larger issues when he noted that these projects were "an ideal way of recommencing . . . cooperation."[21] As welcome as these projects were, Jules Thébaud, Haiti's director of Public Health, was particularly interested in securing support from the RF for medical education in Haiti.

In his ministerial capacity, Thébaud, a forty-four-year-old dentist from Gonaïves, pursued numerous avenues to secure medical fellowships for Haitians. This proved to be a good strategy since RF officers balked at his proposal. The officers expressed an interest in providing assistance, but advised Thébaud that they would not commit prior to conducting a survey of the conditions of Haiti's National School of Medicine and Pharmacy in the years following the occupation. That survey resulted in the RF's denying Thébaud's request to reinstate funding for faculty and staff training, as well as the requests of his successors for supplies, equipment, and the improvement of school facilities.[22] In opposing further investments in Haiti's medical school, RF officers claimed the survey had demonstrated that the school had failed to expand or create initiatives beyond those put in place as a result of the foundation's contributions from the 1920s. It is not apparent whether RF officials were concerned about the circumstances leading to that reality or whether Thébaud sought to further relay the merits of his request. In the end, one foundation officer redirected the petition by asking why cooperation among IIE, CIAA fellows, and the medical school was not in effect.[23] In actuality, the Haitian government was working with the State Department, and because of that funding, by 1943 the medical and dental sciences were among the leading fields for which Haitians were awarded scholarships to study in the United States. Unbeknownst to Haiti's officials, these opportunities would soon narrow with the close of the Second World War. In the post-1945 era, a number of international organizations, such as the American Sanitary Mission, the Pan-American Sanitary Bureau, the United Nations and its specialized agency, the World Health Organization, joined the RF in prioritizing public health missions rather than medical education in Haiti.[24]

And, while disagreements between Haitian and American leaders about approaches to reforming Haitian education were a prominent source of tension during the occupation, both sides appear to have been much more successful at forging cooperative relations during the post-occupation years. Recognizing that "most Haitian students would not be able to travel outside the country," Maurice Dartigue worked to arrange short and longer-term visits to Haiti by American lecturers and artists.[25] Without the fiscal and political obstacles that former Minister of Public Instruction Dantès Bellegarde faced when he tried to collaborate with U.S. occupation officials during the early occupation years, Dartigue was able to pursue a number of self-directed initiatives including welcoming faculty from the United States, France, and the Caribbean to participate in his reform programs.

One such program was a summer school sponsored by the Ministry of Public Instruction in 1944, which served 122 Haitian educators. From August 16 to September, nine teachers from Haiti's secondary schools met at the School of Law to attend courses and lectures offered by both foreign and local educators and intellectuals. Between August 21 and September 14, eight women who taught at Haiti's urban primary schools met at the Girls' Normal School in Martissant for another series of special courses. At the Law School, the teachers were "grouped according to their specialties: literature, math, physical and natural science, social science, and English." The summer sessions enlisted local and visiting instructors. The Haitian educators included former boursier Félix Morisseau-Leroy and prominent intellectuals such as Lucien Hibbert and Dantès Bellegarde. The list of visiting instructors included educators and intellectuals from the United States (Joseph K. Sonntag, Max Bond, Mercer Cook, W.E.B. Du Bois) and the French Caribbean island of Martinique (Aimé Césaire). On other occasions, popular European intellectuals also joined the roster of guest lecturers.[26]

The Preparation of Professional Cadres

Haitians who traveled to study in the United States and those who worked with the Americans who came to Haiti as experts helped constitute new forms of social prestige and a new understanding of the value of ties to the United States for mid-twentieth-century Haitian society. Jeanne C. Sylvain, a prominent member of Haiti's Ligue Féminine d'Action Sociale, was able to expand educational and voluntary aid services in Haiti following her studies of "les questions sociales" at the University of Chicago in 1942. Jeanne was one of four accomplished activist women in Haiti who were all daughters of Georges Sylvain, a prominent Haitian poet, lawyer, and political activist who had lobbied internationally for the end of the U.S. military occupation through such actions as founding the nationalist organization, l'Union Patriotique. Working with the Ligue, Jeanne Sylvain founded a School of Social Work in Haiti,[27] to promote a sense of collective responsibility for meeting society's needs, as well as advancing professional training in social work. She also helped coordinate the work of different aid organizations based in Haiti. By 1954, the Ligue was offering six evening courses in the major cities of Port-au-Prince, Port-de-Paix, Saint Marc, and Les Cayes. It was, in addition, engaged in many other social work activities, including the promotion of hygiene in Jacmel and efforts to secure public funds for needy youth and elders.[28]

When boursiers such as Sylvain returned to Haiti after periods of study in the United States, they came to be known as "les Master's of" because many boursiers secured master's degrees while abroad. At times, the identifier "les Master's of" elicited prejudice toward these individuals, whether as a backlash against the privilege of being able to study at institutions in the United States or a resistance to assumptions that boursiers may have had about their own superiority following a period of higher education in the United States. On the other hand, as boursiers emerged as a distinct elite group, they also came to enjoy heightened status—in terms of respectability for the professional training they garnered and/or the employment opportunities they were now better able to secure in Haiti.[29]

The chance to stand apart from one's peers and, in the best scenarios, generate heightened social respect, secure employment, a promotion, or a new means of generating income, was also available to Haitians who participated in the trade and arts programs instituted through Haitian-U.S. cooperation during the 1940s. In addition to the performing and visual arts, Haiti's ties to the United States during the post-occupation years also encompassed manual arts, which were encouraged as a form of promoting industrial innovations among other developments in Haiti.[30] Grete Franke taught a range of manual arts at the Centre d'Apprentissage to Haitian schoolteachers, some of whom became leading practitioners in their fields. Franke emphasized the practical value of arts and crafts education, as her students advanced in the knowledge of "making . . . articles of clothing and equipment for the home." During special summer sessions and the regular school year, Haitian schoolteachers participated in courses sponsored by the Inter-American Education Foundation (IAEF) in manual arts. Supervised by Franke, the Haitian teachers studied arts and crafts at the Normal School each afternoon during the

1944–45 academic year and for the first trimester of the 1945–46 session. These cohorts included elementary school craft teachers who came from several towns, including Port-au-Prince, to train directly with Franke each morning. Teachers who traveled any distance "were granted time from their teaching to attend" the classes. The course curriculum soon expanded to a curriculum in which art, pottery, and fiber-work (most likely with sisal) were added to instruction in weaving.[31]

Toward the end of Franke's program, she "instituted a new course in color and design with the assistance of Mr. [Glen] Lukens," a ceramics professor from the University of Southern California who headed the IAEF's arts education programs on-site. Eventually, a few Haitian participants were enlisted to lead four distinct working groups, which Franke designed. And, teachers who traveled to Port-au-Prince from other towns were charged to "return . . . to their respective communities to supervise arts and crafts study in their schools." In at least two cases, former students held "official positions in the arts and crafts programs of Haitian schools," allowing for further dissemination of the methods.[32] Marcus Douyon and fellow ceramicist Jean Jacques were among the apprentices that Lukens employed. Through their ties with Lukens both Douyon and Jacques traveled to the United States to study, teach, and exhibit their expertise as ceramicists (Figure 4.2).[33]

Lukens noted the enthusiasm his Haitian apprentices demonstrated for developing skills in the arts industries. Besides courses at the Normal School, Lukens offered training opportunities at a new workshop created in Bois St. Martin in conjunction with the Department of Rural Education, at the School of Agriculture in Damien, and at the Center for Apprenticeship (Centre d'Apprentissage). The IAEF described the workshop as a "central laboratory" that served as "a place of meeting for all kinds of craft interests." Given Lukens's expertise as a ceramicist, he emphasized that craft by working with "leaders in the ceramic work" three times a week at the laboratory. Additionally, Lukens made special efforts to reach and stay connected to Haitian students who did not reside in the immediate areas of the workshops. He worked to keep

You and your friends are cordially invited to the
HILL TOP STUDIO OF CLARE CRONENWETT
Monrovia, California
Sunday Afternoon, **MARCH 24th** From 2:30 to 9:00

TO MEET **GLEN LUKENS**
(Dr. of Ceramics) and his student-ceramist guest **JEAN JAQUES** of Haiti.

TO HEAR **DR. LUKENS** Talk at 3:30 — **"HAITI SPEAKS THROUGH CLAY"**

TO SEE **HAITIAN ART** . . . produced under the guidance of the master ceramist **GLEN LUKENS.**

ALSO an **EXHIBITION** of his original **AMERICAN DESERT GLASS** . . in gorgeous new forms & colors.

The Republic of Haiti, last month, decorated DR. LUKENS, with the highest award to a foreigner . . . the Medal of the Legion of Honor and Merit . . . with Honorary Citizenship in their Republic . . . as recognition of his great contribution to the people of Haiti in the field of Home Industries and Art.

Directions to Gold Hill Studio . . . From Foothill Blvd. up Alta Vista to end of drive on mesa . . . tall eucalyptus trees or up Myrtle Avenue to top of hill.

Admission $1.00 plus tax

FIG. 4.2 Invitation to event featuring ceramists Glen Lukens and Jean Jaques [*sic*], n.d., circa 1957. (Glen William Lukens Papers, 1931–1983, Archives of American Art, Smithsonian Institution, Washington, D.C.)

laboratories accessible and active, and to secure local scholarships for his students. The IAEF Commission noted these scholarships as their "special project," awarding them to "women and men wishing to learn the ceramics trade." One recipient was a man named Rock Mirabeau, who served as "supervisor and laboratory assistant" to the ceramics workshop in Bois St. Martin, a locality near Gonaïves.[34] According to an IAEF report, the "well-equipped" Bois St. Martin workshop demonstrated "the beginning of a small industry." To further meet the needs of rural residents, Lukens purchased a car, which served as a traveling laboratory, as well as "a means of transportation for students anxious to receive extra lessons."[35]

The prevalence of public and private programs for Haitians to learn American English provided adults and children of various social classes with another significant means of viewing Haiti's ties to the United States as advantageous, for general knowledge as well as the socioeconomic opportunities that came with that knowledge. The Haitian-American Institute and radio station HH3W sought to reach broad audiences by offering courses and broadcasts, sponsored by the Office of Inter-American Affairs. In 1942, the Institute reported that sixty people were enrolled to learn English. The participants were primarily office employees of business firms and government agencies, as well as university and technical school students. Tuition was normally "kept within the reach of clerks and skilled workers."[36] In 1946, a fifteen-minute radio program of oral instruction, "L'Anglais sur les Ondes" (English on the Air), was broadcast every Tuesday and Friday from 6:45 to 7:00 P.M., with lessons printed for further distribution. As a complementary broadcast, every other Sunday from 11:30 A.M. to 12 noon, half-hour cultural programs featuring musical records and readings from the literature of both Haitian and American culture were aired. The aim of those programs was "relating American and Haitian artistic expression in simple English."[37] More individualized study was available for Haitians eager to learn English through private and correspondence courses.[38] In these ways, English language instruction gained a more prominent presence in Haiti, both for those formally engaged in learning English, and for others through mere exposure to the language.

Promoters of English emphasized how learning the language could stimulate inter-cultural awareness and understanding. In an editorial published in the Haitian daily *Le Matin*, the Haitian lawyer Louis Garoute wrote that studying English was an ideal way for Haitians to begin learning about the United States' mentality and culture.[39] The Rev. Henry J. Smith, a Yorkshire missionary who had been teaching English at Haiti's prestigious Christian school Petit Séminaire Collège St. Martial (PSCSM) since 1932, shared his opinion with the Rockefeller Foundation's Humanities Officer John Marshall that fluency in English helped promote a favorable reputation for Haiti internationally. Smith spoke proudly of a St. Martial student named Maurice Kirby who won "the only competition ever run [by a foreign entity] in Haiti for English." After his success in 1946, Kirby traveled to New York City "as a guest of . . . the *New York Herald Tribune*" to represent "Haiti's student body." Smith pitched these facts as part of his petition to Marshall to fund updated teaching materials in St. Martial's classrooms.[40]

But the most significant emphasis on English within Haitian society came at the national level through the Department of Public Instruction. This occurred under the leadership of Minister Maurice Dartigue who oversaw a 1942 policy requiring all students attending Haiti's primary, secondary, and post-secondary schools to study English.[41] What was once an optional extracurricular activity now became part of the national curriculum. To facilitate the execution of the policy, the Lescot administration sought American language teachers who would travel to Haiti. One petition to the Roosevelt administration led seventeen English instructors and ten supervisors to travel to Haiti, for appointments throughout the country.[42] The two governments eventually arranged for the Haitian government to lodge, maintain, and transport these educators throughout their stay. To supplement the Haitian treasury allocations, further agreement was made for the American government to send ten instructors. In July 1942, the Haitian government reported that 18,000 Haitian gourdes (approximately US$8,500 at the time) were allocated to cover the costs associated with hosting American teachers who would teach English in national secondary schools.[43] This policy and fund allocation reveals how the department prioritized the learning of English above Spanish, the other regional language promoted by the department.

The arrival of American educators provided Haitian educators with an avenue for accessing knowledge and enhanced teaching credentials. During the 1943–44 school year, nine American teachers of English worked in Haiti's lycées and trained future Haitian English teachers, under the direction of an American English Language supervisor. They served lycées in major cities across the country, including the Lycée Pétion in Port-au-Prince, the Lycée des Jeunes Filles, and lycées in Cap-Haïtien, Jacmel, Les Cayes, and Jérémie. The supervisor's office helped to produce printed materials. "Mimeographed prepared lessons" were "regularly distributed to the teachers" and were "under press" for publication as a "manual of study." In addition, the supervisor prepared "an anthology of articles and extracts of works on Haiti having appeared in English . . . at the expense of the Office of the Coordinator of Inter-American Affairs and the General Direction of Urban Education." These materials were complemented by "[b]ooks and magazines" sent to the teachers. By the second trimester "Haitian teachers became the assistants of the American teachers in the lycées of Cayes and Jacmel, and in St. Marc they assumed entire responsibility." The visiting instructors stayed in Haiti until July 1944. Afterward, they were "replaced by . . . Haitian teachers who continue[d] to work under the guidance of the American supervisor who remained in Haiti for another year."[44]

A glimpse of what these initiatives meant for the young Haitians being taught by these educators is provided by the gleeful memories of a former student of the Lycée Philippe Guerrier, a public school run by the Brothers of Christian Instruction in the northern city of Cap-Haïtien. In 2002, Charles Manigat fondly recalled his English teacher, Ms. Irene Barksdale. Manigat was a twelve-year-old student when Barksdale, an African American woman, came to Haiti as one of at least three visiting American instructors working in his school between 1942 and 1944. Manigat described the teachers as Black or *mulâtre*, with only one White teacher, a woman he recalled by the name of Mrs. Davis. Manigat remembered receiving English lessons at the school, under the direction of a Haitian man named Max Jean-Jacques, before Ms. Barksdale came on the teaching mission. What changed with Ms. Barksdale, Manigat recalled, was how the language was taught. Barksdale's pedagogical methods included oral expression, singing songs, reading, and repetition. Manigat appreciated these techniques as being less rigid than what he was used to. He also remembered that Barksdale did not punish the students. Instead, the classroom was always animated, especially during Christmas. So impactful was the learning experience of Manigat and his peers with Ms. Barksdale that more than four decades later they continued to reminisce about those days.[45]

Young Haitians could also develop their appreciation for English when they learned that some economic opportunities were only available to those who had English language skills. Beyond the fondness that young schoolboys may have had for an African American woman who used novel instructional methods, learning English meant acquiring marketable language skills. Rev. Smith, the Yorkshire missionary who taught English at Collège St. Martial, observed that "[m]ost of the offices [of U.S.

government agencies] are staffed with our students." In the private sector, Smith pointed out that RCA Communications, "[t]he only American firm which has 100% local personnel is staffed almost entirely by our old boys, including the manager, who is a mechanical trouble shooter for all the Caribbean Area." And, the English language skills may have helped at least two other St. Martial alums, Auguste Bastien and Maurice Borno, secure positions with a community development project (discussed in the next chapter) that the Haitian government was pursuing in the southwestern town of Marbial, in partnership with the United Nations Educational, Social and Cultural Organization (UNESCO), as well as several U.S.-based entities.[46]

English language training was but one of many forms of intellectual cooperation between individuals from Haiti and the United States during the first decade of Haiti's post-occupation period. Haitian officials sought to exploit opportunities for intellectual cooperation with the United States, as well as with other nations in the region and across the Atlantic, in order to achieve bureaucratic, economic, and social advances in Haiti. They did so by entering into formal agreements and dedicating state resources that facilitated the travel of Haitians abroad and foreigners to Haiti for study, advanced training, and mission work in several fields. While such travel between Haiti and the United States during the interwar and Second World War periods encompassed numerous fields, some of the most active exchanges served to extend or revitalize initiatives in the fields of education, military science, public health, and medicine that began during the United States occupation of Haiti. In this way, Haitians interested in professional collaborations welcomed the presence of individuals and institutions from the United States in Haiti after the occupation, albeit under less authoritarian circumstances. Under the direction of Haitian officials, intellectual cooperation with the United States during the post-occupation years was more immediately associated with a Haitian national agenda rather than a U.S. imperial agenda. But, even as Haitian officials made claims that there could be positive synchronicity between a Haitian nationalist agenda and that of

U.S. officials, it was the participation of Haitian citizens in the programs of intellectual cooperation that enabled the visions officials had to gain traction.

The idea that Haiti's ties to the United States could generate advantages for Haitian citizens and Haitian society was not strictly a product of official propaganda or dictates. It was also very much based on the private citizens who participated in the programs. They did so in order to acquire new knowledge and expertise. They sought to play a role in the development of new institutions in Haiti. Others aimed to put themselves in a position to generate income. Increasingly so, a distinct social status became possible with employment opportunities linked to the openness and access that Haitian citizens had to individuals, institutions, or skills from the United States. These developments subtly and explicitly embedded elements of the United States into post-occupation Haitian society. As the Second World War came to an end, and the course of international affairs led public officials and private citizens to emphasize international cooperation as a global and not strictly regional matter, the opportunity for Haitians to accommodate a place for the United States in Haitian affairs expanded and the idea that ties to the United States could contribute to the well-being of Haitians and the elevation of Haiti's international status deepened even with profound changes on Haiti's internal political scene.

5

"Viva UNESCO"

A Subtle Embedding of the United States in Haiti, 1948–1953

In April 1948, the Rockefeller Foundation's Humanities Officer John Marshall traveled to Port-au-Prince, where he met with Haitian president Dumarsais Estimé. During their meeting, Estimé "stressed . . . the need of the Haitian peasant for help, not only from [the Haitian] government, but from outside sources" as well.[1] The help that Estimé was seeking was funding for a pilot project in fundamental education that the Haitian government was pursuing with the United Nations Educational, Social and Cultural Organization (UNESCO) in Haiti's southwestern rural valley known as Marbial. Haiti and the United States were two of fifty nations that chartered the United Nations in June 1945, and thirty-seven countries present at the founding of the UN's specialized agency, UNESCO, in November 1945. Haitian diplomatic representative David Placide attended UNESCO's founding meeting, despite a delay in the verification of diplomatic credentials. By the third day of the meeting, Haiti received formal recognition as part of the body. This was just in time for the first General Conference at the Sorbonne, Paris, November 20–December 10, 1946. In the following year, plans for a pilot project in fundamental education emerged, signaling the dawn of postwar efforts for public-private initiatives in the field of international aid.

UNESCO's mission was to support international agendas that the organization's members believed would promote world peace. It was preceded by bodies affiliated with the League of Nations, which Haiti also joined as a founding member. Those entities included the International Committee of Intellectual Co-operation (1922–46), the International Institute of Intellectual Co-operation (1925–46), and the International Bureau of Education (1925–68). The latter became part of UNESCO in 1969. During UNESCO's first years, the organization's member-nation representatives prioritized what they called fundamental education (FE): the reduction of illiteracy and the promotion of basic knowledge in areas such as health and agriculture, to encourage civic engagement and the ability of citizens to sustain the well-being of their community in social and economic terms, and relatedly, to foster political peace. In essence, FE advocates stressed that literacy and education were central to a community's social, economic, and political standing. The uniqueness of the FE initiative was the emphasis that UNESCO members gave to carrying out the program with attention to the particularities of the local culture.[2] In Haiti, one of those particularities pertained to the relationship between language and literacy, namely whether to promote the use of Haitian Creole rather than the traditional French, for formal instruction.

From current scholarship, we know that European leaders assumed exclusive privileges for themselves as they planned international organizations; yet, the visions and efforts of Haitian statesmen, professional experts, and citizens in seminal projects such as the UNESCO pilot project in Marbial suggest there is more to know about the role that people from "smaller" states (particularly communities of color) played in postwar planning for modernization and development through international organizations. After the Second World War, leaders from nations around the world—big and small—employed the strategy of advancing state projects through worldwide collaborations. Haitian president Estimé was one such leader. Heads of state drew on international resources—such as financing, materials, equipment, and human experts valued for their "scientific" approaches to contemporary issues—to pursue national reforms that could also strengthen the state's authority and influence among citizens. In the eyes of leading European figures, populations and states such as Haitians and Haiti were but marginal or token participants. In truth, however, it was those marginalized participants that lent legitimacy to the idea of using global platforms for postwar development initiatives. The initiatives of leaders from "smaller" states and communities of color, such as Haiti, challenged the assumptions that leaders from "great power" nations had about who ought to be involved in building international organizations.[3]

Many joint postwar efforts, such as the UNESCO/FE pilot project in Marbial, Haiti, were grand utopian schemes that were logistically, financially, and politically hard to actually realize.[4] The failures of such projects have frequently been described as a failure of the "smaller state," in this case Haiti. But a closer look allows us to see the limitations in the process of implementation. Moreover, a look at Haitian efforts to secure Rockefeller Foundation (RF) contributions for the FE project is worthwhile because it can also deepen our understanding of the basis for the grand expectations that some Haitians and foreigners had about postwar internationalism. In particular, the postwar plan for a UNESCO pilot project in Marbial was an extension of the contacts, institutional memory, and programs that began under the auspices of inter-American and international cooperation from the end of the occupation through the early 1940s.[5] Estimé's initiatives helped to sustain the Haiti-U.S. ties that his predecessors, Sténio Vincent and Élie Lescot, had instituted. And, because Estimé sought direct collaboration with the RF, the United Nations, and its specialized agencies, he helped create additional avenues for individuals and institutions from the United States to become embedded in the Haitian state's agenda. Such ties between Haiti and the United States intersected with the interests of Haitian professionals who garnered credentials through training in Haiti and abroad during the early 1940s. Haitians trained in a range of fields, including anthropology, agronomy, and social work, enthusiastically welcomed the opportunity to play a role in the planning and execution phases of international projects, such as the one taking place in Marbial.

The continuity between Vincent's, Lescot's, and Estimé's agendas is worth highlighting because the Estimé administration has mostly been studied for being part of a sharp break in Haiti's political history. That break, commonly referred to as Haiti's Noiriste Revolution, occurred when a popular political uprising in 1946 led to Lescot's ousting and ultimately, Estimé's inauguration. Vincent and, particularly, Lescot, faced criticism for their repressive rulings against anyone who posed seeming threats to their executive authority, for perpetuating local color prejudices by favoring *mulâtres* as superior, and for entering into economic agreements that benefitted Americans but were detrimental for Haitians. However, just as Haiti's first two post-occupation presidents perceived that tapping into U.S. resources could be a viable strategy for advancing reforms that would improve domestic conditions in Haiti, as well as enhance Haiti's participation in international and economic affairs, so did Estimé.[6]

Closely related to the nationalist concerns and efforts to improve Haiti's foreign relationships was the increasing attention that Haitian politicians and intellectuals lent to the conditions of Haiti's urban and rural laborers. During the occupation, nationalists argued that it was the Haitian elite's disregard for the well-being, education, and civic contribution of Haiti's working majority that led Americans to claim that their intervention in Haitian affairs was an act of moral and social justice for Haitians. The post-U.S. occupation efforts of Haitian intellectuals, activists, and politicians to demonstrate their concern for Haiti's most marginalized citizens had encompassed a wide range of activities including literary productions, labor organizing, advocacy through social work, and the promotion of adult literacy programs in Haitian Creole.[7]

Haitian literacy programs during the first half of the twentieth century illuminate the interconnections and tensions between nationalist sentiments, interest in cooperative ties with the United States, and concerns about the Haitian majority during and after the U.S. military occupation of Haiti ended in 1934. These programs involved foreigners from England and the United States who promoted a phonetics-based approach to Creole language instruction that approximated techniques used for teaching English more than the techniques used for teaching French. Consequently, critics of the literacy programs argued that the initiatives threatened the integrity of Haitian national culture because the use of anglophone elements in teaching Haitian Creole would trump what was traditionally associated with the language's francophone elements.[8]

Noiriste revolutionaries proposed to do more to end Haiti's post-occupation dependence on U.S. financial control and fulfill revolutionary ideals of the nationalist movements of the 1920s and 1930s than Presidents Vincent or Lescot. A particular point of critique was the enduring need for the Haitian government to fulfill its obligation to Haiti's working-class and peasant majority. Estimé and his administrators promoted their pursuit of the UNESCO/FE project as a means of leveraging local efforts to improve literacy and other conditions in Marbial. Yet, despite Noiriste efforts to distinguish themselves as establishing a new era in Haitian politics and foreign relations, the agenda set forth by Estimé did not necessarily reduce American involvement in Haitian affairs. As the records of the UNESCO/FE project in Marbial reveal, there would be many continuities, even in the midst of the distinct developments in post-1946 Haiti and international affairs. The continuities between Estimé's reform agenda and that set by his predecessors make sense when we consider that Estimé served as Vincent's minister of public instruction and was succeeded in this post by Vincent's director of Rural Education, Maurice Dartigue. Furthermore, as historians Matthew Smith and Brenda Plummer make clear in their accounts of Estimé's rise to power, Estimé was far from the most progressive among liberal candidates for the Haitian presidency in 1946.[9]

The Viability of the Marbial Valley as a Working Site

Advocates for the Marbial site spoke of the inherent beauty and challenges of the prospective location for an FE pilot project. Addressing delegates at UNESCO's second General Conference in Mexico City in 1947, Haiti's director of Adult Education in Port-au-Prince, Arthur Bonhomme, described Marbial as an ideal site for a pilot project in fundamental education given that the valley was home to "the most crucial problems of Haiti" and of "many under-developed areas" of the world. Located "along a river whose path was up into a range of the Selle Mountains, running southeast between mountains and hills, then into the Caribbean Sea at the port-town, Jacmel," the valley was just south of the capital city of Port-au-Prince. The challenges of the area stemmed from its geographic isolation and the fact that residents depended on Jacmel for food and supplies. Access to the community entailed travel along unpaved roads that crossed the Marbial River at least five times. That river impeded entry into the valley when it flooded twice a year. These factors lay beneath the prevalence of poverty, occasional famine, and widespread illiteracy in Marbial, and were exacerbated by overpopulation, deforestation, soil erosion, and poor agricultural conditions in the region.[10]

The presence on the UNESCO staff of a Haitian professional named Emmanuel Gabriel as a fundamental education specialist influenced the Estimé administration's success at securing an FE pilot project in Haiti, albeit for some conflicting reasons. Alongside Liberia, Egypt, and Ethiopia, Haiti was one of the handful of independent states with predominantly Black populations in the world at the time eligible to be a founding member of the United Nations and UNESCO.[11] Still, Haitian representatives within the international organizations did not present themselves first and foremost as representatives of a race. Rather, given Haiti's historic participation in international organizing, Haitian representatives viewed themselves as members of the international body whose contributions would be of value for the larger global good. By contrast, White members of the UN leadership minimized and outright discriminated against persons of color such as Gabriel within the organization, thereby belying the universal principles they publicly proclaimed to embrace. Referring to Gabriel in his memoirs, UNESCO's first general director, Julian Huxley, described UNESCO's decision to work in Haiti as the result of pressures imposed by "a coloured man on the staff." Huxley described Gabriel's appointment as a token gesture intended to "stress the organization's 'universal character.'"[12]

The biased tendencies of the nineteenth- and early twentieth-century imperial order were being translated into the new structures of the postwar international system. As historian Glenda Sluga has pointed out, people of color working within the UN system had difficulty garnering respect for their contributions and were often paid below the norm. Emmanuel Gabriel, for example, was employed as a program specialist in fundamental education at Grade Level 11, while his European counterparts worked at Grade Level 14. In the midst of a political climate where the contributions of persons of color to the United Nations were devalued, members of the Estimé administration pushed ahead in their efforts to be visible within the UN system. Of the three sites selected by UNESCO for an FE pilot project, Haiti was the only one to move from proposal to working phase. It became the first ever coordination of efforts between the United Nations, its specialized agencies (e.g., UNESCO, the World Health Organization) and collaborating partners such as the Rockefeller Foundation.[13] And, it was a forerunner of what became a long and flourishing history of transatlantic collaborations facilitated by the United Nations, involving countries from the Americas and Europe after the Second World War.[14] But these titles came at a high cost.

The actual FE pilot project work in Haiti was delayed, full of uncertainty, and ultimately, short-lived. A working plan for the pilot project was drafted in early 1948. The plan included teacher training, rural primary schools, an agricultural school, rural clinics, a health education clinic, a rudimentary library, and adult education. Numerous concerns about the proposed working site, however, led UNESCO Secretariat officials to delay signing a formal agreement with the Haitian government until September 6, 1949. Officers from the UN's Food and Agriculture Organization (FAO) who were carrying out their own work in Haiti advised that Marbial was not an ideal working site, given the valley's many needs. The anthropologist Alfred Métraux confirmed much of the FAO report. Métraux's input carried weight since he was the expert whom UNESCO officials contracted to assess the viability of pursuing the pilot project by conducting a preliminary survey of the sociological conditions in Marbial.

Tensions regarding the distribution of local authority in the valley also threatened plans for the pilot project. In the spring of 1948, local peasants gathered to demand the resignation of the UNESCO team's "protestant-communists," perhaps in an attempt to garner favor with the Estimé administration, which had previously forged ties with the local Catholic priest (Father Farnèse Louis-Charles) and with U.S. government officials who supported the administration. Estimé aligned himself with U.S. officials in using anticommunist rhetoric in their campaigns to secure power and influence during the postwar era. This meant suppressing the activities of individuals and organizations that challenged the central authority. Labor organizing was foremost among suppressed activities. Repression by national authorities continued to be a characteristic of post-U.S. occupation Haiti.[15]

The fact that Estimé drew on Haitian leadership from outside the valley to help Métraux assess conditions within it and lay the ground for the UNESCO pilot project was at the heart of local conflict concerning the project. According to Métraux, most of the pilot project's team members were in fact practicing Catholics. Métraux himself was a Protestant and his research interests in Haiti focused on Vodou, though he aimed to be discreet about both. The protests, Métraux noted, appeared to be primarily directed at Arthur Bonhomme, Estimé's director of adult education programs.

Bonhomme came from Port-au-Prince to serve as the Haitian government's representative to UNESCO in the valley and acting director of the pilot project, with Métraux. Bonhomme was Protestant and, perhaps more significantly, his appointment generated conflict when he became responsible for community development activities previously overseen by Father Farnèse Louis-Charles, the parish priest who had been working in Marbial since 1939. Louis-Charles had been leading educational and community-building activities in the valley for the Estimé administration well before the UNESCO project was conceived. When Métraux cautioned the peasants that their protests threatened the commitment UNESCO was seeking to make in the valley, they pointed to Louis-Charles as the chief mobilizer of the demonstration.[16]

In an effort to moderate hopes about what UNESCO would commit to in Haiti, Director Julian Huxley wrote President Estimé in June 1948. "The whole Project is more difficult and complex than at first appeared," Huxley advised. "[I]t would be unwise to proceed further until certain preliminary difficulties have been overcome."[17] Huxley's conclusions were based on his consultations with Métraux, UNESCO experts in fundamental education, potential collaborators from FAO and the UN's World Health Organization, and interested foundations such as the RF. He advised that four major areas lying outside the realm of education needed attention: (1) developing the local infrastructure, including roads, drainage, and accommodations for the UNESCO team; (2) enhancing local food supply, particularly during periods of drought; (3) addressing religious disputes between Protestants and Catholics to avoid interruptions of the on-site work; and (4), demonstrating the preparedness of the Haitian government to invest, in no less than five years, significant funds beyond the $13,200 UNESCO had committed for 1948.[18] While the Estimé administration sought to solicit international support for their efforts, Secretariat officials aimed to emphasize that the operative role that UNESCO had initially taken on in Haiti "put a disproportionate burden on [the international organization's] small staff." They pushed for changes that they claimed would ensure sustainability and long-term Haitian investment in the activities planned for the Marbial Valley, after the termination of the "pilot" phase of the project.[19]

The Central Place of the United States in the Pilot Project

While the input of experts, institutions, funds, materials, and models originating from multiple sites outside the valley were part of the Estimé administration's plans to work with the United Nations in order to advance fundamental education in the Marbial Valley, contributions from the United States were foremost for several reasons. Structurally, the prominence of U.S. citizens, institutions, and resources in UNESCO's plans was consistent with the international organization's policy that member states should contribute according to their various capacities. Because individuals and institutions from the United States were technically and financially involved in Haitian-based and inter-American programs during the 1930s and early 1940s, they were in a position to be key contributors to the UNESCO/Haiti pilot project. The Rockefeller Foundation's experience in Haiti during the previous decades led UNESCO's on-site director and surveyor of the Marbial Valley, Alfred Métraux, to invite John Marshall, humanities officer at the Rockefeller Foundation since 1933, to investigate possibilities for the RF to support the project. As associate director for humanities at the foundation (1940–62), Marshall actively supported efforts to establish a UNESCO pilot project in Haiti, particularly by funding the study and development of Creole language materials for instructional purposes (Figure 5.1).

The experience and networks from within the foundation enabled the philanthropic organization to maintain an influential role in the pilot project's planning.[20] Scholars have drawn attention to the interests of the foundation and its collaboration with U.S. officials. In considering the vantage point of Haitians securing ties with the foundation, we turn our attention to the moments when and the reasons why the foundation was invited to participate. While Marshall himself had no prior personal or

FIG. 5.1 Graduation ceremony for an adult literacy program that preceded the UNESCO/Haiti Pilot Project. The instructor is the gentleman with the blazer. (Photo by John Marshall. Courtesy: Rockefeller Archive Center.)

professional ties to Haiti, he was able to use his contacts at the American Council of Learned Societies (ACLS), an organization that he previously worked for and that the RF frequently funded, to secure contributions for the UNESCO/Haiti project. In particular, Marshall identified linguistic experts from the ACLS's Committee on Language Program with an interest in studying whether it was most appropriate to promote literacy through an individual's maternal language or an auxiliary language. In this case, the two respective languages in question were Haitian Creole and French. The commitment that Marshall made to support the literacy arm of the pilot project led him to secure a $7,500 grant-in-aid for study of printed and visual materials related to the project in 1948. The following year, an additional $2,500 was disbursed for the completion of the study.[21]

Pursuing a Haitian literacy project under the auspices of UNESCO gave U.S.-based linguists a political advantage. The well-published and internationally respected linguist W. F. Twadell, who became affiliated with the pilot project through his ties to the RF, advised, "The American imperialism label is a danger . . . that suggests that UNESCO is a safer sponsoring agency than any specifically American Council or Foundation." His concern was one that other American missionaries working in Haiti during the 1940s had, as they sought to ensure a favorable reputation for themselves in Haiti. Twadell was the chairman of an RF-funded consortium of linguists from prestigious American universities (Brown, Michigan, Cornell, and Texas) who convened on behalf of the education of Egyptian doctoral students and the teaching of languages. That gathering of professionals, along with Twadell's teaching and consulting experiences in Western Europe, Egypt, and the Philippines, among other places, are all factors that could inform Twadell's sensitivity to the value and the prospective challenges of international collaboration.[22]

Prior to the Estimé administration, Haitian officials collaborated with Protestant missionaries to carry out literacy campaigns in Haiti. Frank Laubach, a Christian missionary from the United States who advocated literacy as a mode of salvation, began working in Haiti at the invitation of the Northern Irish Methodist minister the Rev. H. Ormonde McConnell, who had evangelized to rural Haitians since 1933. The Vincent and Lescot administrations officially recognized Laubach's international reputation for promoting literacy and endorsed the McConnell-Laubach system to promote literacy in Haiti. Critics of the system, who were suspicious of the Protestant presence and the anglophone phonetics of the endorsed orthography, cautioned that the McConnell-Laubach program was a tool of U.S. (or at best, Anglo) cultural imperialism. The programs generated added critique when missionaries used their access to local communities to carry out an aggressive and violent campaign to force Vodou practitioners to renounce their beliefs. As an alternative to working with Protestants, the Estimé administration relied on the Catholic Church and, particularly, the leadership of the Marbial Valley's Catholic priest, Father Farnèse Louis-Charles, to educate Haiti's peasantry in Creole and eradicate Vodou in Haiti. Such collaborations were intended to secure the local peasantry's affiliation with Catholicism.[23]

The UNESCO pilot project plan held some prospect for creating distance between historic associations of Creole language instruction and religious missions, if not politics in Haiti. This was possible when Arthur Bonhomme (who was Protestant) became the Haitian government representative to the UNESCO project in Marbial. Furthermore, the emphasis on the role of experts in the UNESCO plans, added to the prospects that the politics of language instruction in Haiti could be neutralized. In an overly optimistic argument, Alfred Métraux projected that an orthographic "system recommended by a trained linguist would have the advantage of settling once and for all the dispute about the scientific character of [Haitian Creole's orthographic] system and of putting the whole problem on an objective basis without the stint of a religious bias." Métraux's expectations were grand. Frank Laubach was actually on UNESCO's original fundamental education board; and, McConnell ended up being a co-author with Métraux and others working on literacy in Marbial. The structures of the UNESCO/FE project in Haiti enabled continuities in the connections between individuals and projects tied to the United States (the McConnell-Laubach method) and Haiti, in direct and indirect ways.[24]

The UNESCO project plans also involved expertise, funds, and programming opportunities with ties to the U.S. State Department. During his time in Haiti, John Marshall reached out to the U.S. cultural attaché to Haiti, and in the months that followed, the U.S. Embassy hosted film screenings in the Marbial Valley pertaining to public health and nutrition topics.[25] One of the most influential connections early on in the project's planning came indirectly through the expertise of Frederick Rex, a former instructor and educational specialist for the Office of the Coordinator of Inter-American Affairs, later known as the Office of Inter-American Affairs (OIAA). As previously discussed, the OIAA was created in 1940 to facilitate public and private linkages, principally within the commercial and cultural spheres in the United States and Latin America, as a means of combatting perceived threats to U.S. national security during the Second World War.

The OIAA operated under close supervision of the Department of State. In fact, the State Department assumed most of the OIAA's functions in 1946 when the wartime office was abolished.[26] Rex's experience with Inter-American Affairs led UNESCO officials to place a high degree of trust in his perspective. Following a field visit to Haiti in July 1948, Rex gave the Rockefeller Foundation's John Marshall the impression that "the situation of the [Marbial] Valley is just about hopeless." Marshall pressed Rex to address the fact that his observations "seemed to indicate an explicit admission on UNESCO's part that there were people in the tropical belt for whom nothing could be done." Earlier that year, Marshall himself had described conditions in the valley as "little short of desperate." However, Marshall's hopes for the project led him to conclude with caution that work in the valley could "bring . . . some . . . relief" to the Haitian people. In contrast, Rex described seemingly impossible conditions that could only be tackled through "a massive operation," essentially confirming what Huxley had relayed to Estimé in June 1948: the operation needed to be "one that would begin well below the level of education."[27]

Drawing insight from his travels across Latin America, Rex also cautioned that due to its linguistic and racial distinctions, Haiti was not a useful model for addressing poverty in the world. This was a challenge to the Pan-American vision that Haitians had been investing in, as a way of positioning themselves on a par with their regional neighbors. Having traveled the region as a field expert for UNESCO, Rex opined, "Virtually all the Latin American countries felt that any demonstration in Haiti would have no effect in Latin America. While Haiti is one of the sister republics, it is not regarded as a really integral member of the Pan American group." Rex explained that such views were "largely because of race differences" between Haitians and other Latin Americans, but also commented that he did not expect "work in Haiti [to] have influence in Africa." Thus, even as Haitians engaged in the FE project attempted to position themselves as equal partners and to promote the Marbial Valley as a site worth studying for its comparative value, the ways that foreigners perceived Haitians and

Haiti in relationship to their own states impeded the realization of postwar international planning ideals. Rex did express concern that the region's nations shared "some degree of responsibility" for the conditions he witnessed in Haiti. However, his uncertainty about Haiti's relevance for those doing work in Latin America or in Africa did little to encourage him, after a first site evaluation, to recommend that UNESCO officials contract with the Haitian government for a pilot project in Marbial.[28]

While questions persisted about the extent to which the UNESCO project might prove to be a useful international model, U.S. officials did not slow down in introducing their programs to Haiti and elsewhere across the region. Consequently, officials in Haiti and from the UNESCO Secretariat sought to take advantage of proposals Harry S. Truman made as early as 1947 and reiterated during his 1949 inaugural speech as president to make "the benefits of [the United States'] scientific advances and industrial progress available for the improvement and growth of underdeveloped areas." The international agenda that U.S. president Truman and his officials set led the U.S. State Department to extend and reorganize the inter-American projects from the 1930s and early 1940s, most notably through the Office of Inter-American Affairs.[29] The technical assistance program, referred to as Point IV (because it was the fourth policy proposal in Truman's speech), extended the Truman administration's earlier efforts to contain the spread of communism in the world. The containment programs began most visibly under the auspices of what came to be known as the Truman Doctrine.

The containment programs were primarily political in intent and economic in form. The doctrine, as emerged from Truman's declaration on March 12, 1947, held that U.S. policymakers ought to provide $400 million in assistance to Greece and Turkey, and to dispatch civilian and military personnel, as well as equipment, in order to support a defense movement against the rise of communism in those territories and nearby regions. Truman's call for direct intervention led to several U.S. foreign aid policies and programs intended to stabilize and stimulate foreign economies around the world for the purposes of impeding the spread of communism. On June 5, 1947, Secretary of State George C. Marshall encouraged Truman's policy by proposing a financing scheme for the reconstruction of postwar Europe. Following Congress's passing of the Economic Cooperation Act in March 1948, the U.S. government dedicated more than $12 billion to restore Western Europe's infrastructure and economy. In the following year, the Point IV proposal led to initiatives aimed at providing technical assistance to Latin America and the Caribbean, as well as in the Middle East, Asia, and Africa. Congress supported these programs by allocating a $25 million budget for the 1950/51 fiscal year through the Foreign Economic Assistance Act.

In many ways, Point IV extended and reorganized the work carried out by the inter-American affairs agencies which pursued technical assistance missions across the Western Hemisphere during the 1930s and early 1940s. According to historian Claude Erb, Point IV "represented a commitment which ultimately made foreign aid a permanent element of [U.S.] national policy." In this way, Truman's aid to Greece and Turkey, Marshall's financing plan for Western Europe, and the technical assistance offered through Point IV collectively facilitated "a continuing and self-perpetuating global mission" for the United States in an array of sites including Haiti.[30]

The resources John Marshall helped pilot project planners secure and the individuals enlisted for the UNESCO project in his role as the officer of a U.S.-based foundation reinforced the importance of the United States to the project. When Marshall first visited the valley in 1948, he witnessed "high excitement . . . about the UNESCO project." As members of the local UNESCO team accompanied him into the valley, they were greeted by "several people by the roadside who shouted, 'Viva UNESCO'" and offered them coconuts, mangoes, and cigarettes.[31] Marbial Valley residents and Haitian professionals involved in the UNESCO/FE project as experts further enabled subtle links between the valley and the United States to form. As local activities advanced in ways that held promise even "quite independent of what UNESCO [might] go on to do," connections between the valley and the United States deepened.[32]

In the months following Marshall's visit, members of the field team sought to encourage UNESCO's investments with more than just the cheers of a well-orchestrated welcoming committee. In response to caveats that Métraux raised and to Arthur Bonhomme's leadership, local residents, with the support of Father Louis-Charles, set up canteens and built a children's playground. To address transportation needs, local cooperatives constructed and maintained a road that shortened and improved the commute into the valley from Jacmel to just over a half hour.[33] Arousing the interests of residents led to a turnout of more than 400 attendees at local screenings of films about intestinal worms, irrigation, and nutritional dieting hosted by the U.S. Embassy's Cultural Division possible.[34] As a result of this interest, Bonhomme wrote to the UNESCO Secretariat to request help with acquiring equipment to present additional films.[35] By the end of the summer, Bonhomme was planning to host another U.S. Embassy–sponsored film session in Marbial, this time as a fundraiser for the local canteen and as a means of encouraging Jacmeliens to visit Marbial.[36]

The Haitian experts who originated from outside the valley, many of whom had experience studying with American experts in Haiti or in the United States, were also central to on-site developments. The leading agronomist on the field team was Edouard Berrouet, who had studied agronomy on the outskirts of Port-au-Prince at Damien, the school founded by U.S. and Haitian officials during the U.S. military occupation of Haiti in 1924. Working in Marbial, Berrouet consulted with Marshall to identify seeds and farming techniques that would improve agricultural production in the Marbial Valley (Figure 5.2).[37] Recent graduates of the Institut d'Ethnologie were on-site and assisted Métraux with the ethnographic research he was conducting on folk traditions in Marbial. Young Haitian ethnologists, such as Michel Lamartinière Honorat, prided themselves on the opportunity to apply their research skills to a local community development initiative, while bolstering their credentials by affiliating with a prominent international

FIG. 5.2 Members of the professional team in the Marbial Valley. Included here are Arthur Bonhomme, Haitian government representative to UNESCO (standing second from the right with necktie); Alfred Métraux (standing third from the right in the same row as Bonhomme) hired by UNESCO to survey conditions in the valley; and the lead agronomist, Edouard Berrouet (first person from the left, kneeling in the front). (Courtesy: Rockefeller Archive Center.)

project.[38] More senior Haitian ethnographers such as Rémy Bastien and Suzanne Sylvain were also on-site deepening their understanding of Haiti's rural social structures and traditions.

Several of the Haitian professionals working with the pilot project in one capacity or another had traveled to the United States under the auspices of exchanges arranged between the Haitian government and the U.S. government, through the U.S. Office of Inter-American Affairs during the early 1940s. The FE specialist Emmanuel Gabriel, who besides working in the UNESCO Secretariat also spent time in Marbial and in the United States working to develop Creole language manuals for the pilot project, had pursued undergraduate studies at Teachers College at Columbia University.[39] Jeanne Sylvain, who studied social work at Columbia University and helped to found the School of Social Work in Port-au-Prince, was also among those working in Marbial. Métraux, who praised Sylvain's "intelligence and . . . her energy," relied on the social worker to motivate other team members and to orient Yvonne Oddon, a French woman, whom he had recruited to work on the literacy arm of the project.[40]

The manual arts training that Haitians and Americans collaborated on earlier in the decade also proved beneficial for activities in Marbial. Haitian artist Georges Remponeau, who had developed his drawing and painting skills at the Centre d'Art in Port-au-Prince and completed additional training as a boursier at Hampton University, contributed his skills to the literacy program by illustrating the teaching manuals. The center was founded in 1944 by Haitian artists, including Remponeau, and Americans, such as DeWitt Peters, who had originally traveled to Haiti to teach in an English program and was interested in Haiti's local arts tradition. With funding from the Haitian and U.S. governments, the center became one of the foremost sites of inter-American collaboration during the 1940s, and a generative complement to the opportunities Haitian artists had to study abroad.[41]

Other Haitian experts with inter-American experience, such as the architect Albert Mangonès and the public health specialist François Duvalier, contributed to the Marbial Valley project through their affiliation with other agencies that were collaborating with UNESCO. Based on his experience with the UN Building Commission, Mangonès was enlisted to design a "base camp" for the pilot project. Mangonès had built his credentials by studying in Belgium and at Cornell University. Duvalier, who had spent time as a public health boursier at the University of Michigan, worked to improve Haitian public health conditions in various capacities such as serving as a section chief for the Inter-American Sanitary Commission's Malaria mission (1945–46) and director general of the Anti-Yaws Campaign. Yaws (*frambesia tropica*) was a disease in the treponematosis family which includes venereal disease, pinta, and endemic syphilis, which was communicable through everyday interactions (such as children playing together or sleeping next to one another) and resulted in disfiguring lesions. During the time of the pilot project, Duvalier worked to extend earlier efforts by Haitian and American medical professionals to eradicate the disease in the valley, by establishing an independent yaws clinic.[42] Through their sponsored studies and other affiliations with individuals and institutions from the United States, Haitian professionals were able to use the credentials and the connections they had from U.S.-based networks to secure a place at the center of major development initiatives on the island.

Hopeful, Not Hopeless in the Valley

The persistent engagement of Haitians working in the Marbial Valley ultimately led to a formal commitment between UNESCO and the Haitian government in September 1949 for the pilot project. The agreement followed positive reviews from a site visit conducted by a commission of representatives from the United Nations and its specialized agencies, the Food and Agriculture Organization (FAO) and the World Health Organization (WHO). Estimé invited the commission to investigate the possibilities for development in Haiti during the summer of 1948. When the UN commission observed the work that residents and Haitian professionals were carrying out in the valley, they concluded that the Marbial Valley project was "essential" to the advancement of social and economic conditions in Haiti.[43]

The developments in Marbial led to a renewed sense of promise among foreigners about the possibilities of working in Haiti. Even the critic Frederick Rex "very happily reverse[d] . . . himself" after a second visit, held in conjunction with the UN Commission, allowed him to witness what locals had accomplished since his earlier report.[44] Rex's newfound favor for the UNESCO/Haiti project led him to express a "general eager[ness] to see the Haitian Project become a center for the study of all kinds of tropical problems." Besides the yaws work, medical professionals from the United States had been working in Haiti throughout the earlier part of the century studying malaria, hookworm, and other diseases in Port-au-Prince and rural Haiti. Rex proposed that the work in Marbial, "should be of a character and quality to be useful elsewhere and to set standards for the preparation of other materials of the same type."[45] In December 1948, UNESCO officials noted the United Nations Commission's opinion that the pilot project was an "integral part of the work" needed for developing Haiti. Attending UNESCO's General Conference in 1948, Marshall confirmed: "[T]he stock of the Haitian project is now high indeed. So far as I know there was no debate whatsoever about UNESCO's continued interest in it: that was simply taken for granted. Everyone was much impressed with the way that Haitian support had materialized, and likewise impressed with the apparent attitude of the UN Commission toward the work."[46]

Contributions from UNESCO, the Haitian government, and U.S.-based partners were pledged for the proposed project in Marbial. The UNESCO Secretariat allocated $13,500 to the project for 1949 to cover the expenses of employing Métraux as a leading specialist on the project.[47] These funds would be added to a matching supplement from the Haitian government, alongside contributions from the Rockefeller Foundation and other partner agencies such as the Inter-American Cooperative Service for Agricultural Production, for a modest budget of less than $50,000 per year.[48] The opportunity for UNESCO to work in Marbial lent truth to a comment Marshall made after his site visit in April 1948: The Marbial Valley is "ideal in one sense: you could hardly have found a spot where there is more to do." The offer of the Haitian government to host a pilot project in the valley was "essentially an international service" by Haiti to UNESCO, in terms of the lessons that work in Haiti could generate for the world. Those lessons were expected to cover the broad areas of focus specified by the 1949 agreement: (1) primary schooling and general adult education; (2) auxiliary language teaching (i.e., basic French); (3) health education and medical services; (4) agricultural and veterinary education and extension work; (5) a community library, museum, and arts center; (6) women's education; and, (7) rural industries and cooperatives.[49]

The formal plans for a pilot project stimulated heightened expectations about the global value of multilateral development planning in Haiti, and about sustaining partnerships with experts from the United States. Estimations about the project's value circulated widely through the commission's report, *Mission to Haiti*, the UN periodical, *Courier*, international media outlets, and personal testimonies.[50] Journalists and broadcasters for *Time* magazine, the *New York Times*, the *Saturday Evening Post*, the U.S. television network CBS, and newspapers in Haiti, as well as individuals in private correspondence, wrote about the challenges and opportunities of the UNESCO pilot project within the context of the newly formed UNESCO and its efforts to tackle some of the world's most pressing issues. Even graduate students based in the United States at New Mexico State University and Columbia were drawn to UNESCO's efforts in Haiti as a topic for their master's projects. Widespread promotion of the project led to a number of visitors traveling to the site who produced accounts for popular interest, as well as official U.S. State Department efforts to advance President Truman's Point IV agenda. Most of the accounts focused on the challenge of traveling into the area and the conditions visitors found upon arrival.[51]

One illustrative example of the surge in foreign enthusiasm and related strides that took place on behalf of the Marbial community was the combined effort of UNESCO, the Rockefeller Foundation, and ACLS linguists based at U.S. universities to promote literacy in the valley. Discussions between Marshall and Métraux about opportunities for foreign linguists to study Haitian Creole in Marbial soon evolved into ideas about using these studies to develop a "world model" for understanding the world's languages and the best way to achieve widespread literacy.[52] Through their joint effort, the Haitian valley became a site for scientific research on Creole. The Rev. McConnell, whose ongoing work with the Methodist Church in Port-au-Prince had him working on Creole earlier in the 1940s, used the Marbial plans to continue his research and writings.[53] According to Métraux, there was a critical need for a scientific study of Haitian Creole. While there were excellent studies of Creole languages in Dutch Guiana and Dominica, "no attempt [had] been made to analyze the Haitian Creole spoken by 4,000,000 people."[54] Besides McConnell, the linguists that

Marshall recruited for the pilot project anticipated incorporating Haitian Creole into existing studies that sought to assess the legitimacy of the world's Creole languages as bona fide languages that could be formally taught. The work that they did in Haiti would help them advance ongoing investigations into whether an individual's maternal tongue or an auxiliary language was best suited for promoting literacy. Writing to Marshall, the English linguist I. A. Richards, then based at Harvard University's Graduate School of Education, expressed enthusiasm for using research in Haiti to disprove that "it is better to teach reading via the mother tongue." He told Marshall, "I would like a chance to prove [the theory] wrong prominently. It is badly misleading the world."[55] Despite Richards's hypothesis, he and other linguists working in conjunction with the pilot project dedicated themselves to creating Creole language materials as a "path to literacy in more international languages such as the endemic French."[56]

A significant portion of the Creole language material development activities tied to the pilot project took place in the United States, particularly with the assistance of Haitians based there, blurring a bit the distinction between foreigners and Haitians. Both Marshall and Métraux noted that contact with the Haitian consul in New York could easily yield "competent writers of Créole." Marshall's familiarity with Haitian Creole speakers in the United States led him to incorrectly presume that these individuals were also adept at writing Creole.[57] Métraux made a case that working with Haitians in the United States would eliminate the costs associated with traveling to Haiti to conduct work on Creole phonetics. In his opinion, "Dialectical differences are slight. They should be disregarded if we want to keep in view the practical matter of the system."[58] Some of this linguistic research was already underway at Cornell University where Professor Robert Hall was gaining familiarity with Creole "with a cultivated Haitian in Ithaca."[59] Hall, like his colleague Twadell, affiliated with the pilot project through the Rockefeller Foundation. Twadell expected that after carrying out a grammatical (rather than phonetic) analysis of Haitian Creole, several weeks would be spent testing the results on what he crassly referred to as "some good laboratory animals." Like Métraux, Twadell anticipated that relying on native speakers could benefit the development of Creole reading materials.[60] One of those native speakers was Emmanuel Gabriel, the educator and UNESCO/FE specialist, who traveled from the UNESCO Secretariat in Paris to work as part of a research team that Richards created at Harvard University.[61] Richards celebrated Gabriel's contributions and an introductory primer that his linguistics team created. He relayed to Marshall his hope that the primer would be a "world model," emphasizing that this ought to be the case for all instruments created by UNESCO.[62]

Despite this surge of enthusiasm and activity, the advances in creating Creole reading materials and the hopeful visions of Haitians, Americans, and other UNESCO affiliates on behalf of fundamental education in Haiti were short-lived as administrative challenges in Paris, compounded by on-site politics, impeded sustained progress in Marbial. In March 1950, Métraux raised concerns about the "inequities" of the United Nations' Technical Assistance missions, as he was preparing to leave his assignment in Marbial. Beyond disparities in compensation, unequal access to leadership opportunities seems to have directly impacted the viability of the pilot project. As Métraux prepared to terminate his role as on-site director of the pilot project, UNESCO officials sent several other experts to direct the project, much to the consternation of the Haitian government's representative to the pilot project, Arthur Bonhomme, who had been intimately engaged in leading the project with Métraux.

The ongoing restructuring that took place as UNESCO sought to identify the best way to pursue its projects, meant the absence of a stable project structure. This negatively impacted the long-term success of the project.[63] Despite all of the initial efforts to pursue the pilot project, UNESCO officials spent time in the earlier part of 1950 pouring their energy for fundamental education into the establishment of a Fundamental Clearing House. The purpose of the new structure was to train educational professionals and support the activities of "associated projects," which were intended to succeed the pilot project phase, as carried out in Haiti. Plans for a Clearing House materialized in Mexico, the home country of UNESCO's new director-general, Jaime Torres Bodet. As Huxley forewarned Estimé in 1948, within five years of the pilot project plans, the Haitian government was now primarily responsible for funding and administering the work in Marbial. In 1953, the Marbial Valley was officially designated as an "associated project." This relieved wealthy member states of the responsibility for providing UNESCO with a majority of resources for fundamental education projects. It also limited the amount of support UNESCO's Fundamental Education Clearing House would be obligated to disburse to the associated projects. Years after his assignment with the pilot project ended, Métraux continued to lament the approach that UNESCO had taken to working in Haiti. Following a visit to the Marbial Valley in 1956, Métraux informed John Marshall that the UNESCO/Haiti pilot project "had virtually no effect. The conditions of life of the Valley have hardly altered and the project itself is virtually defunct."[64] The UNESCO/Haiti pilot project in fundamental education was indeed one of many "great utopian social engineering schemes of the twentieth century." As described by scholar James C. Scott, these plans were "well-intentioned schemes . . . for improving the human condition [that went] tragically awry."[65]

Still, while the hope that Estimé and his administrators placed in UNESCO and in tapping into resources from U.S. partners such as the Rockefeller Foundation and the ACLS linguists was forcibly curtailed, it would not easily be extinguished. The UNESCO pilot project had given activities such as the use of Haitian Creole for instruction, initiated during the occupation and post-occupation years, an opportunity to be extended during the post–World War II years. Although UNESCO was the leading administrative body for the pilot project, the international organization's reliance on its member states for funds and knowledge, whether in the form of records, work experience, professional training, or professional networks, facilitated a principal role for the United States in activities taking place in the Marbial Valley. Estimé and his administrators looked to international collaboration in order to leverage the financial and human capital already present in Haiti to advance projects such as the literacy campaign in Marbial.

While the pilot project was limited in how it advanced, several aspects of the project reinforced the appeal of cultivating ties between individuals and institutions in Haiti and the United States. First, the project provided experts who were from the United States or who trained in the United States with an opportunity to test their ideas and employ models that they embraced. Consequently, the agronomists, the linguists, and the artists, among others working in Marbial, had a platform upon which they could develop credentials that were not specific to the pilot project. Second, Haitians and Americans working on the Creole-language materials had occasion to witness how working in a multilateral context could temper the challenges of collaborating on a politically sensitive project. Moreover, such a context lent itself to encouraging consideration of the orthographic project as a scientific one. Third, and perhaps most significantly, the overlapping interests of individuals from Haiti and the United States had preceded the pilot project, and so they did not cease to exist with the project's demise. Thus, members of the Estimé administration and his successors, the Rockefeller Foundation, the U.S. State Department, professionals based in Haiti and in the United States, and residents of the Marbial Valley, among others affiliated with the UNESCO initiative, could continue to consider the potential value of ties to the United States when making plans for themselves and their communities in the decades that followed.

Epilogue

Enduring Promises

When Pierre Gilbert traveled from Port-au-Prince to East Lansing, Michigan, in 1949, to pursue advanced agricultural studies at Michigan State University, he had no idea that he would be relocating to the United States seventeen years later. Gilbert's decision to live and work in Michigan in 1966 was his attempt to protect himself and, by extension, his family from the political violence being carried out under the leadership of Haitian President François Duvalier, who was elected into office in 1957. As the late Gilbert recalled, when faced with the decision to flee, securing refuge in Michigan seemed logical. He was very familiar with the area, having traveled as a *boursier* in 1949 for two years of college-level studies and then again in 1963 to complete graduate-level studies in agricultural sciences.[1] By 1972, his wife joined him in Michigan.

Before Duvalier became president of Haiti, he was one of Port-au-Prince's most prominent young *indigénistes*. He had traveled as a boursier in 1942 to study at the University of Michigan in Ann Arbor and he had worked for inter-American agencies during the latter part of the 1940s. That work brought him across the Haitian countryside to communities such as the Marbial Valley where he came to be endearingly referred to as "Papa Doc," because of his leadership as a medical doctor working to eliminate yaws in rural communities. Nearly a decade into office, Duvalier, who was ruling Haiti in an increasingly authoritarian manner, kept his eye on Washington officials who were even more invested in the allegiance of state leaders across the region than during the preceding decades. Aware of the military and political support that U.S. officials extended to Latin American and Caribbean leaders who sought to contain communist movements in their countries, Duvalier gained leverage for using political repression to defend against his detractors whom he sweepingly classified as being communist. Because individuals across social classes—whether politically active or not—faced the risk of assault, imprisonment, or death if they were suspected to be opposed to Duvalier's rule, those who were able to relocated to destinations across the globe.[2]

Many, like Gilbert, chose the United States because it was a place where they had specific connections established during the post-occupation years. Living outside of Haiti was not necessarily an ideal choice for many; it was a practical one. The decision to move his wife and family from Haiti was one that Gilbert neither anticipated nor initially felt inclined toward. Yet, the Gilberts would live full lives in Michigan where they raised their children, were active in building the local Haitian community, worked until they retired, and eventually died. A significant part of their community building was serving as "godparents" for other Haitians who arrived in the area under an array of circumstances, and sometimes collaborating to support communities in Haiti. And, while we have often acknowledged that individuals like the Gilberts moved as a practical response to conditions of hardship and repression in their home country, it is equally important that we consider more explicitly the role that the pre-migration contexts of connections with American citizens and institutions played in the process.[3]

The sizable brain and population drain from Haiti to the world following the auspicious era of the immediate post-occupation years was one of the challenges of realizing the possibilities anticipated during the 1930s and 1940s. The promise of tapping into U.S.-based networks, institutional and funding sources to introduce new opportunities to young Haitians, develop Haiti's professional cadres, and improve economic, political, and social conditions in Haiti, was something that figures like Jean Price-Mars and Maurice

Dartigue pursued during the 1930s and 1940s with a particular interest in Haitian governance and society. But it is not likely that the coordinators of programs linking citizens from Haiti and the United States, such as Price-Mars, Dartigue, and their U.S.-based contacts, intended to build a cadre of Haitian experts who would reside outside of Haiti, contribute to advances in other societies, or work to contribute to Haitian society from abroad. Even Dartigue could be counted among those who left with his family for an extended period of time, going into exile after the ousting of the Lescot administration with the Noiriste Revolution of 1946.[4]

It is also unlikely that advocates of intellectual cooperation during the 1930s and 1940s expected that the areas of expertise they emphasized in order to enact critical reforms in Haiti would continue to be areas of need well into the twenty-first century. But that is precisely what happened, alongside many other unanticipated consequences. Large numbers of Haitian professionals residing outside of Haiti, or young Haitians who study abroad, particularly for university studies, have become the norm. Skills initially intended to serve the needs of Haiti's communities have disproportionately benefitted communities elsewhere in the world. Professional opportunities, expertise, financial or material resources, and cultural experiences based in the United States and elsewhere have continued to draw the attention of Haitians seeking betterment for themselves, their communities, or their nation.

As the narratives in the preceding chapters have revealed, historical interpretations that account for the complexity of why some Haitians continue to look to the United States when making plans for themselves or Haitian society make it possible for us to understand with greater accuracy and nuance the expanding American thread in Haitian history. The promise that many Haitians have come to expect from looking abroad, and particularly toward the United States, for solutions has been more than a legacy of the U.S. military occupation of Haiti or continuing domination in its wake. It has also been a product of Haitian efforts to capitalize upon their faith in the promise of foreign ties, even at moments when the role of foreigners in Haitian affairs has been heavily criticized.

And, as the presence of Haitians abroad swelled, leading them to play an increasing role in activities based in or in partnership with Americans who were not of Haitian descent, the lines between foreign and Haitian blurred. It is a blurring that further reinforces the challenge of answering anyone who asks: What is Haitian? What is "foreign" or American? The partnerships and cosmopolitan perspectives explored in the preceding chapters suggest that we establish a fuller account of the ways that what is often identified as "foreign" was created in conjunction with individuals and entities from Haiti.

The programs that Gilbert and other Haitian citizens participated in and promoted during the 1930s and 1940s laid a foundation upon which an ever-expanding Haitian public identified individuals and institutions based in the United States as a way of addressing their civic and personal concerns. Haitian men and women held fast to a message that they heard both in Haiti and abroad, or witnessed firsthand, through inter-American campaigns and multilateral projects: tapping into foreign resources, including those based in the United States, promised to improve conditions across the Haitian nation as well as in their individual lives. And, even though these programs did not fulfill the visions of those who planned, administered, or participated in them, the allure of looking abroad for fruitful connections and to be recognized as integral contributors to the world's affairs has persisted for many Haitians in Haiti and abroad. The enduring promise is rooted in the programs that Haitian men and women like Pierre Gilbert participated in during the first fifteen years after the U.S. occupation of Haiti ended. The promise remains entangled with an awareness of the constraints and costs that come with sustaining ties to the United States. Ultimately, the promise is a belief that there might still be value in trying to reap benefits from those ties once more.[5]

Acknowledgments

All praise and thanks to the amazing Spirit that led me to and through this project. This is the hardest thing I have ever done and for that I am grateful to all who believed in me and this project along the way, offering support in heartfelt, wise, and practical ways. As a connector who cherishes her ties to and ability to serve as a bridge between many brilliant, beautiful people and communities, I consider it fitting that the support and resources that made this book possible move between academic, personal, community, and spiritual spaces. I apologize for any names that I neglect to note below, with hopes that everyone that I've interacted with along the way has felt the depth of my appreciation in real time.

Thank you to all who generously shared stories and information that made this book possible. The first among those storytellers were elders from Haiti's Michigan-based diaspora whose testimonies, beginning in 1999, helped me tune into the historical richness of Haiti's post-U.S. occupation period. Since then, interviews and informal conversations or correspondence with individuals based in Haiti, the United States, Canada, and France continuously reaffirmed that there was a very worthwhile history to draw greater attention to. Sadly, many of these contacts have made their physical transition since we were in touch, making the testimonies and the time they accorded me all the more valuable. Of particular note are Maxime Léon, who shared his skepticism as graciously as he did his insight, encouragement, and library; and Roger Lescot, Esther Dartigue, and Marie-Madeleine

Price-Mars, who generously made available the historical records in the family archives that they passionately dedicated themselves to curating.

Two other people who played a critical role in this book's creation before transitioning to another life are André Elizée and Eddy Jean-Baptiste. I dedicate the book to them to reaffirm my hope that it is of value to scholars and members of an interested general public. Thanks to historian Irma Watkins-Owens, I prioritized meeting André and conducting research at the Schomburg following my interviews in Michigan. André's critical eye helped me navigate the then mostly unprocessed Maurice Dartigue Papers and begin to consider the viability and need for academic writing based on the materials. Thanks to his encouragement, I eventually wrote a PhD dissertation using those records and materials from subsequent research, most notably in Haiti.

Well into revising the dissertation into a book, I befriended fellow Haitian American, Miamian, and New Thought believer Eddy Jean-Baptiste, who as artist, activist, entrepreneur, and spiritual force was eager to learn as much about Haiti as possible. With an unwavering certainty, Eddy affirmed until his very last days that this book would indeed get done, at a time when I deeply questioned that possibility. Both André and Eddy's encouraging words will continue to resonate within me whenever I recall the journey of creating this book.

For the past two decades, I have dedicated myself to defining a professional life for myself as an academic. Mentors, colleagues, and friends along the way inspired me to see this course as an appealing one and to remember that it can be pursued in many different ways. And, whenever I doubted my own place in this community of minds, I found encouragement by embracing the positive feedback they generously offered to me about my unique contributions to the field.

As a graduate student at Michigan State University, I worked with faculty who excelled as scholars and modeled the importance of living a well-rounded life. I continue to learn that lesson and as I do, I see even more clearly how fortunate I have been to work with each of you: Richard W. Thomas, Laurent Dubois, Darlene Clark Hine, Leslie Moch, Peter Beattie, and Michael Largey.

Other graduate school faculty included June Manning Thomas who, with Richard, has continued to embrace me as mentee and spiritual daughter. Memories of the late Ruth Simms Hamilton, who reinforced my charge to be successful when I headed to Haiti for pre-dissertation research before making her transition, are a reminder to press ONWARDS!!! in the direction of my diasporic dreams. Methods work with Peter Vinten-Johansen and Rubén Rumbaut as a master's student, and with Rebecca Scott as a doctoral student helped me establish critical groundwork that gave rise to this book.

The enthusiasm and support of colleagues at Florida International University, where I have served on the faculty since 2005, has been an important experience at a time when far too many worthy candidates have difficulty being hired and tenured. Help came from many especially in the form of a willingness to read, offer feedback and guide me at various stages of the work. Andrea Queeley has been a tremendous source of friendship and positive affirmation through every intellectual and emotional turn through this experience. In the first of many nudges, Aurora Morcillo invited me to develop my book proposal and circulate it for feedback. This was the beginning of several thoughtful and bountiful exchanges at FIU that minimized the isolating nature of the process and maximized my ability to grow as an academic writer. I am grateful for every writing group member and writing partner, especially Moses Shumow, Lynn Barrett, Vrushali Patil, Rebecca Friedman, Alexandra Cornelius, Kirsten Wood, Dionne Stephens, Veronique Helenon, and Lara Kriegel. Mark Szuchman, David Cook, Bianca Premo, Danielle Clealand, Sarah Mahler, Laurie Shrage, Hilary Jones, Okezi Otovo, April Merleaux, Ken Lipartito, Victor Uribe, Liesl Picard, and Brooke Wooldridge also read, commented, served as interlocutors, and/or offered support in the best ways they could. It is a blessing and a challenge, as I face word limitations here, that I can count so many colleagues, administrators, and staff persons as allies, a genuine team of support and friendship. Additionally, our intellectually curious students have helped more than they may know. My heartfelt thanks.

Research and writing seminars, as well as invitations for works-in-progress sessions afforded me funded time to develop the work. The first of these was the four-week summer seminar, Interrogating the African Diaspora (Interad), coordinated by Jean Rahier, Percy Hinzten, and Felipe Smith. Since my undergrad days at Tulane University, Felipe unselfishly encouraged and guided me through the processes of writing, pursuing graduate studies, and earning tenure. The Interad experience also gifted me friendships within a rigorous intellectual community that includes Andrea Queeley, Devyn Spence Benson, Reena Goldthree, and Irmary Reyes Santos, who helped me articulate this book's arguments about *indigénisme*.

I developed those arguments during a visit to Johns Hopkins University, upon invitation from Nathan Connolly and the generous participation of Franklin Knight, an intellectual giant in our field, Melanie Shell Weiss, and others. An exchange with the late Sidney Mintz during my visit and earlier, when I was ABD, encouraged me to stay the course.

Invitations to speak at Dartmouth, thanks to Reena Goldthree; at Swarthmore, thanks to Arturo and Aurora Schmidt; and at Duke, thanks to my ever-generous mentor Laurent Dubois, in 2010, provided a space to develop my historical arguments and ability to relate them to contemporary issues. A special thanks to David Barry Gaspar who always took time to keep our fruitful conversations going. These campus talks, presentations at the meetings of the American Historical Association, American Studies Association, Association for the Study of African American Life and History, Caribbean Studies Association, Haitian Studies Association, Society for the History of American Foreign Relations, and many other generously hosted sessions helped the project mature.

Last but far from least, the National History Center's inaugural 2006 decolonization seminar founded by William Roger Louis gave me room to explore, for the first time, several historiographies that have proven useful for this and future projects. The insights from my conversations with and/or the work of seminar leaders and fellow participants, especially Yasmin Khan, Lucy Chester, Jason Parker, and Daniel Branch, continue to reverberate. Thanks to Toyin Falola for prompting me to attend.

I am richer in life because of the intellectual community I became a part of during this process. Nadève Ménard has journeyed with me since I collected interviews and archival documents in Haiti in 2001. Matthew Smith, Kate Ramsey, and Millery Polyné are a "post-occupation trio" who, besides their individual magnificence, shared with me intrigue about the previously understudied 1934–57 period in Haitian history. What a joy to witness what they each bring as true scholars and to celebrate the fact that "we are the historiography," or at least a catalyst for its growth. In Haiti, powerhouse scholars such as Laënnec Hurbon, Jean Casimir, Évelyne Trouillot, Suzy Castor, Michel Hector, and Pierre Buteau created a welcome space for me to pursue my research interests within the Haitian academy. And, Watson Denis, Jhon Picard Byron, and Wien Weibert Arthus, who were also very supportive along the way, are doing noteworthy work to create more bridges for scholars across generations and geographic boundaries. Added support came from Nirvah Jean-Jacques, Marie-Lourdes Elgirus, Marie-Carmel Lafontant, Max Penette, Jacques Thébaud, Georges Condé, Consuela and Ronald Mevs, Michlet Divers, and three other giants who have passed: Lamartinière Honorat, Gérard Pierre-Charles, and Ernest Léveillé. I am also grateful to Ishtar Govia, Shawn Christian, Harley Etienne, Grace Sanders, Jacqueline McLeod, Frank Guridy, Yveline Alexis, and Aims McGuinness for being true angels along the way.

There are so many others whose time, words, model scholarship, and/or feedback on various iterations of the manuscript also made a positive difference in this process. Thank you Edmund Abaka, Carol Anderson, Sarah Arvey, Patrick Bellegarde-Smith, Mark Bradely, Frank Costigliola, Pero Dagbovie, Marlene Daut, Robin Derby, Alex Dupuy, Robert Fatton, Susan Ferber, Ada Ferrer,

Carolyn Fick, Pierre Michel Fontaine, Gisela Fosada, Cary Fraser, Julia Gaffield, Mark Gilderhaus, Paul Kramer, Lester Langley, Jana Lipman, Bob Maguire, Jacqueline McLeod, Elaine Maisner, Louis Herns Marcelin, Minkah Makalani, Michael J. McGandy, Claudine Michel, Harvey Neptune, Guitèle Nicoleau, Nathalie Pierre, Brenda Gayle Plummer, Emily Rosenberg, Guido Ruggiero, Elena Sabogal, Ricardo Salvatore, Julius Scott, Jim Sweet, Clarence Taylor, Bettye Collier Thomas, the late Michel-Rolph Trouillot, Gina Ulysse, Ashli White, Erica Windler, and my fellow Feminarians. I am also grateful to the generosity and recommendations of each blind reviewer who over the years read a range of manuscripts that have come together as this book. And, special thanks to all who have taught and encouraged me since my ABCLand days, especially my junior high school history teacher, Mrs. Donnelly, and my undergraduate advisor, the late Judith Schafer: the seeds you've planted continue to blossom.

Several institutions funded the research, writing, and editing for this book. At the graduate level, these included Michigan State University's Graduate School, College of Arts and Science, Urban Affairs Programs, and International Studies Programs, as well as the Social Science Research Council's Pre-Dissertation Research program and the Rockefeller Archive Center's Grant-in-Aid program. Postdoctoral sources included Florida International University (Office of the Provost, Department of History, Department of Politics and International Relations, Kimberly Green Latin American and Caribbean Center, African and African Diaspora Studies Program), the University of Miami (College of Arts and Sciences and Department of History), and the University of Florida Libraries (Latin American and Caribbean Collection Research Travel Grant). Thanks to all of the administrators and staff persons who made securing these funds possible. And, for holding many of the pieces together day in and day out, a special thanks to Emily Carreras, Hayat Kassab-Gresham, and Madelyn Tirado.

Librarians, archivists, and staff persons who helped along the way, when I was on-site, communicating long-distance, or simply browsing online resources, have made navigating and accessing materials to complete such a project feasible. Special thanks to those in Haiti, where I benefitted from the help of Patrick Tardieu at the Bibliothèque Haïtienne des Frères du Saint Esprit at the Petit Séminaire Collège Saint Martial, Frère Evans Ernest and staff at the Bibliothèque Haïtienne des Frères de L'Instruction Chrétienne, Guerlita Joseph, Johnny Saintelus, Patrick Multidor and other staff members at the Ancien Fonds d'Archives, Archives Nationales, Françoise Thybulle and staff at the Bibliothèque Nationale. In addition to Henri and his late brother, Roger Lescot, I am grateful to Claudinette Fouchard-Bonnefil and the late Marie Madeleine Price-Mars for welcoming me into their homes and trusting me with their father's papers. Thanks to all who made introductions and accommodations so that I could take advantage of these rich collections. I was able to work so comfortably because my brothers-from-another-mother, Fedo Boyer and David Desrouleaux, instilled in me a *no fear* approach to working in Haiti; and so much family, especially Jean and Maguy Emeran, hosted me with tremendous generosity. Stateside, I must also thank Max Manigat and Joachim Levy who shared whatever insights and contacts they had, as well as their private libraries. And while the staff members of several research libraries and archives were all very helpful, Diana Lachatenere, Steven G. Fullwood, Tom Rosenbaum, Amy Fitch, and Maureen Hogan were particularly gracious with their support. And, through the dedicated email practice of Frantz Voltaire, I benefitted from a few items held in the Centre International de Documentation et d'Information Haïtienne, Caribéenne et Afro-canadienne (CIDIHCA) which he curates in Montreal.

For their assistance with oral history transcriptions and a wide range of research assistance, I thank Grace Sanders, Mary Antelo, Adam Silvia, Elysée Yhuel, Casey Stegman, Patrick Multidor, Fedo Boyer and staff at CreoleTrans, staff at FIU's Broadcast services. Martine Cameau was relentlessly selfless and generous in helping with graphic design. In a category of his own is John Dartigue who, picking up his mother's mantle, has been a dedicated keeper of his family's archives. He always went above and beyond to help me fill research gaps at many critical junctures during the final stretches of this process including image help with John Eakin.

For guiding me in becoming a clearer, more confident, convincing and joyful writer, I thank each of the professionals I worked with over the years, especially Cassie Premo Steele, Linda Shopes, Janell Walden Agyeman, and editors at pré-Texte. Colleagues that I connected to via the Detroit-based, virtually run National Center for Faculty Development and Diversity community created and led by Kerry Ann Rockquemore have provided a lifeline that is available 365 days a year, 24–7. Much love to my die-hard "small group" members, Sherry, Heidi, Peggy, Enid, and from '12, Carla Badia, you led us well and continue to be a gem.

To Kimberly Guinta, Kristen Bonnano, Marilyn Campbell, Anne Hegeman, Laura Kopp and all other members of the Rutgers University Press team: thank you for your patience, enthusiasm, and care in helping me see this through.

Life and connections outside of the academy helped me stay sane, positively spirited, and ever-growing in my ability to overcome all sorts of challenges. Thank you Catherine Boland, Star Hansen, Michele Berger, Christine Kane and the Uplevel community, especially Sara Arey, Robbin Jorgensen, Christine Springer, and Wendy Limbert. In South Florida, Dr. C and Dr. D, Alon Weir, Juan Carlos Muguercia, Julia Pace, Yasmin Valdes, Monique Blake, Glenda Hudson, Solomon Lallouz and Jodi Jainchill were literally life-savers. Universal Truth Center, Delou Africa, and Ayama Yoga were havens for restoration along the way. Thank you to all who bring love and life to those community spaces. I've been blessed with sister-friends and dear hearts far and wide, who have cheered and offered whatever they could during this journey: Muslima Lewis, Alita Anderson, ED, Mary Mwiandi and her beautiful daughters, Joy and Sheila plus son-in-law Guy, Charmagne Andrews, Vera Benedito, Melise Huggins, Amy Hereford Richardson, Karie Williams, Gina Rudan, Maya Gayle Shaw, Nerissa Street, Regine Rigal, Leslie Casimir, Jhon Charles, Michael Henry, Léonce Limousin, Jean Caze, Cassandra Honorat have been steadfast supporters! Tawnicia Ferguson Rowan and James

Rowan, Paulette Hicks, Lizbeth Niezen and Pat LaSota, Amy Sarnow, Beatriz Raydo made the Cove home. To my original sisters in academic & life prayer: Anne Heutsche, Cecilia Samonte, LaTrese Adkins, Monique Chism, and Pam Martin—Amen! And, from the very early years to now, Sandra Ossé, Odalys Perez, and Judy Polyné have seen me through this.

To my humungous *familia*—finally! I know that after me, you are the ones who will be most relieved and proud that I've made it through this journey. Thank you to members of the Baron, Verna, Roséfort, Paris, Aubry, Baptiste, Cameau, Emeran, Fish, Levy, Marc-Charles, Pun, Surpris, Weir, Boyer, Léon, Mahler, Ossé, Chin-Glemaud, Collazo-Perez, Smith, and Thébaud families for your unwavering faith, encouragement, and support. Monique Baron, Alex Verna, María Verna: what a blessing to have you as parents. I am grateful for my siblings Xavier and Alexis, and army of cousins (especially Marc-Antoine, whom I called upon more times than my data plan could keep up with). To all the precious lil' ones in my life who are growing every day—the world is yours; claim your deepest desires! To my ninety-nine-years-old-and-counting grandfather, Techlerr Baron—thank you for all your wisdom, including the reminder to always do what I can, nothing more, nothing less. I remember Clara Baron, Frances Marrero, Paula and Cephas Célestin, Max Cameau, and Ulrick Fish who also poured much love into this process. And, my heart is glowing, Mitchoun Alusma: you continuously affirm my faith in magnetic energy. Namaste!

In the end, I am keeping a promise I made to so many: let the *konpa*, salsa, soukous, soca, and all the world's most joyous rhythms play. It's that time . . .

Abbreviations

ANH	Ancien Fonds d'Archives, Archives Nationales d'Haïti
FC	Jean Fouchard Collection
JM	John Marshall
LC	Élie Lescot Collection
MAE	Ministère des Affaires Étrangères, Port-au-Prince, Haiti
MDP	Papers of Maurice Dartigue, Schomburg Center for Research on Black Culture, New York Public Library
NAR	Nelson A. Rockefeller
NARA	National Archives Records Administration
PMC	Jean Price-Mars Collection
PSCSM	Bibliothèque Haïtienne, Petit Séminaire Collège Saint Martial
R	Register
RAC	Rockefeller Archive Center
RF	Rockefeller Foundation
RG	Record Group
SLG	Bibliothèque Haïtienne, Saint-Louis de Gonzague
UF	University of Florida, Special Collections
UNESCO	United Nations Educational, Scientific and Cultural Organization

Notes

Introduction

1. Jean Price-Mars, "Discours prononcé le 28 novembre 1944 à l'Institut Haïtiano-américain et enregistré sur disque," Jean Price-Mars Collection (hereafter cited as PMC), Frères, Haiti. On Price-Mars's background and his status within Haitian society, see Emmanuel C. Paul and Jean Fouchard, eds., *Témoignages sur la vie et l'œuvre de Jean Price-Mars, 1876–1956* (Port-au-Prince: Imprimerie de l'État, 1956); Jacques C. Antoine, *Jean Price-Mars and Haiti* (Washington, DC: Three Continents Press, 1981); Magdaline Shannon, *Jean Price-Mars, the Haitian Elite and the American Occupation, 1915–1935* (New York: St. Martin's Press, 1996).

   On Rockefeller's background and his work with the OIAA, see Cary Reich, *The Life of Nelson A. Rockefeller: Worlds to Conquer, 1908–1958* (New York: Doubleday, 1996); Darlene A. Rivas, *Missionary Capitalist: Nelson Rockefeller in Venezuela* (Chapel Hill: University of North Carolina Press, 2002), especially chapter 3; Gisela Cramer and Ursula Prutsch, "Nelson A. Rockefeller's Office of Inter-American Affairs (1940–1946) and Record Group 229," *Hispanic American Historical Review* 86, no. 4 (2006): 785–806.
2. Jean Price-Mars, "Discours prononcé le 28 novembre 1944."
3. Widely cited texts that emphasize the theme of domination and resistance in the history of Haiti-U.S. relations include Hans Schmidt, *The United States Occupation of Haiti, 1915–34* (New Brunswick, NJ: Rutgers University Press, 1971); Brenda Gayle Plummer, *Haiti and the United States: The Psychological Moment* (Athens: University of Georgia Press, 1992); Paul Farmer, *The Uses of Haiti* (Monroe, ME: Common Courage

Press, 1994); Mary A. Renda, *Taking Haiti: Military Occupation and the Culture of U.S. Imperialism: 1915–1940* (Chapel Hill: University of North Carolina Press, 2001); Leon D. Pamphile, *Clash of Cultures: America's Educational Strategies in Occupied Haiti, 1915–1934* (Lanham, MD: University Press of America, 2008). Recent examples of the enduring appeal of this approach: Alan McPherson, *The Invaded: How Latin Americans and their Allies Fought and Ended U.S. Occupations* (Oxford: Oxford University Press, 2014) and Jeffrey Sommers, *Race, Reality and Realpolitik: U.S.-Haiti Relations in the Lead Up to the 1915 Occupation* (Lanham, MD: Rowman and Littlefield, 2015).

On the importance of producing alternative narratives about Haiti, Michel-Rolph Trouillot, *Silencing the Past: Power and the Production of History* (Boston: Beacon Press, 1990); Millery Polyné, *The Idea of Haiti: Rethinking Crisis and Development* (Minneapolis: University of Minnesota Press, 2013); Gina Ulysse, *Why Haiti Needs New Narratives: A Post-Quake Chronicle* (Middleton, CT: Wesleyan University Press, 2015).

4. Michel Hector, "Intellectuels et pouvoir politique en Haïti (XIXe–XXe siècle)," *Revue Haïtienne d'histoire, géographie et géologie* 240 (July–December 2010): 29–38.
5. Jean Price-Mars, "Enquête sur la préparation de l'élite," Appendix to *La vocation de l'élite* (Port-au-Prince: Imprimerie Edmond Chenet, 1929). On the fragmented nature of this group, see Hector, "Intellectuels et pouvoir politique en Haïti." On the category Haitian elite, see Jean Casimir, "Haïti et ses élites: L'interminable dialogue de sourds," *Worlds and Knowledges Otherwise* 2, dossier 3 (Fall 2008), https://globalstudies.trinity.duke.edu/wko-v2d3. On elite, urban Haitians during the 1930s and 1940s, see David Nicholls, *From Dessalines to Duvalier: Race, Colour and National Independence in Haiti* (Basingstoke: Macmillan Caribbean, 1988), chapters 5–7; Matthew J. Smith, *Red and Black in Haiti: Radicalism, Conflict and Political Change, 1934–1957* (Chapel Hill: University of North Carolina Press, 2009); and Georges Corvington, *Port-au-Prince au cours des ans*, vols. 5 and 6 (Port-au-Prince: Imprimerie Henri Deschamps, 1987 and 1991).

   On the historically cosmopolitan character of elite Haitian society, see Nicholls, *From Dessalines to Duvalier* and Gordon K. Lewis, *Main Currents in Caribbean Thought* (Baltimore: Johns Hopkins University

Press, 1983). See also Brenda Gayle Plummer, *Haiti and the Great Powers* (Baton Rouge: Louisiana State University Press, 1988), and Glenda Sluga, "UNESCO and the (One) World of Julian Huxley," *Journal of World History* 21, no. 3 (September 2010): 393–418.

6. Brenda Gayle Plummer used the term semi-foreign elites to discuss families in Haiti produced through intermarriage (e.g., Haitian-German, Haitian-Syrian) and individuals with dual nationality, "The Metropolitan Connection: Foreign and Semiforeign Elites in Haiti, 1900–1915," *Latin American Research Review* 19, no. 2 (1984): 119–142.
7. Liping Bu, *Making the World Like Us: Education, Cultural Expansion, and the American Century* (Westport, CT: Praeger, 2003). Few scholars have dedicated more than a few lines, if any, to Haiti's post-occupation period. Notable exceptions of scholars that discuss the historical significance of Haiti-U.S. relations after the occupation, particularly during the 1930s and 1940s, include Smith, *Red and Black in Haiti*; Millery Polyné, *From Douglass to Duvalier*: U.S. African-Americans, Haiti, and Pan-Americanism, 1870–1964 (Gainesville: University Press of Florida, 2010); Kate Ramsey, *The Spirits and the Law:* Vodou and Power in Haiti (Chicago: University of Chicago Press, 2011); Michael Largey, *Vodou Nation: Haitian Art Music and Cultural Nationalism* (Chicago: University of Chicago Press, 2006); Renda, *Taking Haiti*; Plummer, *Haiti and the United States*; J. Michael Dash, *Haiti and the United States: National Stereotypes and the Literary Imagination*, 2nd ed. (Basingstoke: Palgrave Macmillan, 1997).

   On U.S. cultural engagements and legacies, see Haldore Hanson, *The Cultural-Cooperation Program, 1938–1943* (Washington, DC: U.S. Government Printing Office, 1944); Frank Ninkovich, *The Diplomacy of Ideas: U.S. Foreign Policy and Cultural Relations, 1938–1950* (Cambridge: Cambridge University Press, 1981); Emily Rosenberg, *Spreading the American Dream: American Economic & Cultural Expansion, 1890–1945* (New York: Hill and Wang, 1982); Ricardo Salvatore, "Enterprises of Knowledge," in *Close Encounters of Empire: Writing the Cultural History of U.S.-Latin American Relations*, ed. Gilbert Joseph, Catherine M. LeGrand, and Ricardo D. Salvatore (Durham, NC: Duke University Press, 1998); Mark T. Gilderhaus, *The Second Century: U.S.-Latin American Relations Since 1889* (Wilmington, DE: Scholarly Resources, 2000);

David Engerman, "American Knowledge and Global Power," *Diplomatic History* 31, no. 4 (September 2007): 599–622; Paul A. Kramer, "Is the World Our Campus? International Students and U.S. Global Power in the Long Twentieth Century," *Diplomatic History* 33 (2009): 775–806; Bu, *Making the World Like Us*.

8. Frederick Cooper, "Development, Modernization, and the Social Sciences in the Era of Decolonization: The Examples of British and French Africa," *Revue d'Histoire des Sciences Humaines* 1, no. 10 (2004): 9–38; quotes from pp. 29, 33. Also, see Frederick Cooper and Randall M. Packard, *International Development and the Social Sciences: Essays on the History and Politics of Knowledge* (Berkeley: University of California Press, 1997). For an example of the dynamic that Cooper describes see Todd Shepard, "Algeria, France, Mexico, UNESCO: A Transnational History of Anti-Racism and Decolonization, 1932–1962," *Journal of Global History* 6, no. 2 (July 2011): 273–297.
9. John A. Britton, "Redefining Intervention: Mexico's Contribution to Anti-Americanism," in *Anti-Americanism in Latin America and the Caribbean*, ed. Alan McPherson (New York: Berghahn Books, 2006), 37–60; Harvey R. Neptune, *Caliban and the Yankees*: Trinidad and the United States Occupation (Chapel Hill: University of North Carolina Press, 2007); Jason Parker, *Brother's Keeper: The United States, Race, and Empire in the British Caribbean, 1937–1962* (Oxford: Oxford University Press, 2008); Polyné, *From Douglass to Duvalier*; Eric Paul Roorda, *The Dictator Next Door: The Good Neighbor Policy and the Trujillo Regime in the Dominican Republic, 1930–1945* (Durham, NC: Duke University Press, 1998).
10. Quote from Gilbert Joseph, Catherine M. LeGrand, and Ricardo D. Salvatore, eds., *Close Encounters of Empire: Writing the Cultural History of U.S.-Latin American Relations* (Durham, NC: Duke University Press, 1998), 4, emphasis mine. For a useful discussion of these developments in U.S. foreign relations with Latin America and the greater Caribbean see works discussed in Max Paul Friedman, "Retiring the Puppets, Bringing Latin America Back In," *Diplomatic History* 27, no. 5 (November 2003): 621–636 and Stephen G. Rabe, "Marching Ahead (Slowly): The Historiography of Inter-American Relations," *Diplomatic History* 13 (Summer 1989): 297–316. For other examples, particularly in African and

Asian contexts, Frederick and Ann Laura Stoler Cooper, eds., *Tensions of Empire: Colonial Cultures in a Bourgeois World* (Berkeley: University of California Press, 1997); Frederick Cooper, "Conflict and Connection," in *The Decolonization Reader*, ed. James Le Sueur (New York: Routledge, 2003), 23–42; Frederick Cooper, "Networks, Moral Discourse, and History," in *Intervention and Transnationalism in Africa: Global-Local Networks of Power*, ed. Thomas Callaghy, Ronald Kassimir, and Robert Latham (Cambridge: Cambridge University Press, 2001), 23–46; Mark Bradley, *Imagining Vietnam and America: The Making of Postcolonial Vietnam, 1919–1950* (Chapel Hill: University of North Carolina Press, 2000); Erez Manela, *The Wilsonian Moment*: Self-Determination and the International Origins of Anticolonial Nationalism (Oxford: Oxford University Press, 2007).

11. The popularity of Paul Farmer's *The Uses of Haiti* and Mary Renda's *Taking Haiti* illustrates the wide reception of such narratives. For a recent critique of this trend, see Ulysse, *Why Haiti Needs New Narratives* and Polyné, *The Idea of Haiti*.
12. Classic texts include David Nicholls, *From Dessalines to Duvalier* and "Ideology and Protest in Haiti, 1930–1946," *Journal of Contemporary History* 9, no. 4 (1974): 3–26; Michel-Rolph Trouillot, *Haiti, State against Nation:* The Origins and Legacy of Duvalierism (New York: Monthly Review Press, 1990); Schmidt, *The United States Occupation of Haiti*; Plummer, *Haiti and the United States*. More recently, Matthew J. Smith discusses the importance of nuance in studies of color, power, and privilege in post-occupation Haiti in *Red and Black in Haiti*.
13. Friedman, "Retiring the Puppets"; Britton, "Redefining Intervention"; Neptune, *Caliban and the Yankees*; Parker, *Brother's Keeper*; Polyné, *From Douglass to Duvalier*; Roorda, *The Dictator Next Door*.
14. Smith, *Red and Black in Haiti*; Polyné, *From Douglass to Duvalier*; Ramsey, *The Spirits and the Law*.
15. Plummer, *Haiti and the Great Powers* and "The Metropolitan Connection"; Nicholls, *From Dessalines to Duvalier* and "Ideology and Protest in Haiti."

    On tensions related to U.S. control of Haitian national finances following the occupation, see Shannon, *Jean Price-Mars*, 123–135, and Schmidt, *The United States Occupation*, 222–229. For those concerning the

1937 massacre, see Plummer, *Haiti and the United States*, chapter 8, and Smith, *Red and Black*, 28–37. And, on critiques of SHADA, see Plummer, *Haiti and the United States*, 145–148; Smith, *Red and Black*, 43–47, 93; and Myrtha Gilbert, *Shada: Chronique d'une extravagante escroquerie* (Port-au-Prince: L'imprimeur, 2011).

16. The dates for the interwar and World War II years are in keeping with more current scholarly efforts to acknowledge the warfare taking place beyond the confines of Europe and the United States.
17. Plummer, *Haiti and the Great Powers*, 40. On the nature and prominence of internationalism, see Akira Iriye, *Cultural Internationalism and World Order* (Baltimore: The Johns Hopkins University Press, 1997); Manela, *The Wilsonian Moment*; Leila J. Rupp, "Constructing Internationalism: The Case of Transnational Women's Organizations, 1888–1945," *American Historical Review* 99, no. 5 (December 1994): 1571–1600.
18. For a classic model of paying attention to Haitian history within a broader geopolitical framework, see Plummer, *Haiti and the Great Powers*. Newer works include Marlene Daut, "The 'Alpha and the Omega' of Haitian Literature: Baron de Vastey and the US Audience of Haitian Political Writing," *Comparative Literature* 64, no. 1 (2012): 49–72; Deborah Jenson, "Dessalines's American Proclamations of the Haitian Independence," *The Journal of Haitian Studies* 15, nos. 1–2 (2010): 72–102; Julia Gaffield, "Haiti and Jamaica in the Remaking of the Early Nineteenth-Century Atlantic World," *The William and Mary Quarterly* 69, no. 3 (2012): 583–614; Ada Ferrer, *Freedom's Mirror* (Cambridge: Cambridge University Press, 2014); Matthew J. Smith, *Liberty, Fraternity, and Exile: Haiti and Jamaica after Emancipation* (Chapel Hill: University of North Carolina Press, 2014). Paul Kramer, "Power and Connection: Imperial Histories of the United States in the World," *American Historical Review* (December 2011): 1348–1391, provides a useful discussion for understanding the significance of such global dynamics and contexts from the vantage point of United States history.

Chapter 1. The Promise and Peril of Foreign Ties, 1791–1915

1. Solon Ménos, *L'affaire Luders* (Port-au-Prince: Imprimerie J. Verrollot, 1898), quoted in Antoine, *Jean Price-Mars and Haiti*, 87–88; Gusti

Gaillard-Pourchet, *L'expérience haïtienne de la dette extérieure (ou) la production caféière pillée, 1875–1915* (Port-au-Prince: Imprimerie Henri Deschamps, 2001); Ménos, *L'affaire Luders*, 233–234.

2. Ménos, *L'affaire Luders*, 88; Paul A. Kramer, *The Blood of Government: Race, Empire, the United States, and the Philippines* (Chapel Hill: University of North Carolina Press, 2006); Louis A. Pérez, Jr., "Cuba between Empires, 1898–1899," Pacific Historical Review 48, no. 4 (November 1979): 473–500. On U.S. expansionism, see Gilderhaus, *The Second Century*; Lester D. Langley, *America and the Americas: The United States in the Western Hemisphere* (Athens: University of Georgia Press, 1998, 2010); Rosenberg, *Spreading the American Dream.*
3. Laurent Dubois, *Haiti: The Aftershocks of History* (New York: Metropolitan Books, 2012), 78–84; 97–105; Victor Bulmer-Thomas, *The Economic History of the Caribbean since the Napoleonic Wars* (Cambridge: Cambridge University Press, 2012), sections 7.1, 7.3–7.4. For more on the character of the revolution and the related impact on early Haitian foreign relations, see David Barry Gaspar and David Patrick Geggus, eds., *A Turbulent Time: The French Revolution and the Greater Caribbean* (Bloomington: Indiana University Press, 1997); David Patrick Geggus, *Haitian Revolutionary Studies* (Bloomington: Indiana University Press, 2002); David Patrick Geggus, ed., *Impact of the Haitian Revolution in the Atlantic World* (Columbia: University of South Carolina Press, 2001); Laurent Dubois, *Avengers of the New World: The Story of the Haitian Revolution* (Cambridge: Harvard University Press, 2005); Ferrer, "Talk About Haiti," in *Tree of Liberty: Cultural Legacies of the Haitian Revolution in the Atlantic World*, ed. Doris L. Garraway (Charlottesville: University of Virginia Press, 2008), 21–40; Ashli White, *Encountering Revolution: Haiti and the Making of the Early Republic* (Baltimore: Johns Hopkins University Press, 2010); Maurice Jackson and Jacqueline Bacon, eds., *African Americans and the Haitian Revolution: Selected Essays and Historical Documents* (New York: Routledge, 2010).

   On Haiti's early national period, see Nicholls, *From Dessalines to Duvalier*; Pedro L. San Miguel, *The Imagined Island: History, Identity, & Utopia in Hispaniola*, trans. Jane Ramírez (Chapel Hill: University of North Carolina Press, 2005); Anne Eller, "'All would be equal in the effort': Santo Domingo's 'Italian Revolution,' Independence and Haiti,

1809–1822," *Journal of Early American History* 1 (2011): 105–141; Plummer, *Haiti and the Great Powers*; Trouillot, *State Against Nation*, 51–53.

4. White, *Encountering Revolution*; Deborah Jenson, *Beyond the Slave Narrative: Politics, Sex, and Manuscripts in the Haitian Revolution* (Liverpool: Liverpool University Press, 2011); Tim Matthewson, *A Proslavery Foreign Policy: Haitian-American Relations during the Early Republic* (Westport, CT: Praeger, 2003); Julia Gaffield, "'So many schemes in agitation': The Haitian State and the Atlantic World" (PhD diss., Duke University, 2012); Ferrer, "Talk About Haiti."
5. Karen Racine, "Imported Englishness: Henry Christophe's Educational Programme in Haiti, 1806–1820," in *Imported Modernity in Post-Colonial State Formation: The Appropriation of Political, Educational, and Cultural Models in Nineteenth-Century Latin America*, ed. Eugenia Roldan and Marcelo Caruso (Frankfurt am Main: Peter Lang, 2007), 210; Dubois, *Haiti*, 68–71.
6. Bolivar quoted in Judith Ewell, "Bolívar's Atlantic World Diplomacy," in *Simón Bolívar: Essays on the Life and Legacy of the Liberator*, ed. David Bushnell and Lester D. Langley (London: Rowman and Littlefield, 2008), 46.
7. Collier, "Simón Bolívar," in *Simón Bolívar*, ed. Bushnell and Langley, 27.
8. Quotes from Ewell, "Bolívar's Atlantic World Diplomacy," 49 and 35. Jenson, *Beyond the Slave Narrative*, chapter 4; Hermes Tovar Pinzón, "Bolívar and the Future of Democracy," in *Simón Bolívar*, ed. Bushnell and Langley; Paul Verna, *Petión y Bolívar: Una etapa decisiva en la emancipación de hispanoamérica, 1790–1830* (Caracas: Ediciones de la Presidencia de la República, 1980); Richard W. Slatta and Jane Lucas De Grummond, *Simón Bolívar's Quest for Glory* (College Station: Texas A&M University Press, 2003).

   For more on inter-island alliances and threats, see San Miguel, *The Imagined Island*; Luis Martínez-Fernández, "El anexionismo dominicano y la lucha entre imperios durante la primera república, 1844–1861," *Revista/Review Interamericana* 22, nos. 1–2 (Spring–Summer 1992): 168–190; Eller, "All would be equal."
9. Daut, "The 'Alpha and Omega," 54.
10. Jenson, *Beyond the Slave Narrative*, chapters 1–4; Daut, "The 'Alpha and Omega,'" 50, 53, 67.

11. Racine, "Imported Englishness." Joseph Lancaster, *Improvements in Education* (London, 1803; New York, 1807). On these and other investments by Christophe and, to a lesser extent, Pétion, see Louis Auguste Joint, "L'école dans la construction de l'état," in *Genèse de l'état haïtien (1804–1859)*, ed. Michel Hector and Laënnec Hurbon (Port-au-Prince: Éditions Presses Nationales d'Haïti, 2009), 240–245 and Dubois, *Haiti*, chapter 2.

Prince Saunders, *A Memoir Presented to the American Convention for Promoting the Abolition of Slavery, and Improving the Condition of the African Race* (Philadelphia, 1818); Dubois, *Haiti*, 74–75. For more on African American emigration to Haiti, see Chris Dixon, *African Americans and Haiti: Emigration and Black Nationalism in the Nineteenth Century* (Westport, CT: Greenwood Press, 2000); Leslie Alexander, *African or American? Black Identity and Political Activism in New York City, 1784–1861* (Urbana: University of Illinois Press, 2008), chapter 2.

12. James G. Blaine, *Political Discussions: Legislative, Diplomatic, and Popular, 1856–1886* (Norwich, CT: Henry Bill Publishing Company, 1887), 404.

13. Enrico Mario Santí, "'Our America,' the Gilded Age, and the Crisis of Latinamericanism," in *José Martí's "Our America": From National to Hemispheric Cultural Studies*, ed. Jeffrey Belnap and Raúl A. Fernandez (Durham, NC: Duke University Press, 1998), 218–227; Blaine, *Political Discussions*; Minutes of the International American Conference (Washington, 1890), 683; Senate Executive document 135, 51st Congress, 1st session, SPECIAL REPORT of the COMMITTEE on CUSTOMS REGULATIONS, 129.

14. Karen Salt, "The Haitian Question" (PhD diss., Purdue University, 2011).

15. Jenson, *Beyond the Slave Narrative*, 11, 195–206. On the indemnity agreement and subsequent financial ties: Pourchet, *L'expérience haïtienne*, chapter 1; Dubois, *Haiti*, 76–84; 97–105. On educational ties: Mercer Cook, *Education in Haiti* (Washington, DC: Federal Security Agency, United States Office of Education, 1948), 16; Charles Tardieu, *L'éducation en Haïti: De la période coloniale à nos jours* (Port-au-Prince: Imprimerie Henri Deschamps, 1990), 137–140.

16. Racine, "Imported Englishness"; Lancaster, *Improvements in Education*; Joint, "L'école dans la construction de l'état," 240–245; Dubois, *Haiti*, chapter 2.

17. Nicholls, *From Dessalines to Duvalier*, 41–46; Largey, *Vodou Nation*, 34–36, 49; Lewis, *Main Currents*, 316–319. For details on Haiti-Vatican relations leading to the Concordat, see Pierre Adolphe Cabon, *Notes sur l'histoire religieuse d'Haïti de la révolution au Concordat, 1789–1860* (Port-au-Prince: Petit Séminaire Collège Saint-Martial, 1933). For a critical discussion of early Haitian-Vatican relations through the Concordat, see Ramsey, *The Spirits and the Law*, 77–83.
18. Joseph-Anténor Firmin, *Lettres de Saint-Thomas: études sociologiques, historiques et littéraires* (Port-au-Prince: Éditions Fardin, 1910), 87.
19. Watson Denis, "Orígenes y manifestaciones de la francofila haitiana: nacionalismo y política exterior en Haití (1880–1915)," *Secuencia* 67 (January–April 2007): 93–139.
20. Kirsten Schultz, *Tropical Versailles: Empire, Monarchy and the Portuguese Royal Court in Rio de Janeiro, 1808–1821* (New York: Routledge, 2001), 104–105; Jeffrey Needel, "Rio de Janeiro at the Turn of the Century: Modernization and the Parisian Idea," *Journal of Interamerican Studies and World Affairs* 25, no. 1 (February 1983): 83–103; idem, *A Tropical Belle Epoque: The Elite Culture of Turn-of-the-Century Rio de Janeiro* (New York: Cambridge University Press, 1987); Dain Borges, "'Puffy, Ugly, Slothful and Inert': Degeneration in Brazilian Social Thought, 1880–194," *Journal of Latin American Studies* 25, no. 2 (May 1993), 235–256; Jean H. Delaney, "Imagining "el Ser Argentino": Cultural Nationalism and Romantic Concepts of Nationhood in Early Twentieth-century Argentina," *Journal of Latin American Studies* 34, no. 3 (2002): 625–658; Claudio Lomnitz, *Deep Mexico, Silent Mexico: An Anthropology of Nationalism* (Minneapolis: University of Minnesota Press, 2001), chapter 9.
21. Janvier quoted in Watson Denis, "La nation comme projet d'intégration socio-économique," *Revue Haïtienne d'histoire, géographie et géologie* 240 (July–December 2010): 44–45.
22. René Depestre, "Problems of Identity for the Black Man in the Caribbean," *Caribbean Quarterly* 3 (September 1973): 55, quoted in Gordon Lewis, *Main Currents*, 319.
23. Nicholls, *From Dessalines to Duvalier*, 41–46; Largey, *Vodou Nation*, 34–36, 49; Lewis, *Main Currents*, 316–319; Carolyn Fluehr-Lobban,

"Anténor Firmin and Haiti's Contribution to Anthropology," *Gradhiva* 1 (2005): 95–108.

24. On the tradition of Haitian intellectuals' engagement with issues of politico-economic and social development, see Plummer, *Haiti and the Great Powers*.
25. Cook, *Education in Haiti*, 17; Fleury Féquière, *L'éducation Haïtienne* (Port-au-Prince: Impr. de l'Abeille, 1906), 37–38, 119, 45, 57.
26. On Washington's methods, the merits, and the limitations of the Tuskegee model, see James D. Anderson, *The Education of Blacks in the South 1860–1935* (Chapel Hill: University of North Carolina Press, 1988); Donal F. Lindsey, *Indians at Hampton Institute, 1877–1923* (Urbana: University of Illinois Press, 1995); Frank Guridy, *Forging Diaspora: Afro-Cubans and African Americans in a World of Empire and Jim Crow* (Chapel Hill: University of North Carolina Press, 2010). Leon D. Pamphile, *Haitians and African Americans: A Heritage of Tragedy and Hope* (Gainesville: University Press of Florida, 2001), 99; Price-Mars, "La Réforme de l'enseignement primaire," *Haïti littéraire et scientifique*, July 5, 1912, 312–317; Largey, *Vodou Nation*, 45–48.
27. Guridy, *Forging Diaspora*, 18–20, 35; quote from p. 20; Dana Chandler, "List of Foreign Students at Tuskegee" (2012), 029 Foreign Students at Tuskegee Institute, Tuskegee University Archives.
28. Quoted in Salt, "The Haitian Question," 135.
29. Plummer, *Haiti and the Great Powers*, 36, 52.
30. Plummer, *Haiti and the Great Powers*, 49–50, 53–55.
31. Plummer, *Haiti and the Great Powers*, 51, 52, 59; Polyné, *From Douglass to Duvalier*, chapter 1; Dubois, *Haiti*, chapter 5.
32. Trouillot, *State Against Nation*, 44–47; Leslie Manigat, "La Substitution de la prépondérance américaine à la prépondérance française en Haïti au début du XXe siècle: la conjoncture de 1910–1911," *Revue d'histoire moderne et contemporaine* 14, no. 4 (October–December 1967): 321–355; Gaillard Pourchet, *L'expérience haïtienne*, 45–47; Schmidt, *The United States Occupation*, 36–38; Georges Michel, *Les chemins de fer d'île d'Haïti* (Jamaica, NY: Haitiana Publications, 1989).
33. Largey, *Vodou Nation*, 198–230. For more on foreign threats of intervention during the nineteenth century, see Plummer, *Haiti and the Great*

Powers, 87–93; Bulmer-Thomas, *The Economic History of the Caribbean*, section 7.1.

Chapter 2. "With the Spirit of Friendship"

1. Maurice Dartigue and Andre Liautaud, *Géographie locale* (Port-au-Prince: Deschamps, 1931); Maurice Dartigue, "Some Aspects of the Educational Problem in Haiti," [circa 1937], 1, Maurice Dartigue Papers, unprocessed collection, Schomburg Center for Research on Black Culture, New York Public Library, NY, hereafter MDP. For more on Liautaud, see forthcoming work by Nadève Ménard on myths about the "birth" of Haitian literature, as related to indigénisme and the U.S. occupation of Haiti.
2. Shannon, *Jean Price-Mars*; Jean Price-Mars, "La réforme de l'enseignement primaire," *Haïti littéraire et scientifique* (July 1912): 312–317.
3. On the occupation, see Schmidt, *The United States Occupation of Haiti*; Suzy Castor, *L'occupation américaine d'Haïti* (Port-au-Prince: Imprimerie Henri Deschamps, 1988); Plummer, *Haiti and the United States*; Renda, *Taking Haiti*. On the treaty, see "Haiti. Amity, commerce, navigation and extradition, November 3, 1864," in *Treaties and Other International Agreements of the United States, 1776–1949*, ed. Charles I. Bevans (Washington, DC: Government Printing Office, 1971), 8:614; "Haiti. Administration of Haiti (finances and economic development). September 16, 1915," in Bevans, *Treaties*, 8:660. Bevans's *Treaties* is available from HeinOnline Treaties and Agreements Library Collection, http://heinonline.org.ezproxy.fiu.edu/HOL/Index?collection=ustreaties. On Vodou and the occupation, see Ramsey, *The Spirits and the Law*, chapter 3; Castor, *L'occupation*, 74–79.
4. Plummer, *Haiti and the Great Powers*, 228.
5. Ramsey, *The Spirits and the Law*, 124–130.
6. See Bevans, *Treaties*, 8:660–713; Castor, *L'occupation*, 79–82; Schmidt, *The United States Occupation*, 194–196; chapter 9; Pamphile, *Clash of Cultures*, chapters 4 and 5. Quote from page 37.
7. Ary Bordes, *Haïti, médecine et santé publique sous l'occupation américaine, 1915–1934* (Port-au-Prince: Imprimerie Deschamps, 1992); Catherine

C. Choy, *Empire of Care: Nursing and Migration in Filipino American History* (Durham, NC: Duke University Press, 2003); Eileen J. Findlay, *Imposing Decency: The Politics of Sexuality and Race in Puerto Rico, 1870–1920* (Durham, NC: Duke University Press, 1999).

8. Pamphile, *Clash of Cultures*, 32–37; 42–43; Lionel Bourgeois, "Our Relations with Haiti," *Loyola Law Journal* 2, no. 26 (1920).
9. Pamphile, *Clash of Cultures*, chapter 1, 26; Tardieu, *L'éducation en Haïti*, 89–160; Price-Mars, "La réforme de l'enseignement primaire"; J. R. Hawke, *Three Years of Vocational Industrial Education in Haiti* (Port-au-Prince: Department of Printing–Service Technique, 1930), 13; Dantès Bellegarde, *La résistance haïtienne* (Montréal: Éditions Beauchemins, 1937), chapters 4 and 5.
10. Castor, *L'occupation*, 127–158; Ramsey, *The Spirits and the Law*, 140–143; Renda, *Taking Haiti*, 80–88; 135–181; Schmidt, *The United States Occupation of Haiti*, chapter 5; Plummer, *Haiti and the United States*, 101–116; Yveline Alexis, "Nationalism and the Politics of Historical Memory: Charlemagne Peralte's Rebellion against the U.S. Occupation of Haiti, 1915–1986" (PhD diss., University of Massachusetts, 2011), *Doctoral Dissertations Available from Proquest*, Paper AAI3461973. Accessed via: http://scholarworks.umass.edu/dissertations/AAI3461973.
11. U.S. Senate, Select Committee on Haiti and Santo Domingo, *Inquiry into Occupation and Administration of Haiti and Santo Domingo*, 67th Cong., 1st and 2nd sess. (Washington, DC: Government Printing Office, 1922); Manela, *The Wilsonian Moment*; Schmidt, *The United States Occupation of Haiti*, 115–116.
12. Pamphile, *Clash of Cultures*, 73–93; Schmidt, *The United States Occupation of Haiti*, chapter 9; Castor, *L'occupation*, 90–124.
13. Rockefeller Foundation fellowship records, Rockefeller Foundation Papers (RF), Record Group (RG) 10.2 Fellowship Recorder Cards (Medical and Natural Sciences), 1917–1970 (1972), as described in Chantalle F. Verna, "The Role of International Aid in Creating Ties between Haiti and the United States, 1934–1957," *Research Reports Online*, Rockefeller Archives Center. Accessible via: http://archive.rockefeller.edu/publications/resrep/rronlinesub.php?printer=1 NPR. Also, see Ary Bordes, *Évolution des sciences de la santé et de l'hygiène publique en Haïti*,

1915–1934 (Port-au-Prince: Centre d'Hygiène Familiale, 1979); Castor, *L'occupation*, 74–79; David McBride, *Missions for Science: U.S. Technology and Medicine in America's African World* (New Brunswick, NJ: Rutgers University Press, 2002), chapter 3.

14. Kathleen Weiler, "Mabel Carney at Teachers College: From Home Missionary to White Ally," *Teachers College Record* 107, no. 12 (December 2005): 2599–2633.
15. Compiled from Esther Dartigue, *An Outstanding Haitian, Maurice Dartigue: The Contribution of Maurice Dartigue in the Field of Education in Haiti, the United Nations, and UNESCO* (New York: Vantage Press, 1994) and curriculum vitae in MDP; Hawkes, *Three Years of Vocational Industrial Education*, 17.
16. Interview with Max Vieux by the author, May 12, 2002, Tête-de-l'Eau (Pétion-Ville), Haiti.
17. Recent works that highlight this trend and emphasize the limits of this perspective include Largey, *Vodou Nation*, chapter 1; Smith, *Red and Black in Haiti*, especially pages 3–10.
18. Robert N. Seidel, *Progressive Pan Americanism: Development and United States Policy toward South America, 1906–1931* (Ithaca, NY: Cornell University Press, 1973).
19. Maurice Dartigue, *Les problèmes de la communauté* (Port-au-Prince: Imprimerie du Service Technique, 1931), 68, 70.
20. Maurice Dartigue, "Education and General Intelligence (Talk)," 1939, 1, MDP; "The Preparation of Teachers," MDP.
21. Shannon, *Jean Price-Mars*, chapter 4.
22. Schmidt, *The United States Occupation of Haiti*, chapter 10; Castor, *L'occupation*, 168–175; Plummer, *Haiti and the United States*, 118.
23. Kent Melhorn to Dr. W. S. Carter, Associate Director, Rockefeller Foundation, January 6, 1930, "320 A National School of Medicine and Pharmacy, 1926–1931, 1934," Box 1, Series 320 (Haiti), RG 1.1 (Projects), RF, Rockefeller Archive Center, Sleepy Hollow, NY [hereafter RAC]; Schmidt, *The United States Occupation of Haiti*, chapter 10; Shannon, *Jean Price-Mars*, 80–86; Plummer, *Haiti and the United States*, 118; Castor, *L'occupation*, 171–174; Max Vieux, interview with the author, May 17, 2002, Tête-de-l'eau (Pétion-Ville), Haïti.

24. Donald B. Cooper, "The Withdrawal of the United States from Haiti, 1928–1934," *Journal of Inter-American Studies* 5, no. 1 (January 1963): 91; Schmidt, *The United States Occupation of Haiti*, 195–196.

25. Schmidt, *The United States Occupation of Haiti*, chapter 10; Shannon, *Jean Price-Mars*, 80–86; Plummer, *Haiti and the United States*, 118; Castor, *L'occupation*, 171–174.

26. Cooper, "The Withdrawal"; Schmidt, *The United States Occupation of Haiti*, 198–199; Plummer, *Haiti and the United States*, 119–120.

27. On Hoover's efforts to usher in a new era of Good Neighborliness, see Roorda, *The Dictator Next Door*, 27–28; Alexander DeConde, "Hoover's Good Will Tour," *The Historian* 12, no. 2 (1950): 167–181; idem, *Herbert Hoover's Latin-American Policy* (Stanford: Stanford University Press, 1951). Hebert Hoover, "Annual Message to Congress on the State of the Union," December 3, 1929. Available from: Gerhard Peters and John T. Woolley, *The American Presidency Project*. http://www.presidency.ucsb.edu/ws/?pid=22021. Schmidt, *The United States Occupation*, 203–205; chapter 6.

28. Hoover, "Annual Message to Congress on the State of the Union," December 3, 1929.

29. Bellegarde and Lhérisson quoted in Polyné, *From Douglass to Duvalier*, 57–58; Plummer, *Haiti and the United States*, 119–120; Schmidt, *The United States Occupation*, 207–218; DeConde, "Hoover's Good Will Tour" and *Herbert Hoover's Latin-American Policy*, 6–7; Miller Center of Public Affairs, University of Virginia, "Herbert Hoover." Accessed via: http://millercenter.org/president/hoover/essays/biography/5.

30. Shannon, *Jean Price-Mars*, 97–99; Schmidt, *The United States Occupation*, 219; Castor, *L'occupation*, chapter 9; "Haiti's New President," *New York Times*, November 20, 1930, 25.

31. "Haitian Result Fails to Alarm Washington," *New York Times*, November 20, 1930, 1.

32. "Anti-occupationistes, anti-conventionistes, mais pas anti-américains," *Le Nouvelliste*, October 20, 1930, 1.

33. Castor, *L'occupation*, chapter 9; Schmidt, *The United States Occupation*, 219–220; Plummer, *Haiti and the United States*, 120; Smith, *Red and Black in Haiti*, 9–10.

34. October 17, 1930 news article referenced in letter from U.S. High Commissioner to U.S. Secretary of State, October 20, 1930, RG 59, 838.00/2902.
35. Copy and translation of December 20, 1930 letter from Sannon to Munro, enclosed with letter from Munro to U.S. Secretary of State, Port-au-Prince, January 2, 1931, RG 59, 838.00/2925, *Foreign Relations of the United States* [FRUS] 3 (1930): 279; Sannon to Munro, December 2, 1930, translation enclosed with letter to U.S. Secretary of State, December 5, 1931, RG 59, 838.00/2915, FRUS 3 (1930): 263–266; Sannon to Munro, December 20, 1930, FRUS 3 (1930): 277. See Castor, *L'occupation*, chapter 10; Schmidt, *The United States Occupation*, chapter 11.
36. Maurice Dartigue, "On the Eve of the Liberation from the American Occupation, 1934, (Talk)" and "The Merit System of the U.S. (Talk), 1931 or 1932," MDP; Chantalle F. Verna, "Maurice Dartigue and Educational Reform as a Strategy for Haitian National Development 1930–46," *Journal of Haitian Studies* 13, no. 2 (Fall 2007).
37. See Rulx Léon, Directeur General, SNd'HP to Dr. Alan Gregg, Director Education, RF, October 10, 1931; Sténio Vincent to RF, November 9, 1931; Gregg to Léon, December 2, 1931, RF, RG 1.1 (Projects), Series 320 (Haiti), Box 1, folder 1: "320 A National School of Medicine and Pharmacy, 1926–1931, 1934," RAC.
38. Schmidt, *The United States Occupation of Haiti*, 222–229.
39. Frederick Pike, *FDR's Good Neighbor Policy: Sixty Years of Generally Gentle Chaos* (Austin: University of Texas Press, 2010), 131.
40. Jean Desquiron, *Haïti à la une: Une anthologie de la presse haïtienne de 1724 à 1934*, vol. 6, *1931–1934* (Port-au-Prince: l'Imprimeur II, 1997); Conversation with Michel Hector, Port-au-Prince, Haiti, November 2013.
41. Sténio Vincent, "L'entrevue du Cap-Haïtien entre le Président Vincent et le Président F. D. Roosevelt, le 5 juillet 1934," *Sur la route de la seconde indépendance: En compagnie du soldat et du citoyen haïtiens* (Port-au-Prince: Imprimerie de l'État, 1934), chapter 24.
42. Franklin D. Roosevelt: "Remarks at Cape Haitien [sic], Haiti," July 6, 1934. Online by Gerhard Peters and John T. Woolley, *The American Presidency Project*. Accessed via: http://www.presidency.ucsb.edu/ws/?pid=14721.
43. Vincent, *Sur la route*, 74.

Chapter 3. Pan-Americanism in Port-au-Prince

1. *Le Temps*, September 8, 1934, 20. Jerome S. Berg, *The Early Shortwave Stations: An Early Broadcasting History through 1945* (Jefferson, NC: MacFarland and Company, 2013).
2. The 1937 start date for WWII is in keeping with more current scholarly efforts to acknowledge the global warfare that was taking place in Asia. Whereas 1939 is the start date when European history is at the center of the narrative, 1941 is the start date when U.S. history is at the center of the narrative.
3. Hanson, *The Cultural-Cooperation Program*; J. Manuel Espinosa, *Inter-American Beginnings of U.S. Cultural Diplomacy: 1936–48* (Washington, DC: US Government Printing Office, 1976); Claude C. Erb, "Prelude to Point Four: The Institute of Inter-American Affairs," *Diplomatic History* 9, no. 3 (Summer 1985): 249–269; Gilderhaus, *The Second Century*; Ninkovich, *The Diplomacy of Ideas*; Rosenberg, *Spreading the American Dream*.
4. Jeffrey Sommers, "Haiti and the Hemispheric Imperative to Invest: The *Bulletin* of the Pan American Union," *Journal of Haitian Studies* 9, no. 1 (2003): 68–94; Stephen M. Streeter, "The Myth of Pan Americanism: United States Policy toward Latin America during the Cold War, 1954–1963," in *Beyond the Ideal: Pan Americanism in Inter-American Affairs*, ed. David Sheinin (Santa Barbara, CA: Greenwood, 2000).
5. Lescot to Vincent, May 9, 1938, Jean Fouchard Collection (hereafter cited FC); "This week," *Radio Guide* 7, no. 32 (May 28, 1938), 1. Retrieved via: http://www.americanradiohistory.com/Archive-Radio-Guide/1938/Radio-Guide-38-05-28.pdf. On Lescot's heavy reliance on ties with the U.S. for his political-economic agenda, see Smith, *Red and Black in Haiti*, chapter 2. On the U.S. fiscal representative in Haiti, see Plummer, *Haiti and the United States*, 98, 133, 139; Smith, *Red and Black in Haiti*, 43–47; 113–116; Alex Dupuy, *Haiti in the World Economy* (Boulder: Westview Press, 1989); Karen Richman, *Migration and Vodou* (Gainesville: University Presses of Florida, 2005).
6. Dantès Bellegarde, "Haiti and International Cooperation," in *Haiti and Her Problems: Four Lectures* (Rio Piedras, PR: University of Puerto Rico, 1936), 49.

7. Jean Price-Mars, "La position de la République d'Haïti dans les relations inter-américaines," draft manuscript, n.d. (circa 1939), PMC, 9–10, quotes from pp. 15 and 16. In 1942, Price-Mars published *La contribution haïtienne à la lutte des Amériques pour les libertés humaines* (Port-au-Prince: Imprimerie de l'État).
8. Élie Lescot, *Toussaint Louverture, précurseur de l'amitié américano-haïtienne* (Port-au-Prince: Imprimerie de l'État, 1942).
9. Max Hudicourt, *Haiti Faces Tomorrow's Peace* (New York: L'Association Démocratique Haitienne, 1945), 23–24, 21.
10. Joseph Montllor, "The Test of Panamericanism," *Voz de Haiti en las Americas* (text of a radio broadcast on HH3W, April 13, 1943), 7–8, Bibliothèque Haïtienne, Petit Séminaire Collège Saint Martial [hereafter PSCSM]; Biographical information on Montllor from http://archive.org/stream/departmentofstat240unit/departmentofstat240unit_djvu.txt and http://lcweb2.10c.gov/service/mss/mfdip/2005%20txt%20files/2004hig02.txt. Radio history sketch on Haiti in Alejandra Bronfman, "El Octopus Acústico: Broadcasting and Empire in the Caribbean," in *Radio's New Wave: Global Sound in the Digital Era*, ed. Jason Loviglio and Michele Hilmes (New York: Routledge, 2013), 152–156.
11. Daniel Supplice, *Dictionnaire Biographique des personnalités politiques de la République d'Haïti* (Port-au-Prince: Daniel Supplice, 2001), 589; Max Gustave Chaumette, *Considérations historiques sur l'idéal panaméricain* (Port-au-Prince: printed by author, 1937), 19–23. John Garrigus, "Catalyst or Catastrophe? Saint Domingue's Free Men of Color and the Battle of Savannah, 1779–1782," *Revista/Review Interamericana* 22, nos.1–2 (1992): 110.
12. Supplice, *Dictionnaire Biographique*, 589; Chaumette, *Considérations historiques*; Max Gustave Chaumette, *Le panaméricanisme à travers l'histoire d'Haïti* (Port-au-Prince: n.p., 1944); and Max Gustave Chaumette, *Haïti et les problèmes panaméricaines* (Port-au-Prince: Les Editions de l'Assaut, No. 3, n.d.). Ludovic Rosemond, *Haïti et les États-Unis* (Port-au-Prince: n.p., 1945).
13. Dantès Bellegarde, "La coopération inter-américaine: Haïti, pionnier du panaméricanisme," in *Haïti et ses problèmes* (Montréal: Éditions Bernard Valiquette, 1941), 249–253; Dantès Bellegarde, "Pétion and Bolívar," *Revue de la société d'histoire et de géographie d'Haïti* 12, no. 43 (April 1941): 1–13.

14. René Piquion and Love Léger, *Histoire d'Haïti* (Haiti: n.p., 1938).
15. "De l'esprit panaméricain en Haiti," *Le Nouvelliste*, April 15, 1940, 1.
16. Sténio Vincent, "A L'Union Panaméricaine," n.d. Lescot Family Collection, quotes from pages 1–2. Also see Sénateur Nemours, "Haiti Fète Grandiosement le Panaméricanisme," *Le Nouvelliste*, April 17, 1940, 1, 5. The radio-broadcast speech was also printed in *Le Matin* and *Le Nouvelliste* on the following day.
17. Chaumette, *Considérations historiques*, 22, 21; Max Hudicourt, "Jim Crow Menaces Haiti," *Crisis* 51, no. 11 (1944): 364; *Commémoration du départ des volontaires Haïtiens en 1779* (Port-au-Prince: n.p., 1944), 12–14, rare pamphlet available in Thomas Gamble [mayor of Savannah, 1944–] Collection, City of Savannah, Bull Street Public Library.
18. Price-Mars, "La position de la République d'Haïti."
19. [Kléber] G[eorges] Jacob (Spanish translation [from original] prepared by Ernest Danache), "Breve bosquejo de la historia de la independencia de Haiti y su ideals humano en cuanto al panamericanismo," in *Voz de Haiti en Las Americas* (n.d., early 1940s), 10, copy from PSCSM.
20. For a general discussion of this dynamic, see Trouillot, *Silencing the Past*.
21. Lescot, *Toussaint Louverture*, 5–6. Emphasis mine.
22. Lescot, *Toussaint Louverture*, 3; Neptune, *Caliban and the Yankees*.
23. On emigration, see Dixon, *African Americans and Haiti*. On exile, see Mimi Sheller, *Democracy After Slavery: Black Publics and Peasant Radicalism in Haiti and Jamaica* (London: Macmillan Education, 2000), Matthew J. Smith, *Liberty, Fraternity, and Exile: Haiti and Jamaica after Emancipation* (Chapel Hill: University of North Carolina Press, 2014).
24. Brenda Gayle Plummer, "Firmin and Martí at the Intersection of Pan-Americanism and Pan-Africanism," in *José Martí's "Our America": From National to Hemispheric Cultural Studies*, ed. Jeffrey Belnap and Raúl A. Fernández (Durham, NC: Duke University Press, 1998), 223.
25. See for example David Sheinin, ed., *Beyond the Ideal: Pan Americanism in Inter-American Affairs* (Santa Barbara: Greenwood, 2000); Jerry Dávila, *Diploma of Whiteness: Race and Social Policy in Brazil, 1917–1945* (Durham: Duke University Press, 2003), 160–165; Jana Lipman, *Guantánamo: A Working-Class History between Empire and Revolution* (Berkeley: University of California Press, 2009).

26. Max Charlmers, "L'Union Panaméricaine," *Le Nouvelliste*, April 16, 1940, 1.
27. Smith, *Red and Black in Haiti*; Ramsey, *The Spirits and the Law*, chapter 4; Polyné, *From Douglass to Duvalier*, chapters 3–6.
28. Jean Price-Mars, "Discours prononcé le 28 novembre 1944 à l'Institut haïtiano-américain et enregistré sur disque" (Text), PMC.
29. See for example Brent Hayes Edwards, *The Practice of Diaspora: Literature, Translation, and the Rise of Black Internationalism* (Cambridge: Harvard University Press, 2003); Minkah Makalani, *In the Cause of Freedom: Radical Black Internationalism from Harlem to London, 1917–1939* (Chapel Hill: University of North Carolina Press, 2011); Penny M. Von Eschen, *Race against Empire: Black Americans and Anticolonialism, 1937–1957* (Ithaca: Cornell University Press, 1997); Neptune, *Caliban and the Yankees*; Grace Sanders, "La Voix Des Femmes: Haitian Women's Rights, National Politics and Black Activism in Port-Au-Prince and Montreal, 1934–1986" (PhD diss., University of Michigan, 2013).
30. Lallier C. Phareaux, "Interaméricanisme Haïtien," *Le Matin*, February 3, 1943; Barreau de Port-au-Prince, *Tableau de l'Ordre des Avocats du Barreau de Port-au-Prince, 1938–1939* (Port-au-Prince: n.p., 1939), accessed via Internet Archive: https://archive.org/details/tableaudelordredoobarr.
31. August 1, 1937 Memo (American Republics (Pattee)), no. 3 838.427511935, Record Group 59, National Archives at College Park, College Park, MD.
32. Charles Fernand Pressoir. "Pan-Latinism and Pan-Americanism," Enclosure No. 1 to Despatch No. 569 of October 12, 1937 from the Legation at Port-au-Prince, Haiti (Translation [in original]), Record Group 59, National Archives at College Park, College Park, MD.
33. René Bélance, interviews with the author, Frères (Pétion-Ville), Haïti, April 2002.
34. See numerous examples of correspondence in Registres, Ancien Fonds d'Archives, Archives Nationales d'Haïti (hereafter ANH), Port-au-Prince.
35. "Pan American Day: Paroles prononcées à la Station H.H.BM par M. Max Mossanto," *Le Matin*, April 15, 1941, 6.
36. W. Rayford Logan, "The Possibilities of a Caribbean Federation," in *The Economic Future of the Caribbean*, ed. Edward Franklin Frazier and Eric Williams (Dover, MA: The Majority Press, 1943), 55–58; Cabinet

Particular, ". . . correspondence générale . . . ," 7 February–8 May 1948, 11- Registres 911, Dorsinville to M. Gérard Pierre-Louis, President of the Institute, ANH, Port-au-Prince.

37. *Bulletin du Moniteur*, April 1942, 33–37; and May 1942, available in Haitian Ministry of Foreign Affairs, Port-au-Prince, Haiti.

38. Chaumette, *Le panaméricanisme*; Rosemond, *Haïti et les États-Unis*.

39. UP wire clip, Mar. 1931, Scrapbook 1-Page 1, Box 4, Notebooks, Frank Crumbie Papers, Special and Areas Collections, George A. Smathers Libraries, University of Florida, Gainesville, Florida.

40. Corvington, *Port-au-Prince au cours des ans* (1991), 139.

41. Ibid., 144.

42. U.S. Department of State Records on Microfilm (Dominican Republic), Internal Affairs, 1930–1939, National Archives Microfilm Publication M1272, Roll 11 (University of Florida Libraries, Latin American and Caribbean Collection, Gainesville) includes several items pertaining to street renaming as part of a Dominican public works and diplomatic agenda. Two key examples are: Memo, Sept 16, 1938, prepared by Eugene M. Hinkle, Chargé d'Affaires, of the United States of America re: "Naming of street in Ciudad Trujilo for former president of Haiti, Fabre Geffrard (Calle Fabre Geffrard)," Frame 1580 and Memo, September 16, 1938, "Public Attempt of General to Improve Relations with Haiti," Frame 1582–5; Roorda, *The Dictator Next Door*, chapter 5. For broader context, see Edward Paulino, *Dividing Hispaniola: The Dominican Republic's Border Campaign against Haiti, 1930–1961* (Pittsburgh: University of Pittsburgh Press, 2016).

43. Evidence of this still exists in Pétion-Ville and Port-au-Prince, including l'école nationale République des États-Unis, which was rebuilt, and l'école d'Équateur, which was expanded, after the January 12, 2010 earthquake.

44. Jacqueline Lévy, multiple conversations with the author, Miami, FL, 2001–2002, 2005; Charles Manigat, interview with the author, April 4, 2002, Cap-Haïtien, Haiti.

45. DeConde, *Herbert Hoover's Latin-American Policy*, 118–119; Chaumette, *Le panaméricanisme*; A. Curtis Wilgus, "Pan American Day," *World Affairs* 102, no. 1 (March 1939): 41–43; Élie Lescot, *Le diplomate et l'animateur: Un compte-rendu de la visite officielle, rendue par son excellence le*

président de la république d'Haïti au Canada, aux États-Unis et à Cuba, au Mois d'octobre (New York: IBM, 1943).

46. Jacqueline Levy, multiple conversations with the author, Miami, FL, 2001–2002, 2005.
47. A. Max Chaumette Jr., telephone conversation with the author, June 25, 2009.
48. "Les scouts et le jour panaméricain," *Le Matin*, April 16, 1943, 2.
49. "La promotion dans l'ordre haïtien de Pétion et Bolívar, à l'occasion du 14 avril, Jour Panaméricain," *Le Matin*, April 18, 1940, 1.
50. "La célébration du cinquantenaire de l'Union Panaméricaine," *Le Nouvelliste*, April 16, 1940, 1.
51. Ramsey, *The Spirits and the Law*, 216–218; Largey, *Vodou Nation*, chapter 5.
52. Sénateur Nemours, "Haïti Fête Grandiosement le Panaméricanisme," *Le Nouvelliste*, April 17, 1940, 1, 5.
53. "La célébration du cinquantenaire de l'Union Panaméricaine."
54. "La commémoration du Jour Panaméricain," *Le Matin*, April 15, 1941, 6.
55. "La station de radiodiffusion H.H.B.M. a consacré un festival radiophonique à l'occasion du jour panaméricain," *Le Matin*, April 17, 1942, 1.
56. For other examples of similar radio programs see Pierre Moraviah Morpeau's presentation on HH3W in 1942 ("Festival radiophonique," *Le Matin*, April 12 and 13, 1942, 3); "L'esprit pan-américain: Belles pensées de fameux américains," *Le Nouvelliste*, Saturday, April 18, 1942, 1, 5; "Programme 'idéal de Bolívar' du 14 avril 1943 à la Station HH3W," *Le Matin*, April 13, 1943, 2. Guridy, *Forging Diaspora,* 178–179; Bronfman, "El Octopus Acústico," chapter 9.
57. Jean Coradin, "l'historique de l'Union Panaméricaine," *Le Nouvelliste*, April 18, 1940, 1, 3; Félix Magloire, "Le cinquantenaire de l'Union Panaméricaine," *Le Matin*, April 14 and 15, 1940, 1–2; "L'esprit pan-américain : Belles pensées de fameux américains," 1.
58. "Calendrier inter-américain: (Préparé par la Division de Presse du Bureau du Coordinateur des Affaires Inter-américaines) Éphémérides et faits sensationnels de l'Amérique," *Le Matin*, January 19, 1943, 2; Wednesday, March 17, 1943, 2; Sunday, April 4 and Monday, April 5, 1943, 2. References in 1941, 1942, 1943, 1945, *Bulletin du Moniteur*, available in Haitian Ministry of Foreign Affairs, Port-au-Prince, Haiti.

Chapter 4. *La Nouvelle Coopération*

1. Henri Télémaque is a pseudonym. Confidential interview with the author, 2001, Pétion-Ville; Dép. de l'Instruction Publique, *La préparation des cadres par le gouvernement du président Élie Lescot* (Port-au-Prince: Imprimerie de l'État, October 1945). Inter-American Educational Foundation (hereafter IAEF), *Educational Division Newsletter* (Washington, DC, February 1946) and Correspondence on Marcus Douyon, Glen William Lukens Papers, Chaloner Prize Foundation Records, Secretaries' Files, undated and 1917–1974, Miscellaneous, Archives of American Art, Smithsonian Institution, Washington, DC.
2. Dép. de l'Instruction Publique, *La préparation des cadres* (September 1944); Institute of International Education, *Twenty-seventh Annual Report of the Director*, October 1, 1946 (New York), 89.
3. For a discussion of how the wartime alliance influenced the course of developments in the British Caribbean, see Cary Fraser, *Ambivalent Anti-Colonialism: The United States and the Genesis of West Indian Independence, 1940–1964* (Westport, CT: Greenwood Press, 1994); Parker, *Brother's Keeper*; and Neptune, *Caliban and the Yankees*; Dép. de l'Instruction Publique, *La préparation des cadres* (September 1944). Quote from "The Imperial College of Tropical Agriculture," *Nature* 143 (March 18, 1939): 468, doi:10.1038/143468b0.
4. Bu, *Making the World Like Us*.
5. Jean Price-Mars to Élie Lescot, July 28, 1943, PMC. See for example Gérarde Magloire and Kevin A. Yelvington, "Haiti and the Anthropological Imagination," *Gradhiva* 1 (2005), online edition posted December 10, 2008; Christine Laurière, "D'une île à l'autre," *Gradhiva* 1 (2005), online edition posted December 10, 2008; Katherine Dunham, *Island Possessed* (Chicago: University of Chicago Press, 1969, reprinted 1994); Polyné, *From Douglass to Duvalier*, chapter 5.
6. Laurière, "D'une île à l'autre"; Magloire and Yelvington, "Haiti and the Anthropological Imagination."
7. Maurice Dartigue to Fiorello LaGuardia, April 24, 1942, MDP; Dép. de l'Instruction Publique, *La préparation des cadres* (September 1942).

8. Kramer's discussion of "corporate-internationalist" student migrations begins as early as the 1920s. Kramer, "Is the World Our Campus?" 780; 788–789.
9. Dép. de l'Instruction Publique, *La préparation des cadres* (September 1942, 1943, 1944). On Haitian military pilots who trained at Tuskegee, see Kat, "Haiti History 101: The Haitian Tuskegee Airmen," posted on http://kreyolicious.com/haiti-history-101-the-haitian-tuskegee-airmen/1597/, January 13, 2012.
10. IAEF, *Educational Division Newsletter*, 10.
11. Report on "Cultural Relations-Intellectual Cooperation," 1943–44, MDP; Five-page memo, n.d., folder 40, box 5, series Countries, Record Group III 4, Nelson A. Rockefeller Papers, RAC; Untitled report on the IAEF, folder 40, box 5, series Countries, Record Group III 4, Nelson A. Rockefeller Papers, RAC; "Cooperative Education Program," Agreement signed at Port-au-Prince May 19, 1947, with appendixes. Entered into force May 19, 1947. Bevans, *Treaties*, 8:805–813. Quote from p. 806. Accessed via HeinOnline.
12. See, for example, general correspondence mailed from Haitian government offices including the Secretary of State and Ministry of Foreign Relations, between 1946 and 1950, frequently signed by President Dumarsais Estimé in Registres at the Ancien Fonds d'Archives, ANH.
13. Renda, *Taking Haiti*; Roger Gaillard, *Les Blancs Débarquent*, 8 vols. (Port-au-Prince: Roger Gaillard, 1984); Pamphile, *Clash of Cultures*.
14. Polyné, *From Douglass to Duvalier*.
15. Cynthia Orozco, *No Mexicans, Women, or Dogs Allowed: The Rise of the Mexican American Civil Rights Movement* (Austin: University of Texas, 2009).
16. Nathan D. B. Connolly, *A World More Concrete: Real Estate and the Remaking of Jim Crow South Florida* (Chicago: University of Chicago Press, 2014), 111–112. See also Chanelle Nyree Rose, *The Struggle for Black Freedom in Miami: Civil Rights and America's Tourist Paradise, 1896–1968* (Baton Rouge: Louisiana State University Press, 2015).
17. Lescot to Vincent, May 18, 1939, Élie Lescot Family Collection, hereafter LC.
18. Lescot to Vincent, June 9, 1939, LC.

19. Vincent to Lescot, November 25, 1938, LC; Lescot to Vincent, June 9, 1939, LC; References to specific military boursiers are from *Préparation des cadres.*
20. WAS [Wilbur A. Sawyer] to Porter J. Crawford, Letter dated January 24, 1940, folder 4, "320I Malaria, 1935, 1939–41," box 1, series 320, Record Group 1.1, Rockefeller Foundation Papers, RAC.
21. Ibid.
22. Robert A. Lambert interviews Dr. Jules Thébaud, director of Public Health and Hygiene for Haiti, Monday, April 10, 1944, folder 2 (entitled 320A National School of Medicine and Pharmacy, 1944–1950), RG 1.1 (Projects), RF, RAC; Robert A. Lambert, Inter-office Memo, November 15, 1946, folder 2 (entitled 320A National School of Medicine and Pharmacy, 1944–1950), RG 1.1 (Projects), RF, RAC.
23. Rockefeller Foundation *Annual Reports*; RAL to Crawford, November 14, 1944, folder 2 (entitled 320A National School of Medicine and Pharmacy, 1944–1950), series 320, Record Group 1.1, Rockefeller Foundation Papers, RAC.
24. McBride, *Missions for Science*, 112–114.
25. Maurice Dartigue to Edward Trueblood, April 18, 1941, MDP.
26. "Preparation of Cadres," 1943–1944, MDP.
27. Unsigned letter to J. C. White, April 9 1942, 392–3, R#1468, ANH.
28. Ligue Féminine d'Action Sociale, "Femmes Haïtiennes," brochure, n.d. (1954?), copy in author's files. For more on the history of the Ligue and its activities, see Myriam Chancy, *Framing Silence: Revolutionary Novels by Haitian Women* (New Brunswick, NJ: Rutgers University Press, 1997), 38–43; Chantalle F. Verna, "A Conversation with Paulette Poujol Oriol," *Journal of Haitian Studies* 17, no. 1 (Spring 2011): 246–257 and Grace Sanders, "La Voix des Femmes."
29. This term came up several times in conversations with elders who lived during or were familiar with the period. Also, referenced in Esther Dartigue, *An Outstanding Haitian, Maurice Dartigue*, 56; Tardieu, *L'éducation en Haïti*, 160.
30. On visual and performing arts, see Ramsey, *The Spirits and the Law*, chapter 4; Polyné, *From Douglass to Duvalier*, chapters 4 and 5; Largey, *Vodou Nation.*
31. IAEF, *Educational Division Newsletter*, 9.

32. Ibid.
33. [Exhibition and gallery talk announcement], March 24, 1957, Glen William Lukens papers, 1931–1983, Archives of American Art, Smithsonian Institution, Washington, D.C.
34. IAEF, *Educational Division Newsletter*, 9.
35. Ibid.
36. Hanson, *The Cultural-Cooperation Program, 1938–1943*, 67, 23–24. Quote from p. 24.
37. IAEF, *Educational Division Newsletter*, 8.
38. See for example advertisements in issues of *Le Nouvelliste* and *Le Matin* from the period.
39. Louis Garoute, "l'Importance de l'enseignement de l'anglais," *Le Matin*, April 1, 1943, 4.
40. Henry J. Smith, "Letter to John Marshall," typed, dated 1948, folder 7, box 1, Series 320, RG 1.1, RF, RAC.
41. *Bulletin du Moniteur*, June 1942, 45–44, available in the Ministry of Foreign Affairs, Port-au-Prince, Haiti.
42. Unsigned Letter to J. C. White, August 28, 1942, 310–311, Registres 1061, ANH.
43. Garoute, "l'Importance de l'enseignement de l'anglais," 4.
44. "The Teaching of English," MDP.
45. Charles Manigat, interview with the author, 2002, Cap-Haïtien, Haiti.
46. Henry J. Smith, "Letter to John Marshall," typed letter, dated 1948, folder 7, box 1, Series 320, RG 1.1, RF, RAC.

Chapter 5. "Viva UNESCO"

1. John Marshall Oral History, p. 484, Interview 13, folder 7, box 1, RG II.13, Rockefeller Foundation Archives, RAC; John Marshall interview notes from a meeting with President Dumarsais Estimé, Port-au-Prince, Haiti, April 28, 1948, folder 132, series 100, RG 1.2, RF, RAC.
2. On the centrality of education in general, and literacy in particular, to UNESCO's prominent emergence after the Second World War, see Phillip W. Jones, *International Policies for Third World Education: Unesco, Literacy, and Development* (London: Routledge, 1988); and Charles Dorn and Kristen Ghodsee, "The Cold War Politicization of Literacy:

Communism, UNESCO, and the World Bank," *Diplomatic History* 36, no. 2 (April 2012): 373–398.

3. On the privileges assumed by leaders from "great power" nations in the rise and efforts of UNESCO, the League of Nations, and UN, see Dorn and Ghodsee, "The Cold War Politicization of Literacy"; Manela, *The Wilsonian Moment*; and Marika Sherwood, "The UN: Caribbean and African-American Attempts to Influence the Founding Conference in San Francisco, 1945," *Journal of Caribbean History* 29, no. 1 (1996). On the growing significance of individuals recognized as experts in postwar planning, see Joseph Moran Hodge, "British Colonial Expertise, Postcolonial Careering, and the Early History of International Development," in "Modernizing Missions: Approaches to 'Developing' the Non-Western World after 1945," Special Issue, *Journal of Modern European History* 8, no. 1 (2010): 24–46.
4. James C. Scott, *Seeing Like a State: How Certain Schemes to Improve the Human Condition Have Failed* (New Haven: Yale University Press, 1998).
5. For more on these initiatives, see United Nations, *Mission to Haiti: Report of the United Nations Mission of Technical Assistance to the Republic of Haiti* (Lake Success, NY, 1949); Corvington, *Port-au-Prince au cours des ans*, 326–343; Nick Cullather, "Development? It's History," *Diplomatic History* 24, no. 4 (Fall 2000): 641–653; Glenda Sluga, *Internationalism in the Age of Nationalism* (Philadelphia: University of Pennsylvania Press, 2013). On the culture and practice of transatlantic discourse, debate, and projects, see Engerman, "American Knowledge and Global Power"; Amy L. S. Staples, *The Birth of Development: How the World Bank, Food and Agriculture Organization, and World Health Organization Changed the World, 1945–1965* (Kent, OH: Kent State University Press, 2006); Elizabeth Borgwardt, *A New Deal for the World: America's Vision for Human Rights* (Cambridge: Belknap Press of Harvard University Press, 2005); Shepard, "Algeria, France, Mexico, UNESCO"; Nicole Sackley, "Village Models: Etawah, India, and the Making and Remaking of Development in the Early Cold War," *Diplomatic History* 37, no. 4 (2013): 749–778.
6. On the 1946 transition as revolutionary, Frantz Voltaire, *Pouvoir noir en Haïti: L'explosion de 1946* (Montreal: Éditions du CIDIHCA, 1988). For a discussion of the political transition of 1946, its classic treatment and

the importance of an alternative lens, see Smith, *Red and Black in Haiti*, chapter 3. On the international and economic agendas of Haiti's post-occupation leaders that relied upon connections to the United States, see Polyné, *From Douglass to Duvalier*, chapters 3–6; Smith, *Red and Black in Haiti*; Ramsey, *The Spirits and the Law*, chapter 4.

7. Smith, *Red and Black in Haiti*, chapters 1–2; Ramsey, *The Spirits and the Law*, 4; Sanders, "La Voix des Femmes," chapter 3; Largey, *Vodou Nation*.
8. Bambi B. Schieffelin and Rachelle Charlier Doucet, "The 'Real' Haitian Creole: Ideology, Metalinguistics, and Orthographic Choice," in *Language and Ideologies: Practice and Theory*, ed. Bambi B Schieffelin, Kathryn Ann Woolard, and Paul V. Kroskrity (New York: Oxford University Press, 1998), 285–316; and Chantalle F. Verna, "Haiti's Second Independence and the Promise of Pan-American Cooperation" (PhD diss., Michigan State University, 2005), chapter 3.
9. Smith, *Red and Black in Haiti*, chapter 4; and Plummer, *Haiti and the United States*, 151.
10. John Marshall interview notes on the UNESCO pilot project in fundamental education Marbial Valley, Haiti, April 28–30, 1948, folder 132, box 20, series 100, RG 1.2, RF, RAC. See Arthur Bonhomme, "Avec l'UNESCO," *Les Griots*, May 7, 1948 (Port-au-Prince), p. 1, folder 133, box 20, series 100, RG 1.2, RF, RAC. UNESCO, "Fundamental Education Pilot Project in Haiti Working Plan," February 26,1948 (Paris), p. 2, folder 132, box 20, series 100, RG 1.2, RF, RAC.
11. China and East Asia were the two other proposed sites for the project. On Haiti's presence among founding states, Marika Sherwood, "The UN: Caribbean and African-American Attempts to Influence," 38; On Gabriel's involvement, see Glenda Sluga, "UNESCO and the (One) World of Julian Huxley" and "Imagining Internationalism," *Arts* 32 (2010): 55–68.
12. Historian Glenda Sluga discusses biased tendencies of UNESCO's executive administrators during the organization's early years in "UNESCO and the (One) World of Julian Huxley." Such practices lend credence to the strong critique that Mark Mozwer makes in *No Enchanted Palace: The End of Empire and the Ideological Origins of the*

United Nations (New York: Princeton University Press, 2009). For a discussion of similar challenges when international leaders pursued plans for the post–World War I era, see Manela, *The Wilsonian Moment*.

13. Jones, *International Policies for Third World Development*.
14. On this transatlantic development history, see Engerman, "American Knowledge, Global Power"; Staples, *The Birth of Development*; Borgwardt, *A New Deal for the World*; Shepard, "Algeria, France, Mexico, UNESCO."
15. Quote from Metraux to Marshall, May 11, 1948, Port-au-Prince, RF, RAC; Smith, *Red and Black in Haiti*, chapter 4; Plummer, *Haiti and the United States*, 163–165.
16. On the local situation during the time of the pilot project, see Métraux to Marshall, May 11, 1948, Port-au-Prince, folder 133, series 100, RG 1.2, RF, RAC; Laurière, "D'une île à l'autre," 13–20; Rémy Bastien and Harold Courlander, *Religion and Politics in Haiti* (Washington, DC: Institute for Cross-Cultural Research, 1966). For a biographical sketch of Louis-Charles who served as a priest in Marbial between 1939 and 1955, see P. Patrick Aris, "Farnèse Louis-Charles, Théologien et Prophète," *Moun—Revue de Philosophie* 6 (2007): 285–313.
17. Julian Huxley to Dumarsais Estimé, June 8, 1948, folder 133, series 100, RG 1.2, RF, RAC; UNESCO, *The Haiti Pilot Project, Phase One [1947–1949]* (Paris, 1951), 48–49.
18. Huxley to Estimé, June 8, 1948, folder 133, series 100, RG 1.2, RF, RAC.
19. John Bowers to John Marshall, July 1948, folder 133, box 20, series 100, RG 1.2, RF, RAC.
20. For more on the Rockefeller Foundation's activities in Haiti during and immediately following the occupation, see Chantalle F. Verna, "The Role of International Aid"; McBride, *Missions for Science*. On the prominence of philanthropic organizations in the foreign missions of other major institutions such as the U.S. government and non-governmental agencies such as UNESCO, see Edward H. Berman, *The Ideology of Philanthropy: The Influence of the Carnegie, Ford, and Rockefeller Foundations on American Foreign Policy* (Albany: SUNY Press, 1986); Inderjeet Parmar, *Foundations of the American Century: The Ford, Carnegie, and Rockefeller Foundations in the Rise of American Power* (New

York: Columbia University Press, 2012); Cramer and Prutsch, "Nelson A. Rockefeller's Office of Inter-American Affairs," 785–787; Shepard, "Algeria, France, Mexico, UNESCO."

21. Marshall to Bowers, March 29, 1949, Folder 132–136, Series 100, RG 1.2, RF, RAC.
22. W.F. Twadell to Alfred Métraux, attached to a letter from Twadell to John Marshall November 15, 1948, folder 134, series 100, RG 1.2, RF, RAC. On Twadell's background and career, see Archibald A. Hill, "William Freeman Twaddell," *Language* 59, no. 2 (June 1983): 347–354. For other examples of how U.S. officials expressed and acted with similar sentiment, see Staples, *Birth of Development*, 62–63. Wallace and Eleanor Turnbull (Haiti Baptist Mission), Interview with the author, Fermathe, Haiti, 2002, in author's files.
23. On the relationship between literacy programs and political influence during the Lescot administration, see Chantalle F. Verna, "Haiti's Second Independence," chapter 3. For a discussion of how deeply interwoven contentious religious differences and violent acts of intolerance were with contests for securing political power at the national and local level, see Ramsey, *The Spirits and the Law*, 193–210; Smith, *Red and Black in Haiti*, 48–49. By opening her work during Haiti's revolutionary period, the entirety of Ramsey's text is particularly useful for a longer historical perspective on the 1940s raids on Vodou practitioners.
24. Métraux to Marshall, May 11, 1948, Port-au-Prince, folder 133, series 100, RG 1.2, RF, RAC. Robert Anderson Hall with the collaboration of Suzanne Comhaire-Sylvain, H. Ormonde McConnell, [and] Alfred Métraux, *Haitian Creole: Grammar, Texts, Vocabulary* (Philadelphia: American Folklore Society, 1953).
25. John Marshall interview notes from a visit to Haiti April 28–30, p. 3, folder 132, series 100, RG 1.2, RF, RAC. Seth Fein, "El cine y las relaciones culturales entre México y Estados Unidos durante la década de 1930," *Secuencia* 34 (January–April 1996): 155–195; Fein, "Everyday Forms of Transnational Collaboration: U.S. Film Propaganda in Cold War Mexico," in *Close Encounters of Empire: Writing the Cultural History of U.S.-Latin American Relations*, ed. Gilbert M. Joseph, Catherine C. LeGrand, and Ricardo D. Salvatore (Durham: Duke University Press, 1998).

26. For more on the OIAA and its history, see Cramer and Prutsch, "Nelson A. Rockefeller's Office of Inter-American Affairs," 785–787.

27. John Marshall interview notes from a meeting with Frederick Rex, UNESCO, October 6, 1948, folder 134, series 100, RG 1.2, RF, RAC; John Marshall to John Bowers, May 11, 1948, p.2, folder 133, series 100, RG 1.2, RF, RAC, emphasis mine.

28. John Marshall interview notes from a meeting with Frederick Rex, UNESCO, October 6, 1948, folder 134, series 100, RG 1.2, RF, RAC; John Marshall to [W.] Freeman [Twadell], December 3, 1948, folder 134, box 20, series 100, RG 1.2, RF, RAC. For a useful discussion of the persistent view that Haiti is an anomaly in the international system, see Michel-Rolph Trouillot, "The Odd and the Ordinary: Haiti, the Caribbean and the World," *Cimarrón: New Perspectives on the Caribbean* 2, no. 3 (June 2007): 1–15; Millery Polyné, ed., *The Idea of Haiti: Rethinking Crisis and Development* (Minneapolis: University of Minnesota Press, 2013).

29. RSM [Robert S. Morison, RF director of natural and medical sciences] interview notes from a meeting with John Bowers, March 8, 1949, folder 135, series 100, RG 1.2, RF, RAC; Truman quote from Erb, "Prelude to Point Four," 249; Michael J. Hogan, *The Marshall Plan: America, Britain, and the Reconstruction of Western Europe, 1947–1952* (New York: Cambridge University Press, 1987). Robert Charles Sio, "The United Nations Fundamental, Scientific, and Cultural Organization's Program in Fundamental Education" (M.S. thesis in Education, New Mexico Western College, July 1951), 100; Geir Lundestead, "Empire by Invitation? The United States and Western Europe, 1945–1952," *Journal of Peace Research* 23, no. 3 (September 1986): 264. John Bowers to John Marshall, November 27, 1948, folder 134, series 100, RG 1.2, RF, RAC.

30. Erb, "Prelude to Point Four," 249.

31. John Marshall Oral History, p. 486, Interview 13, folder 7, box 1, RG II.13, RF, RAC.

32. John Marshall interview notes from a meeting with Alfred Métraux, NYC, June 28, 1948, p. 1, Port-au-Prince, folder 133, series 100, RG 1.2, RF, RAC.

33. John Marshall interview notes from a meeting with Alfred Métraux and Yvonne Oddon, NYC, November 3, 1948, p. 1, folder 134, series 100, RG 1.2, RF, RAC. UNESCO, *Haiti Pilot Project*, 48.

34. John Marshall interview notes from a visit to Haiti April 28–30, p. 3, folder 132, series 100, RG 1.2, RF, RAC. Fein, "El cine y las relaciones culturales" and "Everyday Forms of Transnational Collaboration."

35. "Dans les Montagnes de Marbial," unidentified news clip accompanying a letter from Arthur Bonhomme to John Marshall, June 28, 1948, folder 133, box 20, series 100, RG 1.2, RF.

36. Bonhomme to Bowers, September 9, 1948, p. 4, 6, folder 134, box 20, series 100, RG 1.2, RF.

37. John Marshall to John Bowers, May 11, 1948, p. 2, folder 133, series 100, RG 1.2, RF, RAC.

38. Conversations between the author and Michel Lamartinière Honorat, Pétion-Ville, Haiti, 2001, 2008.

39. Sluga, "UNESCO" and "Imagining Internationalism." Gabriel also studied at the University of London's Education Institute.

40. Alfred Métraux to John Marshall, May 11, 1948, folder 133, series 100, RG 1.2, RF, RAC. Alfred Métraux, Edouard Berrout, [Jean and Suzanne] Comhaire-Sylvain, "Making a Living in the Marbial Valley," *Occasional Papers in Education* (Paris: UNESCO, December 7, 1951) and Hall et al., *Haitian Creole*.

41. I. A. Richards to John Marshall, November 18, 1948, folder 134, box 20, series 100, RG 1.2, RF, RAC. Département de l'Instruction Publique, *La préparation des cadres* (1945); George Remponeau, Interview with the author, 2003.

42. John Marshall to John Bowers, May 11, 1948, p.2, folder 133, series 100, RG 1.2, RF, RAC. Also, see François Duvalier, *Oeuvres essentielles* (Port-au-Prince: Presses Nationales d'Haïti, 1968), 1:491–601; McBride, *Missions for Science*, 95–99; 202–205; 210–211; H. Fox, "Yaws (frambesia tropica) as Observed in Haiti," *Archives of Dermatology and Syphilology* 20, no. 6 (December 1929): 820–834.

43. John Marshall interview notes from a meeting with Alfred Métraux and Yvonne Oddon, NYC, November 3, 1948, p. 1, folder 134, series 100, RG 1.2, RF, RAC.

44. Ibid.

45. John Marshall interview notes from a meeting with Alfred Métraux and Yvonne Oddon, NYC, November 3, 1948, p. 2, folder 134, series 100, RG 1.2, RF, RAC. On public health work by medical doctors from the United States in Haiti, see McBride, *Missions for Science*; Chantalle F. Verna, "The Role of International Aid"; and Bordes, *Évolution des sciences de la santé*, vols. 1–3.
46. John Marshall to Alfred Métraux, December 23, 1948, folder 134, series 100, RG 1.2, RF, RAC.
47. John Marshall interview notes from a meeting with C. E. Beeby, UNESCO, December 15, 1948, folder 134, series 100, RG 1.2, RF, RAC.
48. UNESCO, *Haiti Pilot Project*, 53.
49. John Marshall to Alfred Métraux, June 11, 1948, folder 133, series 100, RG 1.2, RF, RAC; UNESCO, *Haiti Pilot Project*.
50. The UNESCO archives file, 375 (729.4) A61 Part 1, Box 375/729.4/A61/ Part 1, UNESCO Archives, Paris, France, contains several clippings about the project, as does UNESCO's organ *Courier*. For example, Symontowne, "UN to Test the Theory" and "The Rebirth of a Valley," Supplement, *Courier* 2, no. 5 (June 1949): 5–8; John Marshall interview notes from a meeting with C. E. Beeby, UNESCO, December 15, 1948, folder 134, series 100, RG 1.2, RF, RAC, emphasis mine; United Nations, *Mission to Haiti*.
51. Marshall's files contain six pages of clippings including "Hope for Backward Areas," *New York Herald Tribune*, March 22, 1949; *Time*, December 6, 1948 (Conferences in the International Section), 25–26 and Ernest O. Hauser, "Doctor Huxley's Wonderful Zoo," *Saturday Evening Post*, October 2, 1948, 16 in folder 40: UNESCO, 1948, Box 3, Series 1: General Files, John Marshall Papers, RAC. Edmund Wilson, *Red, Black, Blond, and Olive: Studies in Four Civilizations Zuni, Haiti, Soviet Russia, Israel* (New York: Oxford University Press, 1956); Dorsey, "Report on a Visit to Marbial," for U.S. State Department; Folder [3], 21/11/1949—31/12/1949, Box 375/729.4/A61/ Part 15, UNESCO Archives, Paris, France; Claire Mali, Acting University Liaison, University Committee on the UN to UNESCO FE Representative, Mr. M.S. Dalton [re: Miss Estades of Columbia University], December 23, 1949; and separate letter dated October 11, 1949, Folder [3], 21/11/1949—31/12/1949, Box 375/729.4/A61/ Part 15, UNESCO Archives, Paris, France; Sio, "The

United Nations Fundamental, Scientific, and Cultural Organization's Program."

52. Excerpt from letter, I. A. Richards to John Marshall, May 16, 1949, folder 135, box 20, series 100, RG 1.2, RF, RAC.
53. Folder [3], 21/11/1949—31/12/1949, Box 375/729.4/A61/ Part 15, UNESCO Archives, Paris, France.
54. Memorandum from Alfred Métraux to John Marshall, November 8, 1948, 1–2, folder 134, series 100, RG 1.2, RF, RAC. Métraux refers to "Taylor" as the author of the second study.
55. Correspondence between I. A. Richards, John Marshall, and Alfred Métraux, November 28, 1948, folder 134, box 20, series 100, RG 1.2, RF, RAC. For more on Richards's prominence in the field, see John Paul Russo, *I. A. Richards: His Life and Work* (Baltimore: Johns Hopkins University Press, 1989).
56. Sluga, "UNESCO," 412–423.
57. John Marshall interview notes from a visit to Haiti April 28–30, p. 4, folder 132, box 20, series 100, RG 1.2, RF, RAC. On the distinction between these Creole writing and reading skills, see Schieffelin and Doucet, "The 'Real' Haitian Creole."
58. Memorandum from Alfred Métraux to John Marshall, November 8, 1948, folder 134, box 20, series 100, RG 1.2, RF, RAC.
59. Twadell did not specify who Hall identified as being a "cultivated Haitian." John Marshall to [W.] Freeman [Twadell], December 3, 1948, folder 134, box 20, series 100, RG 1.2, RF, RAC; Twadell to Alfred Métraux, December 21, 1948, folder 134, series 100, RG 1.2, RF, RAC.
60. Twadell to Alfred Métraux, December 21, 1948 folder 134, series 100, RG 1.2, RF, RAC.
61. Emmanuel Gabriel to John Marshall, April 25, 1949, folder 136, box 20, series 100, RG 1.2, RF, RAC.
62. Excerpt from letter, I. A. Richards to John Marshall, May 16, 1949, folder 136, box 20, series 100, RG 1.2, RF, RAC.
63. John Marshall interview notes from a meeting with Alfred Métraux, March 6, 1950, folder 136, series 100, RG 1.2, RF, RAC; John Marshall interview notes from a meeting with Mr. and Mrs. Alfred Métraux, October 5, 1951, subfolder entitled "January–June 1951," folder 29, series 1, John Marshall Papers, RAC. Sluga, "UNESCO," 413.

64. John Marshall interview notes from a meeting with Mr. and Mrs. Alfred Métraux, October 5, 1951, subfolder entitled "January–June 1951," folder 29, series 1, John Marshall Papers, RAC; JM 'interviews' Alfred Métraux, March 6, 1956, John Marshall Papers, Diaries, January to May 1956 folder.
65. James C. Scott, *Seeing Like a State*, 4. For other examples, see Nick Cullather, *The Hungry World: America's Cold War Battle against Poverty in Asia* (Cambridge: Harvard University Press, 2010); Michael E. Latham, *The Right Kind of Revolution: Modernization, Development, and U.S. Foreign Policy from the Cold War to the Present* (Ithaca: Cornell University Press, 2011).

Epilogue: Enduring Promises

1. Chantalle F. Verna, "Haitian Migration and Community-Building in Southeastern Michigan, 1966–1998," in *Geographies of the Haitian Diaspora*, ed. Regine Ostine Jackson (New York: Routledge, 2011), 163–184.
2. Wien Weibert Arthus, "The Challenge of Democratizing the Caribbean during the Cold War: Kennedy Facing the Duvalier Dilemma," *Diplomatic History* 39 (June 2015): 504–531; Millery Polyné, *From Dessalines to Duvalier*, chapter 6; Jackson, ed., *Geographies of the Haitian Diaspora*; Phillipe Zacair, ed., *Haiti and the Haitian Diaspora in the Wider Caribbean* (Gainesville: University of Florida Press, 2011).
3. See Chantalle F. Verna, "Beyond the Immigration Centers: Haitian Community in Michigan" (M.A. thesis, Michigan State University, 2000); or Chantalle F. Verna, "Haitian Migration and Community-Building."
4. See the memoirs prepared by Dartigue's wife and son: Esther Dartigue, *An Outstanding Haitian, Maurice Dartigue*; and Esther Dartigue and John Dartigue, *Forging Ahead: Recollection of the Life and Times of Esther Dartigue* (n.p.: John Dartigue, 2014).
5. Amy B. Wolfson, "An Examination of South Florida's Haitian Diaspora-led Development initiatives and the Formation of New Spaces of Empowerment" (M.A. thesis, Florida International University, 2010); Michel S. Laguerre, *Diaspora, Politics, and Globalization* (New York: Palgrave Macmillan, 2006) and *Diasporic Citizenship: Haitian Americans in Transnational America* (New York: St. Martin's Press, 1998); Nina Glick-Schiller and Georges Fouron, *Georges Woke Up Laughing: Long-Distance*

Nationalism and the Search for Home (Durham: Duke University Press, 2001); Tatiana K. Wah, *Haiti's Development through Expatriate Reconnection: Conditions and Challenges* (Coconut Creek: Educa Vision, 2003); Tara Hefferan, *Twinning Faith and Development: Catholic Parish Partnering in the U.S. and Haiti* (Bloomfield: Kumarian Press, 2007); Paul Farmer, *Haiti: After the Earthquake* (New York: Public Affairs, 2011); Polyné, ed., *The Idea of Haiti*.

Note on Sources

Haiti and the Uses of America is based on research that I conducted at public and private archives, most notably in Haiti and the United States, where I consulted evidence that had yet to be explored or is underexploited within the existing scholarship. Many of these collections are pending formal and complete processing—that is, they are not catalogued for ease of reference or even accessible to the general public.

The most notable of such collections were held privately in Haiti at the family homes of renowned Haitian scholars and statesmen like Jean Price-Mars and Jean Fouchard, and former Haitian president Élie Lescot. This stands in contrast to most works on Haiti–U.S. relations, which are primarily based on U.S. State Department or presidential library holdings and other U.S.-based records. The family-managed archives of the three distinguished Haitian statesmen that I gained access to included official correspondence, rare books, pamphlets, and memorabilia. Additionally, *Haiti and the Uses of America* features information gathered from underutilized public institutions such as Haiti's National Archives. There, I searched through dozens of bound volumes to identify correspondence and occasional reports from the general office records of the Haitian Secretary of the President, Ministry of Foreign Affairs, and Ministry of the Interior. My findings introduced me to the names of individuals, institutions, publications, or projects related to Haitian national development and Haiti-U.S. relations during the study period.

The book has also been shaped by rich examples and testimonies gathered from rare publications (some found exclusively in Haiti) held at the libraries of the Frères du Saint Esprit and the Frères de L'Instruction Chrétienne. These plentiful congregational collections are well known and often cited (unfortunately, the collections at both libraries were inaccessible immediately following the 2010 earthquake that hit Port-au-Prince; see http://dloc.com/dloc1/haitianlibhelp for details). Additionally, modest holdings at the Haitian-American Institute (Port-au-Prince), Alliance Française (Jacmel), and in private family libraries offered news clippings and reports about educational, commercial, and cultural networks between Haiti and the U.S. at the time. These Haiti-based sources allow *Haiti and the Uses of America* to establish very clearly that there are in fact a number of important Haiti-based sources available for scholars who are willing to work in Port-au-Prince and elsewhere on the island.

My research in Haiti reinforced the significance of U.S.-based findings that scholars are beginning to recognize as vital to developments in Haiti-U.S. historiography. Prime examples are the Papers of Maurice Dartigue (former Haitian Minister of Education, Agriculture and Labor), especially those held at the New York Public Library's Schomburg Center for Research on Black Culture, and the records of the Rockefeller Foundation and Nelson A. Rockefeller held at the Rockefeller Archive Center. The evidence found in the Haitian and U.S. collections also reveals the promise of sources held at lesser-known institutions and in otherwise unexpected collections including the records of Pan American Airways held at the University of Miami, and the archives of the United Nations Educational, Scientific and Cultural Organization in Paris, France.

My archival research was also guided and complemented by insights from more than forty oral histories that I gathered for this project, most of which were conducted anonymously or while not quoted, shaped the final narrative. The interviewees were primarily elders from the period, many of whom have since died.

Bibliography

Primary Sources

ARCHIVAL COLLECTIONS

Haiti

Ancien Fonds d'Archives, Archives Nationales d'Haïti, Port-au-Prince

Bibliothèque Haïtienne, Petit Séminaire Collège Saint Martial, Port-au-Prince

Bibliothèque Haïtienne, Saint Louis de Gonzague, Port-au-Prince

Jean Fouchard Family Collection, Boïs Moquette

Elie Lescot Family Collection, Laboule

Jean Price-Mars Family Collection, Frères

United States

Archives of American Art, Smithsonian Institution, Washington, DC
 Glen William Lukens Papers

National Archives and Records Administration, College Park, MD
 RG 59 Department of State
 RG 229 Office of Inter-American Affairs

Rockefeller Archive Center, Pocantico Hills, NY
 John Marshall Oral History
 Papers of John Marshall
 Papers of Nelson A. Rockefeller
 Rockefeller Foundation Papers

Schomburg Center for Research in Black Culture, New York Public Library, Harlem, NY
 Maurice Dartigue Papers

Teachers College, Columbia University
 Maurice Dartigue Collection
University of Florida Libraries, Gainesville, FL
 Latin American and Caribbean Collection
 Special Collections, Frank Crumbie Papers

INTERVIEWS WITH THE AUTHOR

René Bélance, April 2002, Frères (Pétion-Ville), Haiti
Charles Manigat, April 4, 2002, Cap-Haïtien, Haiti
Odette Roy Fombrun, May 27, 2002, Musseau (Port-au-Prince), Haiti
Max Vieux, May 17, 2002, Tête-de-l'eau (Pétion-Ville), Haiti

PUBLISHED PRIMARY SOURCES

Annuaire des agronomes diplômés de la FAMV [Faculté d'Agronomie et de Médecine Vétérinaire], 1924–1998. Port-au-Prince, 1999.

Balch, Emily Greene. *Occupied Haiti: Being the Report of a Committee of Six Disinterested Americans Representing Organizations Exclusively American, Who, Having Personally Studied Conditions in Haiti in 1926, Favor the Restoration of the Independence of the Negro Republic*. New York: Writers Publishing Company, 1927.

Barreau de Port-au-Prince. *Tableau de l'Ordre des Avocats du Barreau de Port-au-Prince, 1938–1939*. Port-au-Prince: n.p., 1939. Available from Internet Archive. https://archive.org/details/tableaudelordredoobarr.

Bellegarde, Dantès. *Au service d'Haïti: Appréciations sur un haïtien et son œuvre*. Port-au-Prince: Imprimerie Theodore, 1962.

———. "Haiti and International Cooperation." In *Haiti and Her Problems: Four Lectures.* Rio Piedras, PR: University of Puerto Rico, 1936.

———. *Haïti et ses problèmes*. Montréal: Éditions Bernard Valiquette, 1941.

———. "Pétion and Bolívar." *Revue de la société d'histoire et de géographie d'Haïti* 12, no. 43 (April 1941): 1–13.

———. *La résistance haïtienne*. Montréal: Éditions Beauchemins, 1937.

Bevans, Charles I. *Treaties and Other International Agreements of the United States, 1776–1949*. Vol. 8. Washington, DC: U.S. Printing Office, 1971. Available from HeinOnline Treaties and Agreements Library Collection. http://heinonline.org.ezproxy.fiu.edu/HOL/Index?collection=ustreaties.

Blaine, James G. *Political Discussions: Legislative, Diplomatic, and Popular, 1856–1886*. Norwich: Henry Bill Publishing Company, 1887.

Bourgeois, Lionel. "Our Relations with Haiti." *Loyola Law Journal* 2, no. 26 (1920): 26–31.

Chaumette, Max Gustave. *Considérations historiques sur l'idéal panaméricain*. Port-au-Prince: printed by author, 1937.

———. *Haïti et les problèmes panaméricains*. Port-au-Prince: Les Editions de l'Assaut, No. 3, n.d.

———. *Le panaméricanisme à travers l'histoire d'Haïti*. Port-au-Prince: printed by author, 1944.

Cook, Mercer. *Education in Haiti*. Washington, DC: Federal Security Agency, United States Office of Education, 1948.

Dartigue, Maurice. *L'enseignement en Haïti (1804–1938)*. Port-au-Prince: Imprimerie de l'État, 1939.

———. *Les problèmes de la communauté*. Port-au-Prince: Imprimerie du Service Technique, 1931.

Dartigue, Maurice, and André Liautaud. *Géographie locale*. Port-au-Prince: Deschamps, 1931.

Département de l'Instruction Publique. *La préparation des cadres*. Port-au-Prince: Imprimerie de l'État, 1942, 1943, 1944, 1945.

Duvalier, François. *Œuvres essentielles*. Vol. 1. Port-au-Prince: Presses Nationales d'Haïti, 1968.

Féquière, Fleury. *L'Éducation haïtienne*. Port-au-Prince: Impr. de l'Abeille, 1906.

Firmin, Joseph-Anténor. *Lettres de Saint-Thomas: Études sociologiques, historiques et littéraires*. Port-au-Prince: Éditions Fardin, 1910.

———. *M. Roosevelt président des États-Unis et la République d'Haïti*. New York: Hamilton Bank Note Engraving and Printing Company; Paris: F. Pichon et Durand-Auzias, 1905.

"Haiti: Bon Papa," *Time*, February 28, 1954.

Hall, Robert Anderson, with the collaboration of Suzanne Comhaire-Sylvain, H. Ormonde McConnell, [and] Alfred Métraux. *Haitian Creole: Grammar, Texts, Vocabulary*. Philadelphia: American Folklore Society, 1953.

Hanson, Haldore. *The Cultural-Cooperation Program, 1938–1943*. Washington, DC: U.S. Government Printing Office, 1944.

Hawke, J. R. *Three Years of Vocational Industrial Education in Haiti*. Port-au-Prince: Department of Printing–Service Technique, 1930.

Hudicourt, Max Lelio. *Haiti Faces Tomorrow's Peace*. New York: L'Association Démocratique Haïtienne, 1945.

———. "Jim Crow Menaces Haiti." *Crisis* 51, no. 11 (1944): 354, 364.

"The Imperial College of Tropical Agriculture." *Nature* 143 (March 18, 1939): 468. Doi:10.1038/143468b0.

Lancaster, Joseph. *Improvements in Education*. London, 1803; New York, 1807.

Lescot, Élie. *Le diplomate et l'animateur: Un compte-rendu de la visite officielle, rendue par son excellence le président de la république d'Haïti au Canada, aux États-Unis et à Cuba, au mois d'octobre*. New York: IBM, 1943.

———. *Toussaint Louverture, précurseur de l'amitié américano-haïtienne*. Port-au-Prince: Imprimerie de l'État, 1942.

Ligue Féminine d'Action Sociale. "Femmes Haïtiennes." Brochure, n.d.

Logan, W. Rayford. "The Possibilities of a Caribbean Federation." In *The Economic Future of the Caribbean*, edited by Edward Franklin Frazier and Eric Williams, 55–59. Dover, MA: The Majority Press, 1943.

Magloire, Paul Eugène. *Address of his Excellency the President of the Republic of Haiti before a Joint-Session of the Congress of the United States of America, January 27, 1955*. [Printed in French, English, and Spanish.] Port-au-Prince: Imprimerie N. A. Théodore, 1955.

Ménos, Solon. *L'affaire Luders*. Port-au-Prince: Imprimerie J. Verrollot, 1898.

Métraux, Alfred. "L'habitation paysanne en Haïti." *Bulletin de la Société Neuchâteloise de Géographie* 55 (1949–51): 3–14.

———. *Médecine et vodou en Haïti*. Basel: Verlag für Recht und Gesellschaft, 1953.

———. "Mes amis les paysans de Marbial." *Gradhiva* 1 (2005). Posted online December 10, 2008.

———. *Voodoo in Haiti*. New York: Schocken Books, 1959.

Métraux, Alfred, Mr. Édouard Berrouet, and Dr. and Mrs. Jean Comhaire-Sylvain. "Making a Living in the Marbial Valley." In *Occasional Papers in Education*. Paris: UNESCO, December 7, 1951.

Métraux, Rhoda Bubendey. *Kith and Kin: A Study of Creole Social Structure in Marbial, Haiti*. Ann Arbor: University Microfilms, 1951.

Piquion, René, and Love Léger. *Histoire d'Haïti*. Haiti: n.p., 1938.

Price-Mars, Jean. *La contribution haïtienne à la lutte des Amériques pour les libertés humaines*. Port-au-Prince: Imprimerie de l'État, 1942.

———. "La réforme de l'enseignement primaire." *Haïti Littéraire et Scientifique*, July 5, 1912, 312–317.

———. *La vocation de l'élite*. Port-au-Prince: Imprimerie Edmond Chenet, 1919.

Rosemond, Ludvic. *Haïti et les États-Unis*. Port-au-Prince: n.p., 1945.

Saunders, Prince. *A Memoir Presented to the American Convention for Promoting the Abolition of Slavery, and Improving the Condition of the African Race*. Philadelphia, 1818.

Spracher, Luciana M., ed. *A Century of History: Savannah City Hall Centennial, 1906–2006*. Savannah: City of Savannah. Research Library and Municipal Archives, 2006. Available at: http://www.savannahga.gov/DocumentCenter/View/273.

Sylvain-Bouchereau, Madeline G. *Éducation des femmes en Haïti*. Port-au Prince: Imprimerie de l'État, 1944.

United Nations. *Mission to Haiti: Report of the United Nations Mission of Technical Assistance to the Republic of Haiti*. Lake Success, NY, 1949.

UNESCO. *The Haiti Pilot Project, Phase One [1947–1949]*. Paris, 1951.

Vincent, Sténio. *Efforts et résultats*. Port-au-Prince: Imprimerie de l'État, 1938.

———. *Sur la route de la seconde indépendance: En compagnie du soldat et du citoyen haïtiens*. Port-au-Prince: Imprimerie de l'État, 1934.

PERIODICALS

Le Moniteur (Port-au-Prince, Haïti)

Le Matin (Port-au-Prince, Haïti)

New York Times

Le Nouvelliste (Port-au-Prince, Haïti)

Le Temps (Port-au-Prince, Haïti)

Voz de Haití en Las Americas

Secondary Sources

Aguilar, Alonzo. *Pan-Americanism from Monroe to the Present: A View from the Other Side*. Translated by Asa Zatz. New York: Monthly Review Press, 1968.

Alexander, Leslie. *African or American? Black Identity in New York City, 1784–1861*. Chicago: University of Illinois Press, 2008.

Alexis, Yveline. "Nationalism and the Politics of Historical Memory: Charlemagne Peralte's Rebellion Against the U.S. Occupation of Haiti, 1915–1986." PhD diss., University of Massachusetts, 2011.

Anderson, James D. *The Education of Blacks in the South 1860–1935*. Chapel Hill: University of North Carolina Press, 1988.

Andrews, George Reid. *Afro-Latin America, 1800–2000*. New York: Oxford University Press, 2004.

Antoine, Jacques C. *Jean Price-Mars and Haiti*. Washington, DC: Three Continents Press, 1981.

Aris, P. Patrick. "Farnèse Louis-Charles, Théologien et Prophète." *Moun—Revue de Philosophie* 6 (2007): 285–313.

Arthus, Wien Weibert. "The Challenge of Democratizing the Caribbean during the Cold War: Kennedy Facing the Duvalier Dilemma." *Diplomatic History* 39 (June 2015): 504–531.

Basch, Linda, Nina Glick Schiller, and Cristina Szanton Blanc. *Nations Unbound: Transnational Projects, Postcolonial Predicaments, and Deterritorialized Nation-States*. Langhorne, PA: Gordon and Breach, 1994.

Bastien, Rémy, and Harold Courlander. *Religion and Politics in Haiti*. Washington, DC: Institute for Cross-Cultural Research, 1966.

Bellegarde-Smith, Patrick. *In the Shadow of Powers: Dantès Bellegarde in Haitian Social Thought*. Atlantic Highlands, NJ: Humanities Press International, 1985.

Belnap, Jeffrey, and Raúl A. Fernandez, eds. *José Martí's "Our America": From National to Hemispheric Cultural Studies*. Durham, NC: Duke University Press, 1998.

Bender, Thomas. *A Nation among Nations: America's Place in World History*. New York: FSG/Hill & Wang, 2006.

Berg, Jerome S. *The Early Shortwave Stations: An Early Broadcasting History through 1945*. Jefferson, NC: MacFarland and Company, 2013.

Berman, Edward H. *The Ideology of Philanthropy: The Influence of the Carnegie, Ford, and Rockefeller Foundations on American Foreign Policy*. Albany: SUNY Press, 1986.

Bordes, Ary. *Évolution des sciences de la santé et de l'hygiène publique en Haïti, 1915–1934*. Port-au-Prince: Centre d'Hygiène Familiale, 1979.

———. *Haïti, la santé de la république 1934–1957*. Port-au-Prince: Imprimerie Deschamps, 1997.

———. *Haïti, médecine et santé publique sous l'occupation américaine, 1915–1934*. Port-au-Prince: Imprimerie Deschamps, 1992.

Borges, Dain. "'Puffy, Ugly, Slothful and Inert': Degeneration in Brazilian Social Thought, 1880–194." *Journal of Latin American Studies* 25, no. 2 (May 1993): 235–256.

Borgwardt, Elizabeth. *A New Deal for the World: America's Vision for Human Rights*. Cambridge, MA: Belknap Press of Harvard University Press, 2005.

Bory-Adams, Aline. "Educational Policies for Development in the Caribbean: An Analysis of UNESCO's Role and Contribution to Educational Development in Haiti." PhD diss., Florida State University, 1991.

Bradley, Mark. *Imagining Vietnam and America: The Making of Postcolonial Vietnam, 1919–1950*. Chapel Hill: University of North Carolina Press, 2000.

Britton, John, ed. *Molding Their Hearts and Minds: Education, Communications, and Social Change in Latin America*. Wilmington, DE: Scholarly Resources, 1994.

———. "Redefining Intervention: Mexico's Contribution to Anti-Americanism." In *Anti-Americanism in Latin America and the Caribbean*, edited by Alan McPherson, 37–60. New York: Berghahn Books, 2006.

Bronfman, Alejandra. "El Octopus Acústico: Broadcasting and Empire in the Caribbean." In *Radio's New Wave: Global Sound in the Digital Era*, edited by Jason Loviglio and Michele Hilmes, 147–163. New York: Routledge, 2013.

Bu, Liping. *Making the World Like Us: Education, Cultural Expansion, and the American Century*. Westport, CT: Praeger, 2003.

Bulmer-Thomas, Victor. *The Economic History of the Caribbean since the Napoleonic Wars*. Cambridge: Cambridge University Press, 2012.

Bushnell, David, and Lester D. Langley, eds. *Simón Bolívar: Essays on the Life and Legacy of the Liberator*. London: Rowman and Littlefield, 2008.

Butler, Kim D. *Freedoms Given, Freedoms Won: Afro-Brazilians in Post-Abolition São Paulo and Salvador*. New Brunswick, NJ: Rutgers University Press, 1998.

Cabon, Pierre Adolphe. *Notes sur l'histoire religieuse d'Haïti de la révolution au Concordat, 1789–1860*. Port-au-Prince: Petit Séminaire Collège Saint-Martial, 1933.

Casimir, Jean. "Haiti et ses élites: L'interminable dialogue des sourds." *Worlds and Knowledges Otherwise* 2, dossier 3 (Fall 2008). https://globalstudies.trinity.duke.edu/wko-v2d3.

Castor, Suzy. *L'occupation américaine d'Haïti*. Port-au-Prince: Imprimerie Henri Deschamps, 1988.

Catanese, Anthony V. *Haitians: Migration and Diaspora*. Boulder, CO: Westview Press, 1999.

Chancy, Myriam. *Framing Silence: Revolutionary Novels by Haitian Women*. New Brunswick, NJ: Rutgers University Press, 1997.

Chasteen, John Charles. *National Rhythms, African Roots: The Deep History of Latin American Popular Dance*. Albuquerque: University of New Mexico Press, 2004.

Choy, Catherine C. *Empire of Care: Nursing and Migration in Filipino American History*. Durham, NC: Duke University Press, 2003.

Connelly, Matthew. "Taking Off the Cold War Lens: Visions of North-South Conflict during the Algerian War for Independence." *American Historical Review* 105, no. 3 (2000): 739–769.

Connolly, Nathan D. B. "By Eminent Domain: Race and Capital in the Building of an American South Florida." PhD diss., University of Michigan, 2008.

———. *A World More Concrete: Real Estate and the Remaking of Jim Crow South Florida*. Chicago: University of Chicago Press, 2014.

Cooper, Donald B. "The Withdrawal of the United States from Haiti, 1928–1934." *Journal of Inter-American Studies* 5, no. 1 (January 1963): 83–101.

Cooper, Frederick. "Conflict and Connection: Rethinking Colonial African History." In *The Decolonization Reader*, edited by James Le Sueur, 23–42. New York: Routledge, 2003.

———. "Development, Modernization, and the Social Sciences in the Era of Decolonization: The Examples of British and French Africa." *Revue d'Histoire des Sciences Humaines* 1, no. 10 (2004): 9–38.

———. "Networks, Moral Discourse, and History." In *Intervention and Transnationalism in Africa: Global-Local Networks of Power*, edited by Thomas Callaghy, Ronald Kassimir, and Robert Latham, 23–46. Cambridge: Cambridge University Press, 2001.

Cooper, Frederick, and Ann Laura Stoler Cooper, eds. *Tensions of Empire: Colonial Cultures in a Bourgeois World*. Berkeley: University of California Press, 1997.

Cooper, Frederick, and Randall M. Packard, eds. *International Development and the Social Sciences: Essays on the History and Politics of Knowledge*. Berkeley: University of California Press, 1997.

Coronil, Fernando. "Listening to the Subaltern: The Poetics of Neocolonial States." *Poetics Today* 15, no. 4 (Winter 1994): 643–658.

Corvington, Georges. *Port-au-Prince au cours des ans: La ville contemporaine, 1934–1950*. Port-au-Prince: Imprimerie Henri Deschamps, 1991.

Cramer, Gisela, and Ursula Prutsch. "Nelson A. Rockefeller's Office of Inter-American Affairs (1940–1946) and Record Group 229." *Hispanic American Historical Review* 86, no. 4 (2006): 785–806.

Cullather, Nick. "Development? It's History." *Diplomatic History* 24 (Fall 2000): 641–653.

———. *The Hungry World: America's Cold War Battle against Poverty in Asia*. Cambridge: Harvard University Press, 2010.

Curti, Merle, and Kendall Birr. "Prelude to Point Four." In *Prelude to Point Four: American Technical Missions Overseas, 1838–1938*. Madison: University of Wisconsin Press, 1954.

Dartigue, Esther. *An Outstanding Haitian, Maurice Dartigue: The Contribution of Maurice Dartigue in the Field of Education in Haiti, the United Nations, and UNESCO*. New York: Vantage Press, 1994.

Dartigue, Esther, and John Dartigue. *Forging Ahead: Recollections of the Life and Times of Esther Dartigue*. n.p.: John Dartigue, 2014.

Dash, J. Michael. *Haiti and the United States: National Stereotypes and the Literary Imagination*. 2nd ed. Basingstoke: Palgrave Macmillan, 1997.

———. *Literature and Ideology in Haiti 1915–1961*. London: Macmillan Press, 1981.

———. "Nineteenth-Century Haiti and the Archipelago of the Americas: Anténor Firmin's Letters from St. Thomas." *Research in African Literatures* 35, no. 2 (2004): 44–53.

———. *The Other America: Caribbean Literature in a New World Context*. Charlottesville: University Press of Virginia, 1998.

Daut, Marlene L. "The 'Alpha and Omega' of Haitian Literature: Baron de Vastey and the US Audience of Haitian Political Writing." *Comparative Literature* 64, no. 1 (2012): 49–72.

———. *Tropics of Haiti: Race and the Literary History of the Haitian Revolution in the Atlantic World, 1780–1865*. Liverpool: Liverpool University Press, 2015.

Dávila, Jerry. *Diploma of Whiteness: Race and Social Policy in Brazil, 1917–1945*. Durham, NC: Duke University Press, 2003.

———. "Norma Fraga: Growing Up Black in the Estado Novo." In *The Human Tradition in Modern Brazil*, edited by Peter M. Beattie, 165–182. Wilmington, DE: Scholarly Resources, 2003.

DeConde, Alexander. "Herbert Hoover's Good Will Tour." *Historian* 12, no. 2 (1950): 167–181.

———. *Herbert Hoover's Latin-American Policy*. Stanford, CA: Stanford University Press, 1951.

Delaney, Jean H. "Imagining El Ser Argentino: Cultural Nationalism and Romantic Concepts of Nationhood in Early Twentieth-Century Argentina." *Journal of Latin American Studies* 34, no. 3 (2002): 625–658.

Denis, Watson. "La nation comme projet d'intégration socio-économique." *Revue Haïtienne d'histoire, géographie et géologie* 240 (July–December 2010): 44–45.

———. "Orígenes y manifestaciones de la francofila haitiana: nacionialismo y política exterior en Haití (1880–1915)." *Secuencia* 67 (January–April 2007): 93–139.

Desmangles, Leslie G. *The Faces of the Gods: Vodou and Roman Catholicism in Haiti*. Chapel Hill: University of North Carolina Press, 1992.

Desquiron, Jean. *Haïti à la une: Une anthologie de la presse haïtienne de 1724 à 1934*, vol. 6, *1931–1934*. Port-au-Prince: l'Imprimeur II, 1997.

Dixon, Chris. *African Americans and Haiti: Emigration and Black Nationalism in the Nineteenth Century*. Westport, CT: Greenwood Press, 2000.

Dorn, Charles, and Kristen Ghodsee. "The Cold War Politicization of Literacy: Communism, UNESCO, and the World Bank." *Diplomatic History* 36, no. 2 (April 2012): 373–398.

Dozer, Donald Marquand. *Are We Good Neighbors? Three Decades of Inter-American Relations, 1930–1960*. Gainesville: University of Florida Press, 1969.

Dubois, Laurent. *Avengers of the New World: The Story of the Haitian Revolution*. Cambridge, MA: Harvard University Press, 2005.

———. *Haiti: The Aftershocks of History*. New York: Metropolitan Books, 2012.

———. "A Spoonful of Blood: Haitians, Racism, and AIDS." *Science and Culture* 6, no. 26 (1996): 7–43.

Dunham, Katherine. *Island Possessed*. 1969. Reprint, Chicago: University of Chicago Press, 1994.

Dupuy, Alex. *Haiti in the World Economy: Class, Race, and Underdevelopment since 1700*. Boulder, CO: Westview Press, 1989.

———. *The Prophet and Power: Jean-Bertrand Aristide, the International Community, and Haiti*. New York: Rowman & Littlefield, 2007.

Edwards, Brent Hayes. *The Practice of Diaspora: Literature, Translation, and the Rise of Black Internationalism*. Cambridge, MA: Harvard University Press, 2003.

Egerton, Douglas. *Rebels, Reformers, and Revolutionaries: Collected Essays and Second Thoughts*. New York: Routledge, 2002.

Eller, Anne. "'All would be equal in the effort': Santo Domingo's 'Italian Revolution,' Independence, and Haiti, 1809–1822." *Journal of Early American History* 1 (2011): 105–141.

Engerman, David. "American Knowledge and Global Power." *Diplomatic History* 31, no. 4 (September 2007): 599–622.

Engerman, David C., Nils Gilman, Mark H. Haefele, and Michael E. Latham, eds. *Staging Growth: Modernization, Development, and the Global Cold War*. Amherst: University of Massachusetts Press, 2003.

Erb, Claude C. "Prelude to Point Four: The Institute of Inter-American Affairs." *Diplomatic History* 9, no. 3 (Summer 1985): 249–269.

Ewell, Judith. "Bolívar's Atlantic World Diplomacy." In *Simón Bolívar: Essays on the Life and Legacy of the Liberator*, ed. David Bushnell and Lester D. Langley, 35–53. London: Rowman and Littlefield, 2008.

Espinosa, J. Manuel. *Inter-American Beginnings of U.S. Cultural Diplomacy: 1936–48*. Washington, DC: US Government Printing Office, 1976.

Farmer, Paul. *Haiti: After the Earthquake*. New York: Public Affairs, 2011.

———. *The Uses of Haiti*. Monroe, ME: Common Courage Press, 1994.

Fein, Seth. "El cine y las relaciones culturales entre México y Estados Unidos durante la década de 1930." *Secuencia* 34 (January–April 1996): 155–195.

Ferrer, Ada. *Freedom's Mirror*. Cambridge: Cambridge University Press, 2014.

———. *Insurgent Cuba: Race, Nation, and Revolution, 1868–1898*. Chapel Hill: University of North Carolina Press, 1999.

———. "Talk About Haiti." In *Tree of Liberty: Cultural Legacies of the Haitian Revolution in the Atlantic World*, edited by Doris L. Garraway, 21–40. Charlottesville: University of Virginia Press, 2008.

Findlay, Eileen J. *Imposing Decency: The Politics of Sexuality and Race in Puerto Rico, 1870–1920*. Durham, NC: Duke University Press, 1999.

Fischer, Sibylle. *Modernity Disavowed: Haiti and the Cultures of Slavery in the Age of Revolution*. Durham: Duke University Press, 2004.

Fluehr-Lobban, Carolyn. "Anténor Firmin and Haiti's Contribution to Anthropology." *Gradhiva: Revue d'Anthropologie et d'Histoire des Arts* 1 (2005): 95–108.

Fouchard, Jean. *Les Marrons du syllabaire: Quelques aspects du problème de l'instruction et de l'éducation des esclaves et affranchis de Saint-Domingue*. Port-au-Prince: H. Deschamps, 1953.

Fox, H. "Yaws (frambesia tropica) as Observed in Haiti." *Archives of Dermatology and Syphilology* 20, no. 6 (December 1929): 820–834.

Fraser, Cary. *Ambivalent Anti-Colonialism: The United States and the Genesis of West Indian Independence, 1940–1964*. Westport, CT: Greenwood Press, 1994.

Friedman, Max Paul. "Retiring the Puppets, Bringing Latin America Back In." *Diplomatic History* 27, no. 5 (November 2003): 621–636.

Gaffield, Julia. "Haiti and Jamaica in the Remaking of the Early Nineteenth-Century Atlantic World." *The William and Mary Quarterly* 69, no. 3 (2012): 583–614.

———. *Haitian Connections in the Atlantic World: Recognition after Revolution*. Chapel Hill: University of North Carolina Press, 2015.

———. "'So many schemes in agitation': The Haitian State and the Atlantic World." PhD diss., Duke University, 2012.

Gaillard, Roger. *Les Blancs débarquent*. 8 vols. Port-au-Prince: Roger Gaillard, 1984.

Gaillard-Pourchet, Gusti. *L'Expérience haïtienne de la dette extérieure (ou) une production caféière pillée, 1875–1915*. Port-au-Prince: Imprimerie Henri Deschamps, 2001.

Garrigus, John D. "Catalyst or Catastrophe? Saint Domingue's Free Men of Color and the Battle of Savannah, 1779–1782." *Revista/Review Interamericana* 22, nos. 1–2 (1992): 110.

Gaspar, David Barry, and David Patrick Geggus, eds. *A Turbulent Time: The French Revolution and the Greater Caribbean*. Bloomington: Indiana University Press, 1997.

Geggus, David Patrick. *Haitian Revolutionary Studies*. Bloomington: Indiana University Press, 2002.

———, ed. *Impact of the Haitian Revolution in the Atlantic World*. Columbia: University of South Carolina Press, 2001.

Gilbert, Myrtha. *Shada: Chronique d'une extravagante escroquerie*. Port-au-Prince: l'Imprimeur, 2011.

Gilderhaus, Mark T. "An Emerging Synthesis? U.S.-Latin American Relations since the Second World War." In *America in the World: The Historiography of American Foreign Relations Since 1941*, edited by Michael J. Hogan, 424–461. New York: Cambridge University Press, 1995.

———. *Pan American Visions: Woodrow Wilson in the Western Hemisphere, 1913–1921*. Tucson: University of Arizona Press, 1986.

———. *The Second Century: U.S.-Latin American Relations since 1889*. Wilmington, DE: Scholarly Resources, 2000.

Gonzales, Michael J. "Imagining Mexico in 1910: Visions of the Patria in the Centennial Celebration in Mexico City." *Journal of Latin American Studies* 39, no. 3 (August 2007): 495–533.

Guridy, Frank. *Forging Diaspora: Afro-Cubans and African Americans in a World of Empire and Jim Crow*. Chapel Hill: University of North Carolina Press, 2010.

Hector, Michel. "Intellectuels et pouvoir politique en Haïti (XIXe–XXe siècle)." *Revue Haïtienne d'histoire, géographie et géologie* 240 (July–December 2010): 29–38.

Hector, Michel, and Laënnec Hurbon, eds. *Genèse de l'état Haïtien (1804–1859)*. Port-au-Prince: Éditions Presses Nationales d'Haïti, 2009.

Hefferan, Tara. *Twinning Faith and Development: Catholic Parish Partnering in the U.S. and Haiti*. Bloomfield, MI: Kumarian Press, 2007.

Hill, Archibald A. "William Freeman Twaddell." *Language* 59, no. 2 (June 1983): 347–354.

Hodge, Joseph Moran. "British Colonial Expertise, Postcolonial Careering, and the Early History of International Development." In "Modernizing Missions: Approaches to 'Developing' the Non-Western World after 1945," edited by Andreas Eckert, Stephan Malinowski, and Corinna Unger. Special Issue, *Journal of Modern European History* 8, no. 1 (2010): 24–46.

Hogan, Michael J. *The Marshall Plan: America, Britain, and the Reconstruction of Western Europe, 1947–1952*. New York: Cambridge University Press, 1987.

Holt, Thomas C. *The Problem of Freedom: Race, Labor, and Politics in Jamaica and Britain, 1832–1938*. Baltimore: The Johns Hopkins University Press, 1992.

Hunt, Alfred N. *Haiti's Influence in Antebellum America: Slumbering Volcano in the Caribbean*. Baton Rouge: Louisiana State University Press, 1988.

Hurbon, Laënnec. "American Fantasy and Haitian Vodou." In *Sacred Arts of Haitian Vodou*, edited by Donald J. Consentino, 181–197. Los Angeles: UCLA Fowler Museum of Cultural History, 1995.

Inter-American Educational Foundation. *Educational Division Newsletter* (February 1946).

Iriye, Akira. *Cultural Internationalism and World Order*. Baltimore: The Johns Hopkins University Press, 1997.

Jackson, Maurice, and Jacqueline Bacon, eds. *African Americans and the Haitian Revolution: Selected Essays and Historical Documents*. New York: Routledge, 2010.

Jenson, Deborah. *Beyond the Slave Narrative: Politics, Sex, and Manuscripts in the Haitian Revolution*. Liverpool: Liverpool University Press, 2011.

———. "Dessalines's American Proclamations of the Haitian Independence." *The Journal of Haitian Studies* 15, nos. 1 and 2 (2010): 72–102.

Jones, Hilary. *The Métis of Senegal: Urban Life and Politics in French West Africa*. Bloomington: Indiana University Press, 2013.

Jones, Phillip W. *International Policies for Third World Education: UNESCO, Literacy, and Development*. London: Routledge, 1988.

Joseph, Gilbert, Catherine M. LeGrand, and Ricardo D. Salvatore, eds. *Close Encounters of Empire: Writing the Cultural History of U.S.-Latin American Relations*. Durham, NC: Duke University Press, 1998.

Joseph, Gilbert, and David Nugent, eds. *Everyday Forms of State Formation: Revolution and the Negotiation of Rule in Modern Mexico*. Durham, NC: Duke University Press, 1994.

Kat. "Haiti History 101: The Haitian Tuskegee Airmen." Posted online January 13, 2012. http://kreyolicious.com/haiti-history-101-the-haitian-tuskegee-airmen/1597/.

Katz, Jonathan. *The Big Truck That Went By: How the World Came to Save Haiti and Left Behind a Disaster*. New York: St. Martin's Press, 2013.

Kelly, Robin D. G. "'But a Local Phase of a World Problem': Black History's Global Vision, 1883–1950." *Journal of American History* 86 (1999): 1045–1077.

Kramer, Paul A. *The Blood of Government: Race, Empire, the United States, and the Philippines*. Chapel Hill: University of North Carolina Press, 2006.

———. "Is the World Our Campus? International Students and U.S. Global Power in the Long Twentieth Century." *Diplomatic History* 33 (2009): 775–806.

———. "Power and Connection: Imperial Histories of the United States in the World." *American Historical Review* (December 2011): 1348–1391.

LaFeber, Walter. *Inevitable Revolutions: The United States in Central America*. New York: W. W. Norton, 1984.

Laguerre, Michel S. *American Odyssey: Haitians in New York City*. Ithaca, NY: Cornell University Press, 1984.

———. *Diaspora, Politics, and Globalization*. New York: Palgrave Macmillan, 2006.

———. *Diasporic Citizenship: Haitian Americans in Transnational America*. New York: St. Martin's Press, 1998.

Langley, Lester D. *America and the Americas: The United States in the Western Hemisphere*. Athens: University of Georgia Press, 1998, 2010.

Largey, Michael. *Vodou Nation: Haitian Art Music and Cultural Nationalism*. Chicago: University of Chicago Press, 2006.

Latham, Michael E. *The Right Kind of Revolution: Modernization, Development, and U.S. Foreign Policy from the Cold War to the Present*. Ithaca: Cornell University Press, 2011.

Laurent, Gérard. *Haïti et l'indépendance américaine*. Port-au-Prince: Imprimerie Séminaire Adventiste, 1976.

Laurière, Christine. "D'une île à l'autre." *Gradhiva* 1 (2005). Posted online December 10, 2008. http://gradhiva.revues.org/359.

Le Grand, Catherine M. "Living in Macondo: Economy and Culture in a United Fruit Company Banana Enclave in Colombia." In *Close*

Encounters of Empire: Writing the Cultural History of U.S.-Latin American Relations, edited by Gilbert Joseph, Catherine M. LeGrand, and Ricardo D. Salvatore, 333–369. Durham, NC: Duke University Press, 1998.

Lescot, Élie. *Avant l'oubli: Christianisme et paganisme en Haïti et autres lieux*. Port-au-Prince: Imprimerie Henri Deschamps, 1974.

Lewis, Gordon K. *Main Currents in Caribbean Thought: The Historical Evolution of Caribbean Society in Its Ideological Aspects, 1492–1900*. Baltimore: The Johns Hopkins University Press, 1983.

Lindsey, Donal F. 1995. *Indians at Hampton Institute, 1877–1923*. Urbana: University of Illinois Press, 1995.

Lipman, Jana K. *Guantánamo: A Working-Class History between Empire and Revolution*. Berkeley: University of California Press, 2009.

Lomnitz, Claudio. *Deep Mexico, Silent Mexico: An Anthropology of Nationalism*. Minneapolis: University of Minnesota Press, 2001.

Lundestead, Geir. "Empire by Invitation? The United States and Western Europe, 1945–1952." *Journal of Peace Research* 23, no. 3 (September 1986): 264.

Magloire, Gérarde, and Kevin A. Yelvington. "Haiti and the Anthropological Imagination." *Gradhiva* 1 (2005). Posted online December 10, 2008. http://gradhiva.revues.org/335.

Maurel, Chloé. "L'Unesco: Un âge d'or de l'aide au développement par l'éducation (1945–1975)." *Cahiers d'histoire*: *Revue d'histoire critique* 108 (2009). Posted online April 1, 2012. Accessed November 19, 2013. http://chrhc.revues.org/1819.

Makalani, Minkah. *In the Cause of Freedom: Radical Black Internationalism from Harlem to London, 1917–1939*. Chapel Hill: University of North Carolina Press, 2011.

Manela, Erez. *The Wilsonian Moment: Self-Determination and the International Origins of Anticolonial Nationalism*. Oxford: Oxford University Press, 2007.

Manigat, Leslie. "La Substitution de la prépondérance américaine à la prépondérance française en Haïti au début du XXe siècle: La conjoncture de 1910–1911." *Revue d'histoire moderne et contemporaine* 14, no. 4 (October–December 1967): 321–355.

Martínez-Fernandez, Luis. "El anexionismo dominicano y la lucha entre imperios durante la Primera República, 1844–1861." *Revista/Review Interamericana* 22, nos. 1–2 (Spring–Summer 1992): 168–190.

Matthewson, Tim. *A Proslavery Foreign Policy: Haitian-American Relations during the Early Republic*. Westport, CT: Praeger, 2003.

McBride, David. *Missions for Science: U.S. Technology and Medicine in America's African World*. New Brunswick, NJ: Rutgers University Press, 2002.

McCrocklin, James H. *Garde d'Haiti: Twenty Years of Organization and Training by the United States Marine Corps*. Annapolis, MD: Naval Institute Press, 1956.

McGuinness, Aims. *Path of Empire: Panama and the California Gold Rush*. Ithaca, NY: Cornell University Press, 2009.

McPherson, Alan, ed. *Anti-Americanism in Latin America and the Caribbean*. New York: Berghahn Books, 2006.

———. *The Invaded: How Latin Americans and Their Allies Fought and Ended U.S. Occupations*. Oxford: Oxford University Press, 2014.

Michel, Georges. *Les chemins de fer d'île d'Haïti*. Jamaica, NY: Haitiana Publications, 1989.

Mignolo, Walter D. "The Geopolitics of Knowledge and the Colonial Difference." *South Atlantic Quarterly* 101, no. 1 (Winter 2002): 56–96.

———. *The Idea of Latin America*. London: Wiley-Blackwell, 2005.

———. "The Many Faces of Cosmo-polis: Border Thinking and Critical Cosmopolitanism." *Public Culture* 12, no. 3 (Fall 2000): 721–748.

Miller, Francesca. "The International Relations of Women of the Americas, 1890–1928." *The Americas* 43, no. 2 (October 1986): 171–182.

Mintz, Sidney, and Michel-Rolph Trouillot. "The Social History of Haitian Vodou." In *Sacred Arts of Haitian Vodou*, edited by Donald J. Cosentino, 123–147. Los Angeles: UCLA Fowler Museum of Cultural History, 1995.

Mozwer, Mark. *No Enchanted Palace: The End of Empire and the Ideological Origins of the United Nations*. New York: Princeton University Press, 2009.

Needel, Jeffrey. "Rio de Janeiro at the Turn of the Century: Modernization and the Parisian Idea." *Journal of Interamerican Studies and World Affairs* 25, no. 1 (February 1983): 83–103.

———. *A Tropical Belle Epoque: The Elite Culture of Turn-of-the-Century Rio de Janeiro*. New York: Cambridge University Press, 1987.

Nemours, Auguste. *La Charte des Nations Unies: Étude comparative de la Charte avec les propositions de Dumbarton Oaks, le covenant de la Société des Nations, les conventions de la Haye, les propositions et doctrines inter américaines*. Port-au-Prince: H. Deschamps, 1945.

———. *Haïti et la guerre de l'indépendance américaine*. Port-au-Prince: H. Deschamps, 1952.

Neptune, Harvey R. *Caliban and the Yankees: Trinidad and the United States Occupation*. Chapel Hill: University of North Carolina Press, 2007.

Nicholls, David. *From Dessalines to Duvalier: Race, Colour, and National Independence in Haiti*. Basingstoke: Macmillan Caribbean, 1988.

———. "Ideology and Protest in Haiti, 1930–1946." *Journal of Contemporary History* 9, no. 4 (1974): 3–26.

Ninkovich, Frank. *The Diplomacy of Ideas: U.S. Foreign Policy and Cultural Relations, 1938–1950*. Cambridge: Cambridge University Press, 1981.

Orozco, Cynthia. *No Mexicans, Women, or Dogs Allowed: The Rise of the Mexican American Civil Rights Movement*. Austin: University of Texas, 2009.

Pamphile, Leon D. *Clash of Cultures: America's Educational Strategies in Occupied Haiti, 1915–1934*. Lanham, MD: University Press of America, 2008.

———. *Haitians and African Americans: A Heritage of Tragedy and Hope*. Gainesville: University Press of Florida, 2001.

Parker, Jason. *Brother's Keeper: The United States, Race, and Empire in the British Caribbean, 1937–1962*. Oxford: Oxford University Press, 2008.

Parmar, Inderjeet. *Foundations of the American Century: The Ford, Carnegie, and Rockefeller Foundations in the Rise of American Power*. New York: Columbia University Press, 2012.

Paul, Emmanuel C., and Jean Fouchard, eds. *Témoignages sur la vie et l'œuvre de Jean Price-Mars, 1876–1956*. Port-au-Prince: Imprimerie de l'État, 1956.

Paulino, Edward. "Birth of a Boundary: Blood, Cement, and Prejudice and the Making of the Dominican-Haitian Border, 1937–1961." PhD diss., University of Michigan, 2001.

———. *Dividing Hispaniola: The Dominican Republic's Border Campaign against Haiti, 1930–1961*. Pittsburgh: University of Pittsburgh Press, 2016.

Pérez, Louis A., Jr. "Cuba between Empires, 1898–1899." *Pacific Historical Review* 48, no. 4 (November 1979): 473–500.

———. *On Becoming Cuban: Identity, Nationality, and Culture*. Chapel Hill: University of North Carolina Press, 1999.

Pike, Fredrick B. *FDR's Good Neighbor Policy: Sixty Years of Generally Gentle Chaos*. Austin: University of Texas Press, 2010.

Plummer, Brenda Gayle. "Firmin and Martí at the Intersection of Pan-Americanism and Pan-Africanism." In *José Martí's "Our America": From*

National to Hemispheric Cultural Studies, edited by Jeffrey Belnap and Raúl A. Fernández, 218–227. Durham, NC: Duke University Press, 1998.
———. *Haiti and the Great Powers, 1902–1915*. Baton Rouge: Louisiana State University Press, 1988.
———. *Haiti and the United States: The Psychological Moment*. Athens: University of Georgia Press, 1992.
———. "The Metropolitan Connection: Foreign and Semiforeign Elites in Haiti, 1900–1915." *Latin American Research Review* 19, no. 2 (1984): 119–142.
Polyné, Millery. *From Douglass to Duvalier: U.S. African-Americans, Haiti, and Pan-Americanism, 1870–1964*. Gainesville: University Press of Florida, 2010.
———, ed. *The Idea of Haiti, Rethinking Crisis and Development*. Minneapolis: University of Minnesota Press, 2013.
———. "Modernizing the Race: Political and Cultural Engagements between African Americans and Haitians, 1930–1964." PhD diss., University of Michigan, 2003.
Rabe, Stephen G. "Marching Ahead (Slowly): The Historiography of Inter-American Relations." *Diplomatic History* 13 (Summer 1989): 297–316.
Racine, Karen. "Imported Englishness: Henry Christophe's Educational Programme in Haiti, 1806–1820." In *Imported Modernity in Post-Colonial State Formation: The Appropriation of Political, Educational, and Cultural Models in Nineteenth-Century Latin America*, edited by Eugenia Roldan and Marcelo Caruso, 205–230. Frankfurt am Main: Peter Lang, 2007.
Ramsey, Kate. "Legislating 'Civilisation' in Postrevolutionary Haiti." In *Race, Nation, and Religion in the Americas*, edited by Henry Goldschmidt and Elizabeth McAlister, 231–258. Oxford: Oxford University Press, 2004.
———. "Prohibition, Persecution, Performance." *Gradhiva* 1 (2005). Posted online December 15, 2008. http://gradhiva.revues.org/352.
———. *The Spirits and the Law: Vodou and Power in Haiti*. Chicago: University of Chicago Press, 2011.
———. "Without One Ritual Note: Folklore Performance and the Haitian State, 1935–1946." *Radical History Review* 84 (Fall 2002): 7–42.
Reich, Cary. *The Life of Nelson A. Rockefeller: Worlds to Conquer, 1908–1958*. New York, Doubleday, 1996.
Renda, Mary. *Taking Haiti: Military Occupation and the Culture of U.S. Imperialism, 1915–1940*. Chapel Hill: University of North Carolina Press, 2001.

Richman, Karen. *Migration and Vodou*. Gainesville: University Presses of Florida, 2005.

Rivas, Darlene. *Missionary Capitalist: Nelson Rockefeller in Venezuela*. Chapel Hill: University of North Carolina Press, 2002.

———. "US-Latin American Relations, 1942–1960." In *A Companion to American Foreign Relations*, edited by Robert D. Schulzinger, 230–254. Malden, MA: Blackwell Publishing, 2003.

Robinson, Ronald. "Non-European Foundations of European Imperialism: Sketch for a Theory of Collaboration." In *Studies in the Theory of Imperialism*, edited by Roger Own and Bob Sutcliffe, 117–140. London: Longman Group, 1972.

Roorda, Eric Paul. *The Dictator Next Door: The Good Neighbor Policy and the Trujillo Regime in the Dominican Republic, 1930–1945*. Durham, NC: Duke University Press, 1998.

Rose, Chanelle Nyree. "Neither Southern nor Northern: Miami, Florida, and the Black Freedom Struggle in America's Tourist Paradise, 1896–1968." PhD diss., University of Miami, 2007.

———. *The Struggle for Black Freedom in Miami: Civil Rights and America's Tourist Paradise, 1896–1968*. Baton Rouge: Louisiana State University Press, 2015.

Rosenberg, Emily. *Spreading the American Dream: American Economic and Cultural Expansion, 1890–1945*. New York: Hill and Wang, 1982.

Rupp, Leila J. "Constructing Internationalism: The Case of Transnational Women's Organizations, 1888–1945." *American Historical Review* 99, no. 5 (December 1994): 1571–1600.

Russo, John Paul. *I. A. Richards: His Life and Work*. Baltimore: The Johns Hopkins University Press, 1989.

Sackley, Nicole. "Village Models: Etawah, India, and the Making and Remaking of Development in the Early Cold War." *Diplomatic History* 37, no. 4 (2013): 749–778.

Said, Edward W. *Orientalism*. New York: Vintage Books, 1979.

Salisbury, Richard V. "Good Neighbors? The United States and Latin America in the Twentieth Century." In *American Foreign Relations: A Historiographical Review*, edited by Gerald K. Haines and J. Samuel Walker, 311–344. Westport, CT: Greenwood Press, 1981.

Salt, Karen. "The Haitian Question." PhD diss., Purdue University, 2011.

Sanders, Grace. "La Voix des Femmes: Haitian Women's Rights, National Politics, and Black Activism in Port-Au-Prince and Montreal, 1934–1986." PhD diss., University of Michigan, 2013.

San Miguel, Pedro L. *The Imagined Island: History, Identity, and Utopia in Hispaniola.* Translated by Jane Ramírez. Chapel Hill: University of North Carolina Press, 2005.

Schieffelin, Bambi B., and Rachelle Charlier Doucet. "The 'Real' Haitian Creole: Ideology, Metalinguistics, and Orthographic Choice." In *Language and Ideologies: Practice and Theory*, edited by Bambi B. Schieffelin, Kathryn Ann Woolard, and Paul V. Kroskrity, 285–316. New York: Oxford University Press, 1998.

Schiller, Nina Glick, and Georges Eugene Fouron. *Georges Woke Up Laughing: Long-Distance Nationalism and the Search for Home*. Durham, NC: Duke University Press, 2001.

Schmidt, Hans. *The United States Occupation of Haiti, 1915–34*. New Brunswick, NJ: Rutgers University Press, 1971.

Schoultz, Lars. *Beneath the United States: A History of U.S. Policy toward Latin America*. Cambridge, MA: Harvard University Press, 1998.

Schultz, Kirsten. *Tropical Versailles: Empire, Monarchy and the Portuguese Royal Court in Rio de Janeiro, 1808–1821*. New York: Routledge, 2001.

Schulzinger, Robert, ed. *A Companion to American Foreign Relations*. Malden, MA: Blackwell Publishing, 2003.

Scott, David. *Conscripts of Modernity: The Tragedy of Colonial Enlightenment*. Durham, NC: Duke University Press, 2004.

Scott, James C. *Seeing Like a State: How Certain Schemes to Improve the Human Condition Have Failed*. New Haven: Yale University Press, 1998.

Seidel, Robert N. *Progressive Pan Americanism: Development and United States Policy toward South America, 1906–1931*. Ithaca, NY: Cornell University Press, 1973.

Seth, Sanjay. *Subject Lessons: The Western Education of Colonial India*. Durham, NC: Duke University Press, 2007.

Shannon, Magdaline W. *Jean Price-Mars, the Haitian Elite, and the American Occupation, 1915–1935*. New York: St. Martin's Press, 1996.

———. "The U.S. Commission for the Study and Review of Conditions in Haiti and Its Relationship to President Hoover's Latin American Policy." *Caribbean Studies* 15, no. 4 (January 1976): 53–71.

Sheinin, David, ed. *Beyond the Ideal: Pan Americanism in Inter-American Affairs*. Santa Barbara, CA: Greenwood, 2000.

Sheller, Mimi. *Democracy After Slavery: Black Publics and Peasant Radicalism in Haiti and Jamaica*. London: Macmillan Education, 2000.

Shepard, Todd. "Algeria, France, Mexico, UNESCO: A Transnational History of Anti-Racism and Empire, 1932–1962." *Journal of Global History* 6, no. 2 (June 2011): 273–297.

Sherwood, Marika. "The UN: Caribbean and African-American Attempts to Influence the Founding Conference in San Francisco, 1945." *Journal of Caribbean History* 29, no. 1 (1996).

Sio, Robert Charles. "The United Nations Fundamental, Scientific, and Cultural Organization's Program in Fundamental Education." M.S. thesis, New Mexico Western College, July 1951.

Skidmore, Thomas E. *Black into White: Race and Nationality in Brazilian Thought*. New York: Oxford University Press, 1974.

Slatta, Richard W., and Jane Lucas De Grummond. *Simón Bolívar's Quest for Glory*. College Station: Texas A&M University Press, 2003.

Sluga, Glenda. "Imagining Internationalism." *Arts* 32 (2010): 55–68.

———. *Internationalism in the Age of Nationalism*. Philadelphia: University of Pennsylvania Press, 2013.

———. "UNESCO and the (One) World of Julian Huxley." *Journal of World History* 21, no. 3 (September 2010): 393–418.

Smith, Jenny M. *When the Hands Are Many: Community Organization and Social Change in Rural Haiti*. Ithaca, NY: Cornell University Press, 2001.

Smith, Matthew J. "From Dessalines to Duvalier Revisited: A Quarter Century Retrospective." *Journal of Haitian Studies* 13, no. 1 (Spring 2007): 27–39.

———. *Liberty, Fraternity, and Exile: Haiti and Jamaica after Emancipation*. Chapel Hill: University of North Carolina Press, 2014.

———. *Red and Black in Haiti: Radicalism, Conflict and Political Change, 1934–1957*. Chapel Hill: University of North Carolina Press, 2009.

———. "Shades of Red in a Black Republic: Radicalism, Black Consciousness, and Social Conflict in Post-occupation Haiti, 1934–57." PhD diss., University of Florida, 2002.

Smith, Peter. *Talons of the Eagle: Dynamics of U.S.-Latin American Relations*. New York: Oxford University Press, 1996.

Socolow, Susan. "Economic Roles of the Free Women of Color of Cap Français." In *More than Chattel: Black Women and Slavery in the Americas*, edited by Darlene Clark Hines and Barry Gaspar, 279–297. Bloomington: Indiana University Press, 1996.

Sommers, Jeffrey. "Haiti and the Hemispheric Imperative to Invest: The *Bulletin* of the Pan American Union." *Journal of Haitian Studies* 9, no. 1 (2003): 68–94.

———. *Race, Reality and Realpolitik: U.S.-Haiti Relations in the Lead Up to the 1915 Occupation*. Lanham, MD: Rowman and Littlefield, 2015.

Spivak, Gayatri Chakravorty, and Rosalind C. Morris. *Can the Subaltern Speak? Reflections on the History of an Idea*. New York: Columbia University Press, 2010.

Staples, Amy L. S. *The Birth of Development: How the World Bank, Food and Agriculture Organization, and World Health Organization Changed the World, 1945–1965*. Kent, OH: Kent State University Press, 2006.

Supplice, Daniel. *Dictionnaire biographique des personnalités politiques de la République d'Haïti*. Port-au-Prince: Daniel Supplice, 2001.

Tardieu, Charles. *L'éducation en Haïti: De la période coloniale à nos jours*. Port-au-Prince: Imprimerie Henri Deschamps, 1990.

Trouillot, Henock. *M. Dantès Bellegarde: Un écrivain d'autrefois*. Port-au-Prince: Imprimerie N.A. Theodore, 1957.

Trouillot, Michel-Rolph. *Haiti, State Against Nation: The Origins and Legacy of Duvalierism*. New York: Monthly Review Press, 1990.

———. "The Odd and the Ordinary: Haiti, the Caribbean, and the World." *Cimarrón: New Perspectives on the Caribbean* 2, no. 3 (June 2007): 1–15.

———. *Silencing the Past: Power and the Production of History*. Boston: Beacon Press, 1990.

Turits, Richard. "A World Destroyed, A Nation Imposed: The 1937 Haitian Massacre in the Dominican Republic." *Hispanic American Historical Review* 82, no. 3 (2002): 589–635.

Ulysse, Gina. *Why Haiti Needs New Narratives: A Post-Quake Chronicle*. Middleton, CT: Wesleyan University Press, 2015.

Verna, Chantalle F. "Beyond the Immigration Centers: Haitian Community in Michigan." M.A. thesis, Michigan State University, 2000.

———. "A Conversation with Paulette Poujol Oriol." *Journal of Haitian Studies* 17, no. 1 (2011): 246–257.

———. "Haitian Migration and Community-Building in Southeastern Michigan, 1966–1998." In *Geographies of the Haitian Diaspora*, edited by Regine Ostine Jackson, 163–184. New York: Routledge, 2011.

———. "Haiti's Second Independence and the Promise of Pan-American Cooperation." PhD diss., Michigan State University, 2005.

———. "Maurice Dartigue and Educational Reform as a Strategy for Haitian National Development 1930–46." *Journal of Haitian Studies* 13, no. 2 (Fall 2007): 24–38.

———. "The Role of International Aid in Creating Ties between Haiti and the United States, 1934–1957." *Research Reports Online*, Rockefeller Archives Center. http://archive.rockefeller.edu/publications/resrep/rronlinesub.php?printer=1 NPR.

Verna, Paul. *Petión y Bolívar: Una etapa decisiva en la emancipación de Hispanoamérica, 1790–1830*. Caracas: Ediciones de la Presidencia de la República, 1980.

Voltaire, Frantz. *Pouvoir noir en Haïti: L'explosion de 1946*. Montréal: Éditions du CIDIHCA, 1988.

Von Eschen, Penny M. *Race Against Empire: Black Americans and Anticolonialism, 1937–1957*. Ithaca, NY: Cornell University Press, 1997.

Wah, Tatiana K. *Haiti's Development Through Expatriate Reconnection: Conditions and Challenges*. Coconut Creek: Educa Vision, 2003.

Weiler, Kathleen. "Mabel Carney at Teachers College: From Home Missionary to White Ally." *Teachers College Record* 107, no. 12 (December 2005): 2599–2633.

White, Ashli. *Encountering Revolution: Haiti and the Making of the Early Republic.* Baltimore: The Johns Hopkins University Press, 2010.

Wilson, Edmund. *Red, Black, Blond, and Olive: Studies in Four Civilizations Zuni, Haiti, Soviet Russia, Israel.* New York: Oxford University Press, 1956.

Wolfson, Amy. "An Examination of South Florida's Haitian Diaspora-led Development Initiatives and the Formation of New Spaces of Empowerment." MA thesis, Florida International University, 2010.

Zacair, Phillipe, ed. *Haiti and the Haitian Diaspora in the Wider Caribbean.* Gainesville: University of Florida Press, 2011.

Index

Page numbers in italics indicate figures.

About the Author

CHANTALLE F. VERNA is an associate professor of history and international relations at Florida International University. She is coeditor with Laurent Dubois, Kaiama Glover, Nadève Ménard, and Millery Polyné of the forthcoming book *The Haiti Reader: History, Culture, and Politics*.

About the Author

CHANTALLE F. VERNA is an associate professor of history and international relations at Florida International University. She is coeditor with Laurent Dubois, Kaiama Glover, Nadève Ménard, and Millery Polyné of the forthcoming book *The Haiti Reader: History, Culture, and Politics.*